Deliverance from Slavery

Historical Materialism Book Series

The Historical Materialism Book Series is a major publishing initiative of the radical left. The capitalist crisis of the twenty-first century has been met by a resurgence of interest in critical Marxist theory. At the same time, the publishing institutions committed to Marxism have contracted markedly since the high point of the 1970s. The Historical Materialism Book Series is dedicated to addressing this situation by making available important works of Marxist theory. The aim of the series is to publish important theoretical contributions as the basis for vigorous intellectual debate and exchange on the left.

The peer-reviewed series publishes original monographs, translated texts, and reprints of classics across the bounds of academic disciplinary agendas and across the divisions of the left. The series is particularly concerned to encourage the internationalization of Marxist debate and aims to translate significant studies from beyond the English-speaking world.

For a full list of titles in the Historical Materialism Book Series
available in paperback from Haymarket Books, visit:
https://www.haymarketbooks.org/series_collections/1-historical-materialism

Deliverance from Slavery

*Attempting a Biblical Theology
in the Service of Liberation*

Dick Boer

Translated by Rebecca Pohl

Haymarket Books
Chicago, IL

First published in 2015 by Brill Academic Publishers, The Netherlands
© 2016 Koninklijke Brill NV, Leiden, The Netherlands

Published in paperback in 2017 by
Haymarket Books
P.O. Box 180165
Chicago, IL 60618
773-583-7884
www.haymarketbooks.org

ISBN: 978-1-60846-700-6

Trade distribution:
In the US, Consortium Book Sales, www.cbsd.com
In Canada, Publishers Group Canada, www.pgcbooks.ca
In the UK, Turnaround Publisher Services, www.turnaround-uk.com
In all other countries, Ingram Publisher Services International,
intlsales@perseusbooks.com

Cover design by Jamie Kerry of Belle Étoile Studios and Ragina Johnson.

This book was published with the generous support of Lannan Foundation
and the Wallace Action Fund.

Printed in Canada by union labor.

10 9 8 7 6 5 4 3 2 1

Library of Congress Cataloging-in-Publication data is available.

For Ton Veerkamp,
friend and comrade

..
.

We are currently witnessing the collapse of two major interpretative traditions focused on history, or at least their loss of significance: Socialism and Christianity. Nobody can deny the part these two interpretative traditions have played in insulting life. But Christianity could always challenge Christians just as the idea of socialism could probe real socialism. Rosa Luxemburg and Francis of Assisi could never be buried entirely. Their subversive songs and stories survived, and were dug up again and again by different groups. A canon was in place, as were obligatory texts, even if they were frequently distorted or withheld. These texts demanded the world be interpreted from the perspective of the victims and the injured. But what happens when the culture that houses these texts declines? What happens when the groups who read and know such texts disappear?

STEFFENSKY 2007

Contents

Translator's Note

I have chosen a literal approach for the translation of this biblical theology in an attempt to preserve the rhythm and the tone of the source text as closely as possible. Crucially, though, the text is itself concerned with the process of both linguistic and conceptual translation, and the author privileges careful attention to etymology and concordance in his own translations from Hebrew and Greek. It seems only just to continue this practice in this further step of translation.

Bible quotations have been translated by me based on the author's own translations rather than making use of any existing Bible translation. The few instances where comparative work between authoritative versions grounds the analysis are marked as such. Where authorised English translations of other cited material were available, these have been used; all other instances have been translated by me. The bibliographic information at the end elucidates this case by case.

I would like to express my gratitude to Dick Boer for the conversations that have marked this translation process.

Rebecca Pohl
Manchester, 2014

Foreword

> For better or worse, we will be Communists, letting ourselves be led forth from Christianity into an extraordinarily questionable movement, one which barely even still exists at the moment, but which might recur at any time.

.·.

Dick Boer may properly be described as a theologian of the revolution, or rather, as a biblical theologian of the revolution. This title was first bestowed by Ernst Bloch on Thomas Müntzer, the theologico-political leader of the Peasant Revolution in the German states of the sixteenth century.[1] I make this point, since some readers of earlier volumes of the Historical Materialism Book Series may be surprised to see an overtly theological, even biblical, work appear in the series. What has historical materialism to do with theology? Is theology not an esoteric practice, speaking of what does not exist? Is not religion the response to an alienated condition, so that our attention should instead be focused on those real, social and economic conditions?

By now, it should not be necessary to argue for the importance of theology for historical materialism, but let me outline some basic facts before introducing this work by Dick Boer. First, theology is as much concerned with this world as any world beyond our sensory experience. As Dick Boer puts it, Christianity, like communism, is 'the practical recognition that this new world cannot be found in castles in the air, but can be found in the old world as the active hope for the "kairos"'. In other words, theology is both secular and anti-secular – understanding 'secular' (from *saeculum*) as belonging to this world and this age. Theology's traditional concerns with anthropology, the human condition, society, politics and history should make it clear that it has much to do with this human world. At the same time, it gives voice to dissatisfaction with the status quo: injustice persists, oppression continues, economic exploitation is still very much of our daily lives. So theology seeks a better world, one of justice, freedom and economic equality. Often that world is assumed to belong in a heaven, to which we go upon death. But that misses the resolutely theological focus on a renewed socio-economic formation here in this world.

---

1   Bloch 1969.

Second, theology is often torn politically between reaction and revolution. The very same system that easily supports tyrants and empires (Constantine was the first) also provides the means and inspiration for overthrowing such despots and their regimes. The most detailed exposition of the revolutionary side of Christianity remains Karl Kautsky's under-studied *Forerunners of Modern Socialism*.[2] Kautsky explores in impressive breadth the tradition of revolutionary Christianity, through from the earliest Christians to his own day. After Kautsky, perhaps the most well-known recent expressions of this much longer tradition are the Latin American, black, feminist and queer liberation theologies, which arose in the 1960s and 1970s. Dick Boer clearly belongs to this revolutionary tradition, with its long and inspiring pedigree.

Third, Boer is not merely a fellow-traveller with the socialist Left, a political theologian who is also a member of the communist party. He does not restrict himself to urging a politics of alliance, but rather argues that in the biblical theological tradition we may find one of the key influences and inspirations for the Left. In other words, revolutionary Christianity is actually the core of the biblical tradition. Thus, the ease with which the church and its ideologies have fallen in line with tyrannical regimes is a betrayal of that core. Boer challenges the assumption that theology and its institutions are by default reactionary and that resistance must come from the edges. Instead, he seeks to seize the centre and argue that it comprises the revolutionary truth of theology.

With these three principles in mind, let us explore how Dick Boer goes about his task. Early on in the book, he writes:

> The purpose of the present biblical theology is to follow the canon and to follow it as *regula fidei* ('the rule of faith'), as a guideline for what we can believe with respect to the story, when necessary – and it is often necessary – contradicting the factual course of history. This biblical theology follows the canon and hence proceeds from the Torah, in the sequence of the canon, which is also a hierarchy, the constitution, which founds the existence of the Liberator-God's people. The 'story' (re)told by this biblical theology is that of the project 'Israel', which is conceived in the Torah, and the real Israel, called to execute this project.

One's initial impression is that such an approach is extraordinarily conventional (theologically speaking): the Bible in its canonical order is a guideline,

---

2 Kautsky 1976a [1895–7]; 1976b [1895–7]; Kautsky and Lafargue 1977 [1922]. This work has been only partially translated (Kautsky 1897).

the rule of faith – so one must follow its dominant narrative, which has been constructed by the framers of the canon. But now Boer gives this conventional approach a distinct twist, for the canonical biblical message is one of liberation, led by a liberator-God! The last sentence indicates the basic structure of Boer's argument, which begins by tracing the plan of the 'project' called 'Israel', which subsequently must be enacted by the real or actually existing Israel. That the latter will make many mistakes and fail many times is to be expected, but the echo of 'real' or 'actually existing socialism' should not be missed. Marx and Engels and those who followed them may have provided the basics of the revolutionary communist project, but it fell to the socialist countries of Eastern Europe and then the proper East to find the path that no one had trodden before to actual, real socialism.

Dick Boer's bid, then, is that the core message of the Bible is liberation. Most of his attention is focused on the Hebrew Bible (Old Testament), for as a Christian theologian he must face – in textual form – the persistent question of the relation between Jews and Christians. The long relationship between the two has been fraught with difficulties, polemic and sheer barbarism. But it is also one of profound common ground, worshipping the same God whom Christians came to know belatedly, and presenting a path to liberation that Boer seeks to trace in those scriptures. So it should be no surprise that he focuses on the most significant section of the Hebrew Bible, the Torah or first five books – Genesis, Exodus, Leviticus, Numbers and Deuteronomy. Here Boer finds an outline for a liberated Israel, in which 'Israel' is not an ethnic identity but a name for a liberated community. I would add that detailed historical and archaeological research has persuasively proposed that Israel was by no means an identifiable ethnic unit when it first appeared on the scene of ancient Southwest Asia (the ancient Near East, as it used to be called) in the first millennium BCE. Instead, it was a profound mix of peoples from different ethnic groups. So it was the theological-political project that brought them together.

However, in the Torah we are not with any real Israel, for the Torah presents not an actual society, but the outlines of one to come. It is a liberated society in waiting, before the revolution, if I may put it that way. One needs at least some idea, usually a combination of careful planning and inspiring political myths, so as to tap into the need for both the 'cold' and 'warm' streams of any liberation movement. The head and the heart, scientific planning and deep-felt hope – these are the two necessary sides of preparing for the revolution. In developing these two dimensions, the text tells us of creation ('and it was good'), offers guidelines and laws for a liberated community, and presents in some detail how one deals with threats to the project.

For me, the more interesting time comes after the revolution, after the gaining of power when one needs to put into action one's hopes and plans. Before turning to this part of Boer's argument, I need to raise a problem with the approach that he takes: if one opts for the canonical and arguably main stream of the biblical material, how do we deal with its negative aspects? These include the story of the conquest of a land and dispossession of its inhabitants, the establishment of kingship, the often arbitrary and absolutist role that God plays in the text, and the idea of 'total war' or the 'ban' (the complete destruction of every living creature among the enemy).

Not every text can fit into Boer's reading. Indeed, he insists that an interpreter should not attempt to smooth over contradictions posed by troublesome texts. So let me take the final two items I listed above, namely, the questions of God and of total war. As for God, is this figure all too often not a despot writ large, full of power that is wielded arbitrarily and jealously? Yes, says Boer, but this is not the figure of liberation, for that one has the name that is not really a name, 'I am' (YHWH):

> This is why this name is also superordinate to the term 'God'. For 'God' ... is a title, an office, a function. It signifies a highest Being, the beginning and end of all wisdom, elevated above all critical doubt. As such, 'God' says nothing – except that his power knows no boundaries: he is capable of everything, knows everything, sees everything, is everywhere and always – omnipotent, omniscient, all-seeing, omnipresent, eternal. In general, 'God' is the absolutisation and hence the sanctioning of the earthly power that condemns the majority of people to servitude. As such, 'God' can have a number of faces again – but as it turns out, it is always the face of a bog-standard ruler.

So 'God' can easily become the mask behind which the aspiring despots of the ancient world (and ours for that matter) hide in order to carry out their well-known and ultimately petty plans. We should not see every 'God said' as the word of the liberating divine figure of the Bible. But what about the 'ban', for this is a more troublesome idea? Initially, Boer argues that an anti-imperialist war is necessary, waged by a weaker force and only in emergency situations. But a war waged on a weaker power, living nearby and completely opposed to a society without domination, is another story. As some texts make clear, the war to be waged in this case is one of total annihilation – of every living creature. Boer cannot accept this position. 'This "final solution" is too terrible to be true', he writes. 'A different solution has to be found'. Boer suggests it may be read – metaphorically perhaps – in terms of the hope that evil will one day be abolished, or that the 'ban' plays a minor key in biblical stories and is challenged even there. In the end, he leaves the question open, discomfited by the idea and practice. Necessary evils remain, such as kingship and the military, for any project of liberation must live in a very imperfect world. 'If you want peace, prepare for war', is the realistic counsel, with all its dangers. Nonetheless, Boer might have made more of the voices of resistance to kingship and total war. He does mention King Saul's questioning of the divine ban on Amalek, and wishes that Saul had protested more insistently. But the text also reveals that such a ban is actually ineffective – Amalek is wiped out on more than one occasion and yet they return, more numerous than ever. Further, Boer does not mention the judge Samuel's dire warnings against a king and his rapaciousness (1 Samuel 8) or the continual voices of murmuring, protest and outright rebellion against despotism. I for one would have liked to hear a little more about these forms of resistance to the despotism that appears too easily even within a liberation project.

This last point brings me back to the question of what happens after the revolution, the 'real Israel' I have already mentioned. This is the time of 'travails of the plain', as Brecht puts it, and is the most important part of Boer's work. The task of climbing the mountain is now past and we are on the plateau where the real task begins. Lenin and Mao too expressed similar thoughts after the revolution: winning power through a revolution is the easy part; far more difficult is the task of actual construction. It is a time of many mistakes, of steps backward, of reshaping the approach in light of changing and unexpected circumstances. So also the 'real Israel' makes many mistakes and certainly does not live up to the project as it was outlined in the Torah. As a result, many would argue that it 'failed', especially when the project came to an end. Too soon did it succumb to imperial powers of the first millennium BCE, becoming a province – Yehud – under the Persians and Greeks and Romans. But 'failure' is a harsh term, beloved of right-wing critics who deploy an impossible benchmark for what counts as success: perfect realisation and eternity. Anything less than eternally perfect is a failure. Of course, in their eyes this applies only to the Left (for they conveniently ignore the disaster of their own project). In response we need to resist such a verdict, insisting that any liberating project which achieves power and which is able to begin the process of construction is a success, especially if it is able to see off the counter-revolution. It may come to an end before its time, leading to profound disappointment. But the experience is enough to foster hope and energy for yet another effort.

I write these words with a deliberate slippage between the biblical theology Boer proposes and the real problems of 'actually existing socialism', especially in Eastern Europe in the twentieth century. The reason I do so is that it was the experience of such socialism that inspired many aspects of Boer's biblical theology. In 1984, he was called to East Berlin to be a minister in the Dutch Ecumenical Congregation in the DDR [*Niederländische Ökumenische Gemeinde in der DDR*]. He was minister for six years, until 1990, after the fall of the wall and the end of the DDR. Why did this congregation call Dick? At the time, he was a professor of theology at the University of Amsterdam, but he was also a member of the communist party. In short, he is a minister of the church, a professor and communist. As for the congregation, it was a small (100 members) communion of left-wing Christians in the DDR. It was established in October of 1949, when the DDR was itself founded in response to the establishment of West Germany. At that time, the church was made up of Dutch citizens who had come to Germany as foreign workers [*Fremdarbeiter*] during the Second World War and who lived in what became both East Berlin and West Berlin. After the construction of the wall in August of 1961, the part of the congregation in the new DDR grew into a community of left-wing Christians. They became deeply committed to political readings of the Bible, especially the Hebrew Bible. They also developed a liturgy that included elements one may describe as 'secular' or 'non-religious'. Or rather, the liturgy saw the work of God in the world outside the walls of the church, outside what had become the acceptable zones of Christianity. For example, the hymnbook contained not only the best examples of church music, but also the 'Internationale' and 'Vorwärts und nicht vergessen'. All of which meant that the Dutch Ecumenical Congregation took a step further than the Federation of Evangelical Churches of the DDR, which defined itself as 'not against and not outside but within socialism' [*nicht gegen, nicht neben, sondern im Sozialismus*]. By contrast, the Dutch Ecumenical Congregation saw itself as a communion of 'Christians for socialism'. That is, they were both 'within socialism and for the DDR'.

The challenge for Dick Boer, as the minister and as a theologian, was to find ways to preach within the context of actually existing socialism. In the liberation and political theologies that arose in Western and Southern contexts – Latin America, North America, Europe – a key biblical narrative is the Exodus out of slavery, as is the Gospel promise of the 'Kingdom of God' that will provide healing, release from hunger and freedom from exploitation. In these cases, the moment of the Exodus or the new world is yet to come at a hoped-for future moment. But what does a minister do when the Exodus has, so to speak, already happened? How does one go about the difficult task of constructing the new society? To preach the Exodus in the DDR would mean to speak of liberation from slavery in the DDR. So Boer became interested in the time after liberation, after the Exodus. He discovered the importance of the 'historical' books (or 'first prophets' as the Jewish canon calls them) of the Hebrew Bible, such as Joshua, Judges, and the books of Samuel and Kings. He also rediscovered Ezra and Nehemiah, with their accounts of rebuilding a 'Torah Republic', when the exile to Babylon (sixth century BCE) was over. This was the problem of the 'travail of the plains' which I mentioned earlier, and the experience led Dick to develop his theory of 'actually existing' or 'real' Israel.

Further, since the government of the DDR recognised the congregation as an organisation with a special relationship to the Netherlands, the church was allowed to organise seminars with Dutch speakers who entered into discussion with Marxists from the DDR. The topics of these seminars included: 'The alliance of Communists and Christians'; 'Faith and Atheism'; 'Socialism and the Third World'; 'The New Economic World-Order'; 'Media'; and 'Gay Theology'. The Marxists who partook in these seminars actually felt free to engage in a robust critique of the official communist positions of the state – in the spirit of the tradition and theory of Marxism itself. Further, even though the government of the DDR officially forbade a 'Christian-Marxist dialogue', here that dialogue took place, regularly.

Since it was Boer's task to find and invite Marxist speakers for these seminars, he also had the opportunity to meet and speak with them in private. He became friends with many of them, a friendship enhanced by their common experience of being members of communist parties. They shared their hopes for a renewal of socialism and their despair concerning the apparent impossibility, at the time, of such a renewal.

These contacts also encouraged Boer to undertake an initiative to 'save' the DDR in the time of the 'Wende' [turn]. He was inspired by the Dutch peace movement's project to 'Stop the N-bomb': one starts with a manifesto, which is signed by prominent figures without explicit political commitments. In the Netherlands, this action led to the largest mass-movement since the Second World War. So he proposed a similar action in the DDR: organise a manifesto, signed by well-known people from the new civic movements [*Bürgerbewegungen: Neues Forum, Demokratischer Aufbruch*], the church and the party (the section working for renewal and not related to the state and the ossified party apparatus). This initiative, beginning with the manifesto *For Our Country* [*Für unser Land*], which was written by Christa Wolf and Volker Braun, became the largest mass-action in the period of the *Wende* in the DDR. They obtained no fewer than 1,167,048 signatures. Sadly, the initiative for renewal itself failed, not least because the Soviet Union was no longer able to protect the DDR from the unending efforts of the West to 'overthrow' communism. Yet, as Boer points out, the sheer size of the movement (one among many) shows that, contrary to much propaganda, the DDR was supported by many of its citizens until the end.

Delivery from Slavery is thus a unique work, one that was inspired by the experience of living and working – in a congregation of the church – in a socialist country. Dick is by no means the first to be a believer and a communist. Yet a biblical theology developed in the context of socialism, indeed one that wishes to affirm socialism, is an extraordinary effort. As he writes, if we wish to translate biblical theology (and not only that of Paul), then 'Communism lends itself to the task'. My anticipation is that it will generate much debate, especially among socialists of many persuasions, for we are Boer's preferred interlocutors.

Roland Boer

Acknowledgements

No work is done without help. I have to thank Bara van Pelt, Rinse Reeling Brouwer and Christine Berberich for their helpful commentary on the German version of my text.

My very special gratitude goes out to 'my' translator, Rebecca Pohl. She succeeded in transforming the German text into an admirable, readable English—starting with my not always readable German, but including some quoted poetry as well.

I thank Danny Hayward from the Historical Materialism Book Series for his support during the editing of the text.

Finally I want to thank the Editorial Board for the Historical Materialism Book Series for their willingness to publish a book of theology that seems rather unusual from an historical-materialist point of view. I hope the book itself proves the possibility of this way of considering the matter of both theology and the theory of historical materialism.

Introduction

1

'Delivery from slavery': these words, taken from a Dutch labour movement song, perfectly map onto the Bible's central concern. They are so similar to the Torah's key phrase (Torah designates the first five books of the Bible), they might as well be a quotation. And the Torah acts as the 'Law' for those addressed by the Bible, it tells them what they can believe, what they should do, and what they may hope for.

The key phrase is: 'I am YHWH, your God, who brought you out of Egypt, out of the house of bondage' (Ex 20:2).

It is invoked here, as it were, to serve as an axiom to be introduced into the modern period. For millions of people 'delivery from slavery' became the guiding principle that directed their longing for a better life onto the path of faith in liberation, the hope for it, and the transformation of this hope into action. The watchword 'delivery from slavery' translates the biblical message of the exodus from slavery into the theory and practice of a modern liberation movement. Biblical theology is the attempt to 'update' the 'language of the message'. It is the work of translation: it searches for a language that attends to the concerns of today's world while 'preserving' the concerns that originally motivated biblical language. For the author of the present biblical theology, this language seems particularly prominent in the modern liberation movement, which dared to take account of the exodus initiated by the Liberator-God as a perspective for human – all too human – action.

This liberation movement, which wanted to free labour from the rule of capital, is not 'the' liberation movement, because there is no such thing as 'the' liberation movement. There are only numerous liberation movements and numerous languages with which to express liberation. The labour movement is unthinkable without the language of the bourgeois revolution: it was heated by the slogan 'liberty, equality, fraternity'; it inherited the longing for the 'Kingdom of Freedom' (Kant). All it had to do, in order to actually achieve such universal fraternity, was to liberate that revolution from its bourgeois limitations, join that warm stream with its own cold stream of the ruthless critique of capitalism, specify its 'all *men* will be brothers' to say '*workers* of the world unite'. But even the liberation articulated by the labour movement was limited. What good, for instance, was fraternity to the sisters concerned with their own liberation? And were all oppressed people workers? The delivery from slavery was not that straightforward. This will have to be taken into consideration during the work of translation that biblical theology must perform. The Bible, too, has to endure being sounded out for its potential limitations. The fact that its key phrase reappears in a song from the labour movement, of all things, also raises questions. And these shall be considered.

2

Are there no other languages, though, that might also translate the language of the message, perhaps even do a better job of it? Did not the Reformation's language rightly emphasise man's sinfulness and his pardoning in the Bible's message? And did 'existential' theology not rightly rephrase this focus on sin and mercy as 'the essential question', thus modernising it? Here, sin is the despair when faced with the futility of all efforts to prove oneself human, mercy the announcement that this is not the end of the matter, thank God. Or is the Bible's message best understood as religious, its language ultimately pointing towards the unspeakable? Delivery from enslavement to well-worn phrases and final words? The fact that these languages articulate that which moves humans most deeply, as well as wittily and profoundly treating essential aspects of the 'condition humaine', is unmistakable. However, they are inadequate for the translation of biblical theology in one crucial point: they do not mention the Torah's key phrase as a principal of liberation theology with reference to concrete slavery.

The key phrase is simply absent from Luther's 'Large Catechism'. Here, the 'Ten Commandments' begin with 'You shall have no other gods before me'. They are only 'law', not Gospel. It is not until the son's Gospel that deliverance appears: 'who has delivered me from sin, the devil, from death, and from all evil'. The Heidelberg Catechism does cite the key phrase (in response to the question: 'What is God's law?'), but it too opens the Ten Commandments with the words, 'You shall have no other gods before me'. Only Calvin, in the Catechism of Geneva, cites the key phrase as part of the First Commandment: 'Hear, Israel, I am the Lord your God, who led you out of Egypt, out of the house of bondage. You shall have no other gods before me.' He also explicitly asks: 'Does what is said of the liberation and the breaking of the yoke of the servitude to Egypt not apply only to the people of Israel?' And responds: 'Literally speaking, yes. But there is another kind of deliverance that extends to all humans alike. For he has liberated us all from the spiritual servitude to sin and from the devil's tyranny.' But it is precisely this statement, which 'literally speaking' refers only to the people of Israel, that 'extends' to the deliverance of all humans by promising a society based in equality.

These languages do speak of deliverance in one way or another, but only the language of the labourers' liberation movement links it with slavery, without which the specific notion of deliverance at play cannot possibly be understood. Only by way of this delivery from slavery can we speak of mercy, sin, and purpose. The mercy experienced by the slave people when an unexpected possibility for liberation appears; the sin of abandoning the path of liberation; the despondent questioning of the purpose of the entire enterprise, which threatens to stifle the hope for its success.[1] If this understanding of mercy, sin, and meaning seems 'reductionist', we should consider whether the Bible might not itself be reductive in this respect. In any case, I maintain that it is the Bible's intention to reduce humanity's problem to their delivery from slavery. But why do we speak of reduction, if reduction means deliverance? All tears are dried, there is no more death, drudgery has ended for good (Rv 21:4). The Bible does not necessarily have to be the most profound book in the world, either. But I know of no other book that tackles the issue of a truly human communal life more radically and at the root (radix): precisely, delivery from slavery![2]

3

The linguistic conjunction of the Bible and the modern labour movement is not limited to the identification of the 'climax'. They have also had to find the words to express the problems that arise when this climax makes history, when it has to descend into the lowlands of the everyday. Here, a movement through time sets in, during which the movement has to prove its worth. This changes the question to whether those delivered from slavery can remain faithful to the cause of liberation. Now they have to agonise about their inevitable entanglement in contradictions. Simply invoking delivery from slavery and then allowing it to deteriorate into an empty slogan is not good enough. We require a

---

1   And thus its language is quotable again – as it is quoted by me.

2   'To be radical is to grasp the root of the matter. But for man the root is man himself. The evident proof of the radicalism of German theory, and hence of its practical energy, is that it proceeds from a resolute *positive* abolition of religion. The criticism of religion ends with the teaching *that man is the highest being for man*, hence with *the categorical imperative to overthrow all relations* in which man is a debased, enslaved, forsaken, despicable being' (Marx 1975b, p. 182).

language for the 'travails of the plains' (Brecht).[3] I do not mean to suggest that the modern liberation movement has found this language – it has frequently repressed its problems, glossed over its mistakes, justified its injustices. Perhaps we must even acknowledge (unfortunately too late) that it has failed to be forthright precisely when an awareness of problems was most required. During my own writing process, however, I realised again and again how reliant my translations are on that movement's language. I could not have actualised the problematic of the liberation movement recounted by the Bible in any other way. What other language would have allowed me to refer to the 'travail of the plains'? Or to speak of the 'real' Israel? How could I have analysed the properties of the social relations in which a liberation movement operates any better than through the trinity of 'economy-politics-ideology'? And is there a more appropriate translation of the view of Israel as a society without king and priests (Ex 19:6) than that of the 'withering of the state'? This language also proved open enough to be turned against its own dogmas.

4

There is one point, however, where these two languages appear to be incompatible: the question of God. In the song from the labour movement, delivery from slavery is a task. The preceding line relates that labour must be liberated, and that this liberation is the task of the labourers themselves. The delivery from slavery is hence the perspective of this self-deliverance: 'No saviour from on high delivers | No faith have we in prince or peer. | Our own right hand the chains must shiver', as the Internationale sings. Biblically speaking, delivery from slavery is a gift. The subject of this liberation is an 'I' that is not the slave people but 'their God', so a 'highest Being'. Everything appears to make sense: some people do not need God for their liberation, others cannot imagine their liberation without God. This should not prohibit a coalition, but on the condition that everyone contributes according to their own fashion. Thus, the issue of God is bracketed and no longer disrupts the liberation movement. Biblical theology, then, is either expected to relinquish God and secularise the language of its message (this would mean no longer being a *theo*logy, it would have truly translated the biblical discourse of God into a different language), or to refrain from a translation into the language of modernity which has no use

---

3   'When I returned / My hair was not yet grey / And I was glad / The travails of the mountains lie behind us / Before us lie the travails of the plains' (Brecht 1976, p. 415 f.).

for the word 'God'. This would render biblical theology an 'internal currency',[4] which can only be communicated in a very small sphere (the Christian community).[5]

Now, I believe it is true that the exceptional language of the Bible – not only when it speaks of God – cannot be translated into the general language of modernity without sacrificing substance. When the attachment to the logic of capital has become so ingrained that it is 'naturally' understood, even felt, as freedom, then the delivery from slavery will only be misunderstood as a relic from ancient history, or as having been already accomplished in the 'free world'. However, this does not mean that biblical theology should simply be content with its 'splendid isolation'. Then it really might as well cultivate the strangeness of biblical language without reflection, instead of translating it. Just because a specific language sounds strange to the general public, this does not necessarily prove that it has become hopelessly old-fashioned. It can also suggest resistance to its co-optation by that general public. Biblical language is resistant: protesting against the general regulation of language even in its own time, narrating an exceptional history that 'brushes history against the grain' (Benjamin).[6]

The question of whether the God of the Bible can be translated cannot be answered in general terms. In general, God can mean anything and nothing; the answer to the question of whether he exists or not can be positive or negative or agnostic, according to taste. The Bible's reference to God, though, is concrete. Criticism of religion that ignores this concreteness has missed the point from the very start. This is also true of Marxist criticism of religion. It explains religion as the deification of forces in nature or in history that humanity cannot conquer and hence feels dependent on, forces that make humans feel small and vulnerable. The God of the Bible, however, is not a natural force and he only takes effect in history as the injunction to deify whichever reality may be at issue at the time (be it emperor, Führer, Generalissimo, or Dalai Lama). He is the God of the ban on images, thus radically and fundamentally destroying religion,

---

4 The term 'internal currency' ['*Binnenwährung*'] was coined by Till Wilsdorf. With it, he tries to express the following: the language of the Bible has lost its universality entirely. This loss gives us the opportunity to learn to understand the peculiarities of this language again: 'All that is left is the labour of reading and obeying HIS (YHWH's) scripture, so a kind of Christian Pharisaism that is an act of political resistance' (Wilsdorf 1990, p. 33).

5 This is only a small community even within the Church, because the latter prefers other languages for its biblical theology than that of the liberation movement. This leads to the fact that within the Church, too, God as the deliverer from slavery is barely communicable.

6 Benjamin 2003, p. 392.

which, after all, consists of painting a picture of God.[7] Humans create gods for themselves, make gods of men, too. This God creates humans for himself and humanises them. Only the human is made in his likeness and yet this human should never want to be 'like God'. We are meant to believe him. This belief, however, doubles as the most radical disbelief of what the ruling powers want to lead us to believe is the ultimate truth. This God demands militant atheism, combatting everything that assumes the role of God. Atheism, with its assertion that God does not exist, is harmless. Gods exist in vast numbers. They exist today, even if they are not called gods: capital, the market, but also humanity *à la* Feuerbach, which raises itself above all critique and heedlessly enforces its idea of humanity. This demands practical atheism: these gods are objectionable and must be rejected.

There is also, however, a criticism of religion within the Marxist tradition that comes very close to what the Bible calls God. This is Marx's critique, which does not criticise religion in general, but very specifically that religion which is 'the sigh of the oppressed creature'.[8] Marx knows what he is talking about. It is indeed this 'sigh of the oppressed creature', which evokes a God who accommodates this creature's protestations against and who delivers it from this misery. But Marx, too, misconstrues the point of this deliverance at a crucial moment when he opposes 'the *other-world of truth*' with the injunction 'to establish the *truth of this world*'.[9] For the God of the Bible does not deliver from the world, but liberates a slave people to search for and find their salvation on earth. The movement he initiates knows only one direction: his will be done on earth as it is in heaven. Marx is right: 'the *task of history*, once the *other-world of truth* has vanished, is to establish the *truth of this world*'. This does not contradict the God of the Bible; it is, in fact, spoken in his spirit.

Marx cannot, however, reconcile deliverance as God's deed with the liberation movement as a demand to human action because his criticism of religion abstracts from the Bible precisely where thinking biblically matters most. Generally, it may well be the case that God's power means humanity's impotence, that God and humans are competitors, that the freedom of one precludes the liberation of the other (like the emperor's liberty precludes his subjects' liberation, the free market precludes the liberation of labour). In the Bible this is not

---

7 God takes masculine gender pronouns throughout this monograph, but it would be equally just to use the feminine gender: 'Take good care of your souls for you did not see a figure on the day the Lord spoke to you from the fires of Horeb, so do not condemn yourselves by making an image, be it *male* or *female*' (Dt 4:15–16).

8 Marx 1975b, p. 176.

9 Ibid.

the case. Here, there is no God *per se* whose nature may be embellished at pleasure with everything the human mind might associate with the word 'God'. This is not the God of metaphysics, who takes pleasure in his abstract absoluteness beyond the material world. What the Bible calls 'God' is defined by a name that is fundamentally distinct from everything that might elsewhere be called 'God'. This name is: I will be there, as he who I will be there (Ex 3:14). The *'as he who I will be there'* is crucial. Through it, we are invited to follow the narrative that has him be present as a God who does not want to be *per se* from end to end, but who wants to be with his people. A God for whom the 'with' is so crucial, he does not even *want* to be God without this people. The delivery from slavery initiated by him is a communal enterprise and its success is not only dependent on him. It is *hence* (indeed, Marx!) the historical task of the people to establish the 'truth of this world'. And the Bible tells us: the people set out from bondage, enter the land where they are meant to organise the Kingdom of Freedom, lose their way (abandon their God), convert (find their way back to their God, who lets himself be found). God only appears in *this* (hi)story: as the companion of, or as he who himself abandons the people because they have lost their way, but who in the end cannot bring himself to leave them to their fate, precisely because he *cannot* be God without his people. We might say this God is taken up with his people, he lives in his people, he would no longer be alive without his people. Nevertheless, he remains their critical counterpart, stands in opposition to his people as the 'eternal' demand to do Torah – until the day when all tears have been dried, death is no longer, drudgery has ended (Rv 21: 4).

Even as a critical counterpart, however, he does not exist *per se*, independently of his people, as a regulatory idea that is true one way or another. It all depends on the people *acknowledging* him. You are our God. This avowal alone imbues his being-God with truth, only through the avowal of faith. And avowal means prayer: hallowed be your name, your kingdom come, your will be done, on earth as it is in heaven. This is not the expression of wishful thinking whose fulfilment is left up to the addressee of the prayer. He who prays is engaged: I, too, promise to hallow your name; I, too, accept responsibility for ensuring that your kingdom come; I, too, will do all that I can so that your will be done on earth. Not you alone, God, I too. Prayer is not purely about God, just as it is not purely about humans – humans do not pray without reason – but about the convergence of God and humans in the collaborative project that is the delivery from slavery.

It is not as simple as all that then, to declare their incompatibility. The language of the delivery from slavery starts with 'I am YHWH, your God', and the language of experience starts with 'delivery from misery can only be achieved by us ourselves'. For this God never exists *per se* but only through his effects.

And the effect par excellence is the creation of humanity in his likeness, the creation of a people that is liberated by liberating itself: God sends it forth and it issues forth, the one is impossible without the other. But even more than that, God's actions are constituted in the actions of this people. Let us imagine this people in today's world: resistant, militantly atheist, unbelieving. Biblical theology should not somehow try to locate the God of the Bible in a religious consciousness. Not because the era of religion has passed, but because biblical theology cannot represent its language in the language of religion. Biblical theology needs to talk straight. God's people today would say what they learned in their Egyptian bondage: no highest Being, no god, no pharaoh will save us. God's people today would also have to learn not to be misguided by the religion of the market with its illusory promises of happiness. Just as back then they heard the Torah as the command, 'you shall have no gods before me, your deliverer', today they should demand '[t]he abolition of religion as the illusory happiness of the people' and hear the Torah as the 'call on them to give up their illusions about their condition', which essentially means 'to give up a condition that requires illusions'.[10] Biblical theology needs this language – of the Internationale, of Marxist critique of religion, of modern liberation movements in general – especially when establishing what the God of the Bible effects.

5

But does this language also need the word 'God'? The religious socialists thought it did, and their translation work included driving it home to their comrades in the labour movement – just like they strove to show their fellow Christians that a Christian has to be a socialist. The great theoretician of religious socialism, Leonhard Ragaz, pithily articulated this movement: from Christ to Marx – from Marx to Christ.[11] Can a Marxist's movement towards Christ be turned into a political programme, though? If a person does not need the word 'God' in order to follow the Torah's commandments, who are we to reproach them for that absence? Action, after all, is key; theory (theology) is nothing if not a theory of practice. The Apostle Paul, by contrast, succinctly remarked: When people, who have no Torah, practice what the Torah commands of their own accord, they are the Torah unto themselves (Rom 2:14). It does not, however, follow that we should conceive the language of the modern

---

10   Ibid.
11   Ragaz 1972.

liberation movement in overly simple or one-dimensional terms. As though it were exhausted by analyses and instructions, invokes continual agency, suppresses all despair, believes in nothing but a science that has solved all problems, sees only tasks und refuses to acknowledge the extent to which the successful completion of the tasks depends on whether we are also *given* scope for action. Perhaps it is a typically Christian (even leftist Christian) type of arrogance to think that only we know the highs and lows of human existence, that only we know something that renders the courage to live indestructible, that only we have faith which cannot be shaken by anything (not even the negating nothingness). Does Walter Benjamin transcend the language of Marxism when he writes that 'like every generation that preceded us, we have been endowed with a *weak* messianic power'?[12] Was he not actually intent on adding to this language? And did not the Berlin communist, who prior to his execution exclaimed 'Nobody can touch me!',[13] profess *his* faith? Is it not an insult not to believe his profession of faith, to co-opt him as an 'anonymous Christian'?

There remains, however, a 'residue' that cannot be translated. The God who ensures that humans take their delivery from slavery into their own hands can be appealed to, prayed to, screamed at. God is not just the critical counterpart conceived by humans in order to imbue their revolution with permanence, in order never to be satisfied with current achievements, in order always to attend to the (hence 'eternal') demand to fulfil the Torah. Those who are affected by him cannot settle for the idea that he simply stands across from us. They hope that he advances towards our movement. They pray: Our Father, your kingdom come. They despair when this cannot be felt. And they cry out: my Lord, my Lord, why have you abandoned me? Is not this cry precisely where the two languages rediscover one another, though? Do people for whom the biblical talk of God remains alien need a translation when they hear Jesus's cry, just because he twice cries 'Lord'? Do they hear the voice of a human, who believes in something they, by contrast, simply cannot believe? Or is it, after all, the easily recognisable sigh of the oppressed creature, which is so familiar to them it might be their own?

6

But has the language of the message really found a language to express its currency in the modern liberation movement? Its biggest project, socialism,

---

12   Benjamin 2003, p. 390.

13   I do not remember where I read this communist avowal of faith.

has itself been overtaken by history, after all. Its language has itself turned into a foreign language, a language from the past, which today's generation simply cannot understand. However, I have not been able to find a language that can express the same things, only in a different way. To my mind, the dominant language regime is too much in keeping with the market to be able to operate as a critique of the market economy. A (conceptual) movement that transcends this economic order cannot be expressed with this language. The issues brought about by the attempt to organise a regime of liberation can only encounter incomprehension in this language. The interlinking of freedom and the market to the point at which they become indistinguishable is so subconscious to this language that any alternative can only be declared and vilified as bondage. What this language calls 'the Free World' appears to have become a carbon copy of the Kingdom of Freedom.

Hence, to my mind at least, biblical theology's work of translation remains dependent on a language that is itself now 'outmoded'. All it can do is 'preserve' this language, like that of the Bible, in the hope that its time will come again. And this could be the time when the Bible gains currency again (the spirit blows, where it wants). This language, though it is 'outdated', is at the height of the times: it draws attention to the scandalous discrepancy between that which is technically and organisationally possible – a world in which no human has to live an inhumane life – and what society makes of that possibility.[14] This insight gives the perspective of a delivery from slavery a tremendous uplift: a different world is really possible! It is crucial to seize this opportunity. Here, biblical theology finds the appropriate actualisation of its concrete utopia.

7

By now the fact that the Bible cannot be read while side-lining Jews has begun to permeate Christian consciousness. Jews must be taken seriously as autonomous and authoritative readers of their Holy Scripture. They must be taken seriously above all as a people who are bound to the biblical people of Israel in very special ways: their descendants, their continuation in the synagogue, 'accord-

---

14   Coolly but trenchantly, Karl Marx called this the conflict between the material forces of production and the existing relations of production (Marx 1987, p. 263). Peachum, the king of the beggars in Brecht's *Threepenny Opera*, declared (Bible in hand!): 'Let's practise goodness: who would disagree? | But sadly in this planet while we're waiting | The means are meagre and the morals low | To get one's record straight would be elating | But our condition's such it can't be so' (Brecht 1979, p. 33).

ing to the flesh', as Paul says (Rom 9:3–4)[15] – and he uses the word 'Israel' only with reference to the Jews. We, who are not Israel, can only walk alongside, never pass by, let alone replace them as the 'true Israel'. Any biblical theology, thus every theology of liberation that thinks it can afford a fundamental 'anti' has missed its own point: the persistent relation of solidarity between God and his Israel, a relation of solidarity that Israel, too, never abandoned in the face of its God.

Those who think the appellation of the Liberator-God as 'God of Israel' is mere metaphor must ask themselves: where are we 'leftist Christians' left if we reject the Jews because their materially existent liberation movement has been so disappointingly unsuccessful, not least because they betrayed themselves? Are we so a-historical, then, as to think liberation without disappointment is possible? Is not our rejection of the Jews the historical proof of how disappointingly little the 'Christian' liberation movement has achieved? Just how radically it, in particular, lost its way? Without the Jews, something essential is missing. If they are absent, our talk of liberation becomes questionable in its foundation in the material world. Is it doomed to remain an abstraction? And when we argue that the foundation is not to be found in the material world but in the resistance to that world, then the Jews precede us in this protest, too, in their stubborn, downright obstinate, insistence on the avowal: Hear, Israel, YHWH, our God, YHWH is one and only.

The Jews, though, are not only a 'negative' absence, an admonition not to reject the materially existent liberation movement and not to hope for something beyond it. They also have a positive message for us. While writing this biblical theology Judaism's voice increasingly impressed itself on me as the radical adherence to the correlation of God and human, of the God of Israel and his people. In particular the Protestant church read this as 'works righteousness', a 'self-justification' that derogated from the *sola gratia*, the 'through mercy alone' and hence obscured the exceptionality of this God, this most deeply merciful God.

Is not Judaism's serious practice in response to the mercy bestowed on its people by God, when he allows them to be his people, loyalty to him? Is it self-justification, or is it the opposite: a justification of God manifest in the perseverance of their loyalty to him even when he has broken with them? Is it not Jesus, the Jew, who maintains the correlation through his absolute abandonment by God? Did not the church, which professes him as Christ, relax his project too much when it began to understand his 'It has been

---

15   'Flesh' is the biblical term for 'material'.

done' (Jn 19:30) as a perfect moment, a completed fact? And when it didn't catch the fact that this 'completed' solidarity between God and his people can only be accomplished where it inspires the continuation of the correlation he practices?[16]

This biblical theology could be called 'Jewish'. Except for the fact that I am not Jewish and I do not wish to become Jewish – although I know that that is possible and that the synagogue would be open to this option. I have two reasons. First, it would be impertinent to take up this option: becoming Jewish, for me, would mean a willingness to share their passion. I am not so bold as to claim that for myself. Second, however, I also cannot disavow the Jew Paul, who recognised the 'novelty' constituted by Jews and Goy (non-Jews) coming together in a messianic community without the Goy's messianists turning into Jews, i.e. letting themselves be circumcised.[17] I am well aware that this 'novelty' has been falsified by the church. Nevertheless, I cannot surrender its utopian implications in the spirit of the Torah, and I hope in the spirit of Judaism.

8

The Torah constitutes the core of this biblical theology (chapters three to seven). This is intended less as a restriction than as a concentration on the 'constitution' of the Bible as a whole. It already contains everything that humans require to be biblically articulated in order to know what they can believe, how they should act, and what they may hope for.[18] The Torah is the 'Law' of the project 'Israel', which the God of Israel initiated with his people and which the people are beholden to implement. All subsequent books detail this implementation: how the real Israel attempts to realise a just society without lords

---

16   Ton Veerkamp translates *tetelestai*, which rings with the word *telos* (goal), as: 'the goal has been achieved', and the immediately following *paredoken to pneuma* as: 'he handed over the inspiration'. And remarks: 'The goal of solidarity is realised through death. The realisation of the goal is the handing over of inspiration' (Veerkamp 2007, p. 150).

17   I could also have written that Jews and Goy come together in a *Christian* community, without the *Christian* Goy having to become Jews. For *christos* is the Greek translation of the Hebrew *maschiach* (the anointed one). However, ever since the instantiation of a Christian Church, which no longer is, nor wants to be, the community of Jews and Goy, this Greek word and its derivations have been charged with anti-Jewish ideology to such a degree that it has become useless as a translation of Pauline Messianism.

18   'It is well understood that the gospels did not introduce anything new with respect to what is "other". Without exception, the Torah's structures are the prerequisites of the Kerygma, the Christian message' (Miskotte 1983, p. 385).

and slaves; how it fails and betrays ('sins against') the project; its rare victories and many defeats; the voices of the prophets which are audible time and again and which call for repentance, and speak of the promise that God, too, will return to his people. The real Israel is the topic of Chapter 8. That chapter's biblical foundation is the so-called 'first' (Joshua, Judges, 1 and 2 Samuel, 1 and 2 Kings) and 'second' prophets (Isaiah, Jeremiah, Ezekiel, and the Twelve Minor Prophets[19]).[20] The third part of the Bible (next to Torah and Prophets), the Writings,[21] will not be specifically discussed in the present biblical theology, but they are cited on occasion. This is insufficient, I know. These Writings have their own function, absolutely distinct from Torah and Prophets: to comment on and to criticise Torah and Prophets, but also to praise the God who gave them Torah and Prophets, to pester him with the lamentation of his absence, to cry for revenge, to express scepticism towards mastering the everyday with the help of maxims. Here, I have limited myself to the main issue: Torah and Prophets stand in for the whole, which the Writings presuppose and to which they also 'subordinate' themselves.[22] This subordination is not slavish, though, but on occasion quite candid: a 'critique within the Bible'.[23]

According to the gospels and the messianic community's tracts, too, 'Torah and Prophets' make up the 'whole Scripture' (Lk 24:27) which Jesus said he had not come to dispel, but to fulfil in the way that all Jews are charged with fulfilling it (Mt 5:17). The messianic community shares this Scripture with the synagogue; it quarrels about this Scripture with the synagogue, specifically whether Jesus really did fulfil Torah and Prophets or whether, in the end, he dispelled them. This is a question which can only be resolved in practice, through the practice of this community, its messianic actuality. The voices from

---

19 Hosea, Joel, Amos, Obadiah, Jonah, Micah, Nahum, Habakkuk, Zephaniah, Haggai, Zechariah, Malachi.

20 The common terms are 'former' and 'latter' prophets. However, these terms suggest that the books Joshua–2 Kings were written earlier than Isaiah–Malachi, which is not the case.

21 Psalms, Proverbs, Job, Song of Songs, Ruth, Lamentations, Ecclesiastes, Esther, Daniel, Ezra, Nehemiah, 1 and 2 Chronicles.

22 'The *praise* of Psalms, the *lamentation* of Job, the *scepticism* of Ecclesiastes are ... not just any praise, not some all too familiar lamentation, not an easily comprehensible scepticism. It is the praise of him, who may believe in and follow the Torah, it is the lamentation of him, for whom [the Torah's] promise has been destroyed, it is that man's scepticism, who has seen the *Torah's* light fade and vanish' (Miskotte 1966, p. 148).

23 This is the subtitle of Klara Butting's groundbreaking study of the hermeneutics of the 'scriptures' (Butting 1994).

the messianic community that have been written down are not Scripture; they are *after* Scripture, '*post* script'. The temporality of after Scripture means the witnessing of an event which, according to Scripture, has not yet occurred. It also means normatively: scripturally, as *its* 'not yet', as the fulfilment of *its* promise.

Hence, in the present biblical theology, Torah and Prophets is followed by two postscripts. The first examines Paul and the messianic community. The second offers a reading of the image of the crucified Jesus. The fact that Paul and his idea of community precede Jesus in my discussion is not a chronological matter. Although Paul's letters are older than the gospels, which tell the story of Jesus's life, it is evident that for Paul the life of Jesus is constitutive of the novelty he is testifying. The canon of the New Testament determines this: the story of Jesus the Messiah as the prerequisite for the messianic community – first the gospels, then the letters. Paul, however, is the theoretician of practice without which the life of Jesus is suspended in mid-air, as it were. In the community of Jews and Goy who avow the crucified Jesus as the Jew who did Torah until the end and thus fulfilled the Torah, Paul witnesses the novelty of the rising of the crucified. This is why Paul takes precedence in this biblical theology: so that there is no mistaking that Jesus, like his Lord, exists through his effect: Christ existing as church community.[24] It is this community that hands down the gospels so that the life of Jesus is preserved as an inspiration until the world's end.

Chapters 1 and 2 are concerned with the necessary preliminaries to a content-driven account of biblical theology (prolegomena): context and God's word as an intervention in that context (Chapter 1) and the canon as a guideline for the Bible's logic (Chapter 2).

9

The language of the Bible is not only strange, though, it is also offensive. What can we make of its indisputable violence? The God of Israel is a violent God, who displaces other peoples in order to make room for his own people. And his people are violent when – in the name of their God! – they 'ban' their enemies, which means exterminating everything that lives there: 'from man to woman, from the very young to the very old, to oxen and lambs and donkeys' (Jo 6:21). Is this not a genocidal sermon? Is this not biblical propaganda for

---

24   Bonhoeffer 1998, p. 191.

terrorism dressed up as religion? Are not those proven to be right, who remark that the God of the Old Testament is vengeful and aggressive, cannot possibly be reconciled with the God of Love from the New Testament? Do we not have to simply reject these violations in order to recuperate God as Saviour?

Before we do that, though, we have to consider what that Bible is asking us to consider: there is no space for a people such as Israel in the world as it is. In this world, the project 'Israel' is entirely utopian – there is no topos, no location, where a real Israel can take place. The peoples with which the people of Israel have dealings are also bent on forcibly preventing a real Israel. Can we imagine, here, that criticism suffices as a weapon and a critique of weapons is unnecessary?[25] The Bible cannot imagine it.[26] The exodus itself is already a violent act, which costs the entire Egyptian army, in pursuit of Israel, their lives. The land, where the realm of liberty is to be instituted, has to be conquered. And the people remain a constant, enormous threat – not only militarily, by the way, but also ideologically. Confronted with the strength of these peoples, Israel despairs about the purpose of its project again and again, is threatened again and again with relapsing into the fatalist maxim of the peoples ('hoping for deliverance is futile'). It would be a fundamental misunderstanding to think we are faced with a major power's imperialism, whose need for lebensraum is limitless and who must therefore conquer the entire world ('today Germany is ours, and tomorrow the entire world').[27] Equally, it is a complete misunderstanding to think that this people's violence is terrorism: destroy what destroys you. Its violence most certainly has a limit, which is to gain only as much space as is required to construct the new society. The fact that the violence pushes the boundaries in the narrative of the conquering of land does not contradict this salutary limitation. The extraordinarily violent language is 'mythical': it describes the absoluteness of the confrontation between Israel and the peoples, between YHWH – he is the only God – and the gods. There is nothing in between the realm of liberty and the house of bondage (no *social* market economy).[28] Israel must consider this absolute opposition in its attempts to actualise utopia in its location. This opposition is constitutive of its identity. Israel must always

---

25   Marx 1975b, p. 182.

26   Those who think the New Testament is exclusively affectionate should read Rv 19: 13–15 where Is 63:6 is quoted in support ('I [God] trample peoples in my wrath, in my anger I have shattered them, their juice I let flow to the earth').

27   Though common, this is a misquotation of what really reads: 'Germany hears us today, tomorrow the entire world'.

28   At best, we can speak of 'historical compromise', which might have to be reached as the lesser evil at the time, but nevertheless remains an *evil*.

pledge itself to this opposition, despite the fact that it is ultimately characterised by its *Aufhebung* [sublation]. The fulfilment of the project 'Israel' will not
be a 'final victory' that conclusively kills all other peoples.

And yet: can this realisation reassure us? It does not reassure me. The
horror at the degree to which the delivery from slavery is tied up in a myth of
violence remains the same. The tension between the hardships of the struggle
for freedom and the promised shalom is unbearable, even though I know that
the violence of the oppressed is only the reaction to the fact that they are
not granted freedom. And this tension should be unbearable. We can never
allow ourselves to become inured to violence. It has to be clear: violence is
only permitted in extreme circumstances – no, it is never permitted, but forced.
Even where this violence leads to victory, that victory is a defeat. Yes, it might
well be true that the only way of breaking down tyranny is to forego violence.
And we will keep out of the violence between the ruling echelons anyway. Their
wars are not our wars.

Judaism knew that the festival of the delivery from slavery, Pesach, in particular cannot
be celebrated without commemorating the defeated enemy. Why do the instructions
for Pesach, in distinction to those for other holidays, not include the call to *rejoice*?
The answer is as follows: 'Because that season of the year was a time of death for many
Egyptians. Thus indeed is our practice: All seven days of Sukkot [Feast of Tabernacles]
we recite the prayer of Hallel [joyous praise of the Lord] but on Pesach we recite the
prayer of Hallel in its entirety only on the first day. Why? Because of the verse: "Do not
rejoice in the fall of your enemy, and let not your heart be glad when he stumbles" (Prv
24:17)'.[29] There is also a Haggadah which recounts that the angels began to sing in praise
as the people of Israel made their way towards freedom through the Sea of Reeds while
the Egyptian army drowned. But God interrupted them and said: How can you sing my
praises while my creatures drown?

Liberation may be celebrated self-consciously only, with great sadness for the
defeated, until it encompasses all and the delivery from slavery is complete.

This by way of introduction. Everything else follows in the chapters.

---

29   Hertzberg 1961, p. 126.

Text and Context

Like all human activity, theology is contextual. The theologian's ideas do not fall from the sky (Casalis).[1] The theologian, too, like all human beings, is situated in a given reality, born and raised in a specific place at a specific time – allowed to grow up or infantilised, bourgeois or labourer's wife, white boss or black slave, hetero- or homosexual: these are all different worlds. Reality, however, is slightly more complicated still than the determinacy of the words used to express it. Some bourgeois are kept small, labourer's wives gain influence despite their oppression, the white boss loses his balance, the heterosexual comes out as gay, the gay man is also a white boss. And so on and so forth: life, the saying goes (and it is true), is a complicated matter.

Theology, then, is contextual – this is self-evident. What, however, is the point of this observation? Is it enlightening, so that we can see more clearly what theology is all about? What does 'enlightening' even mean, though? Is it ever more than a simplification? Is it not the Enlightenment – man's emergence from his immaturity (Kant)[2] – that provides the most convincing proof that complexity is simplified into 'survival of the fittest'?[3] Does the primacy of reality offer anything other than the observation that 'survival of the fittest', the right to dominate, is as old as humanity itself? Is it not all, despite seeming extremely complicated, basically very simple: the *condition humaine* a constant struggle for executive control?

There is something in humans, though, that resists this. It cannot truly be the end all of historical wisdom: that the vast majority of humans live, only to have to discover that this life is no (worthy) life, that the deepest insight is the realisation that reality is terribly complex – too complex ever to be released from its ties.

---

1 Casalis 1980. His title 'cites' Mao Tse-tung: 'Where do correct ideas come from? Do they fall from the heavens? No. Are they innate in the mind? No. They come from social practice and from it alone'.

2 This was Kant's reply to the question 'What Is Enlightenment?': 'Enlightenment is man's emergence from self-incurred immaturity' (Kant 2009, p. 1).

3 'The system's principles are those of self-preservation. Immaturity amounts to the inability to survive. The bourgeois in the successive forms of the slave-owner, the free entrepreneur and the administrator is the logical subject of enlightenment' (Adorno and Horkheimer 2002, p. 65).

Reality and Resistance

This 'something' that resists is real, too: so long as there is a dominant order, there is also resistance, its opposite. True, thus far, this resistance has been broken again and again – by the force of the dominant order, from without us, from within us. But it is also true that resistance is raised again and again. Until it is broken once and for all? Who can know? Resistance itself is not without hope that the way things have been will not remain the same forever.

And resistance leads to recognition. This recognition offers no insight into the essence of reality, it does not enable a system in which everything is made knowable. It does, however, enable us to recognise the 'logic' by which capital exploits labourers, for instance. The experience of exploitation is enlightened by a 'critique of political economy'.[4] Not *the* reality, but certainly a determining dimension of reality, which determines the lives of masses of people, is made visible as the 'capitalist mode of production'. Capital is produced by the labour power of those who have nothing else to sell. Resistance gains not only hands and feet, but also the possibility of sensibly moving these hands and feet.

There are, however, also other dimensions of reality that make life difficult for people, and there are also other theories that enable a person to recognise what is going on so that the game can then be played to their own benefit. There are the experiences women have with men, gays have with heterosexuals – shameful experiences that elicit resistance. Here, an analysis that reveals the dominant 'order' as the source (the ur-thing) of this experience is helpful. Psychoanalysis, for instance, reveals the order of sexuality, which is people's organisation according to their sex-characteristics. This order identifies (or sexes) people as men above and women below. Such an order declares people who cannot be classified – gay men and lesbians – as 'out of order', or forces them to integrate themselves into this order as homo-*sexually* inclined.

The experience of people who are pinned down to a specific 'race' or a specific ethnicity or tribe, and are hence defined either as sub-human or as positively super-humanly clever and cunning, but always as an object of abjection, also leads to recognition. The depth of this abjection is made visible, as well as the depth of the victims' tendency to put up with their own objectification.[5]

---

4 This is the subtitle of Marx's *Capital*. 'Political economy' basically means the (bourgeois) study of political economy. Marx's concern, hence, is to fundamentally criticise it.

5 *Black Skin, White Masks* (1952), the title of a book by black psychiatrist and revolutionary Frantz Fanon, is programmatic here: 'Willy-nilly, the Negro has to wear the livery that the white man has sewed for him' (Fanon 1968, p. 34).

Recognising this intensifies resistance: it is good to know how difficult it is, because if it is taken lightly it will also be abandoned easily!

There is yet another dimension of reality, though, that can prompt resistance: nature, as it surrounds and carries us. This resistance is directed not against what people do to each other, but against what they do to the condition of their entire existence: nature's destruction is the end of humanity. If reality's primacy is recognisable anywhere, then it is here. Feuerbach had already recognised this when he wrote both '[t]hat he *is man*, he has to thank *man*', and the preface to this indispensable humanist statement: 'That he *is*, he has to thank *nature*'.[6] A civilisation's discontent (Freud) is short-sighted if it overlooks nature. True, *social* being determines consciousness: something within us bristles at what society does to us, and this something stirs a spirit of resistance. This truth, however, is untrue if we neglect to remember that social being cannot be without the *being*. If we refuse to acknowledge this materialist principle, then we will come to feel its truth. It is insufficient, though, to simply let this stand as an abstract threat. What is needed is an environmental theory that is critical of society, though not concerned with nature *per se*, but with nature as given to us to shape in a sustainable way – as a dimension of social practice. Nature has been turning into a cultural issue for human history. For social practice thus far, this has meant the frequently systematic over-exploitation of nature. Preserving nature cannot be achieved without a shift away from social relations that lead to over-exploitation.

Experience and Insight

The experiences that lead to resistance are manifold, as are the theories engendered by these experiences. There is no *one*, all-encompassing theory, at least not a liberating one: grasping everything with one term is the opposite of liberating. If, however, we say (in postmodern fashion) that reality is so complex that there can only be a plurality of theories that bear no relation to each other, then thought falls short. Complex (from the Latin *complicare* = fold *together*) does not mean side by side, but intertwined. The fact that the man who suffers from the exploitation by capital cannot see the woman's suffering, which he (though not he alone) causes, is a knotty issue. Another knotty issue is the fact that black women (have to) tell white women that their oppression is different and neither grasped nor included in their white sisters' resistance. The coincid-

---

6   Feuerbach 1989, p. 83.

ence of the worry about nature's defilement with the indifference towards the violation of human rights is also a complicated issue. These and other 'entanglements' have to be taken into consideration, in their relations. The different theories are connected to one another; their relation is not a question of tolerance, because the topics they 'address' intersect. Who is beyond the social relations on which Marxist analysis focuses? Who is unaffected by the order of sexuality, the concern of psychoanalysis? Who is entirely immune to racism? Who can claim that nature does not affect them?

Merely remarking that the theories intersect is not going far enough, though. They can also work as ancillary disciplines. Psychoanalysis helps Marxist social analysis to understand that a relation of domination and subordination is consolidated through sexuality before people are even aware of it. Hence, they are 'always already' (Althusser) positioned as rulers and subjects in the field of a capitalist social order. Vice versa, Marxist social analysis helps psychoanalysis recognise that the order of sexuality transmits a disposition (of domination and subordination) that plays into the hands of capitalist society, which is then also continuously reproduced by capitalist society. This is why a revolution will never be able to limit itself to *one* dimension of reality. Revolution concerns *all* of reality; it is the revolutionising of the *whole*: 'to overthrow *all* relations in which man is a debased, enslaved, forsaken, despicable being'.[7]

The different experiences are not necessarily alien to each other, either. The first-hand experience of capitalism can open a person's eyes to the effects of sexism on another person; it can even open a person's eyes to the ways in which sexism affects them themselves. Somebody who knows – not in theory, but from experience – what sexism is, can lend an open ear to the narratives of victims of racism. And when someone who is concerned about the environment deploys the language of the *exploitation* of nature, or speaks of the *exhaustion* of natural resources, then this can lead to a concern for exploited and exhausted human beings. The interlocking of theories can reinforce this potential linkage of experiences; it can contribute to building ties, coalitions, and alliances.

Theology and Biblical Tradition

There is something within the human that resists exploitation, oppression, and discrimination. But what does that have to do with theology (apart from the fact

---

7   Marx 1975b, p. 182. This is the 'categorical imperative', which for Marx constitutes the end, i.e. the climax, of the critique of religion.

that social being also determines theology's consciousness, whether it likes it or not)? Is there a particular reason that forces theology to get involved specifically in this something that resists? What might cause theology to align itself with this resistance when it is a part of its general context anyway? Indeed, there is a reason: it is the text that occasioned this present theology in the first place. This text, or this collection of texts, is the Bible.

The theology in question is not a theology that worries about the (im)possibility of speaking of God in general. The theology in question is engaged, from the outset, in the propagation of a definitive, that is biblical, God. And no matter how utopian the object of its considerations may be – where is this God apart from in the text? – this theology is not without 'topos', without place. Its place is the community, whose critical theory it represents.

By speaking in this fashion, we are not following the path of ideas falling from heaven. The Bible is part of the given reality. The Bible also numbers amongst all the possible factors that humans 'construct' or destroy. We should not generalise this fact – the Bible does not speak, or no longer speaks, to the vast majority of people. But not taking the Bible seriously as a factor – among others! – would mean withholding something from ourselves.

Many people will describe their negative relationship with the Bible in other terms even than, 'It (no longer) has anything to say to me'. For them, the Bible has become a pointless book because it presupposes a worldview that is entirely anachronistic and hence unreasonable to the modern person. Or even worse: the Bible is an ethically questionable book because it propagates a moral that is below the dignity of the (modern) person. And this takes a particular shape (serving God) which prevents people from taking responsibility for their own destiny. Nor should we forget those people who were taught mores by wielding the Bible as a conclusive argument. In that case, the Bible hopefully really does have nothing more to say to them.

However, it is questionable whether they really were being taught the Bible. In all likelihood, this was not the case; though that can hardly be remedied now either. The time of a Christian culture, which albeit fundamentally misunderstanding it, is still at least familiar with the language of the Bible, is over. This has made it impossible to introduce the biblical message as 'a combination of thinking and active intervention' (Brecht).[8] The fact that the Bible does speak to others – speaks of something

---

8 'It [Marxism] teaches a combination of thinking and active intervention as a means of dealing with reality in so far as social intervention is able to deal with it. It is a doctrine that criticizes human action and expects in turn to be criticized by it' (Brecht 1965, p. 36).

extraordinarily liberating – is a coincidence. They got lucky. Or should we say: they experienced mercy?

The Bible is a factor, it 'effects' something. It is this factor that determines the contextuality of theology. The Bible pronounces: Delivery from slavery. It thus obliges theology to partiality: to be a partisan of slaves. As *biblical* theology, theology has to take their side – by definition. Theology is hence forced, not by coincidence but by this precariousness, to search for an analysis of reality that will provide insights and then perhaps also exit routes to those people who suffer from this reality. Hence it will gratefully make use of the existing analyses, such as Marxist theory and psychoanalysis, which trace the mechanisms of oppression.

And the theologian is not a free-floating intellectual, though hopefully free enough to be truly partisan. In other words, she is an 'organic intellectual' (Gramsci),[9] bound to the party of those who rely on resistance.

The likelihood that the theologian turns into such an 'organic intellectual' from his own position in society is rather slim. However, the text to which he has bound himself moves him toward 'class betrayal'. Biblical theology itself is unthinkable without class betrayal: the God of whom it speaks betrays the 'class' of gods by turning to face a slave people; his 'servant' Moses, adopted by the pharaoh's daughter, betrays the 'class' of his Egyptian court in order to lead the slave people into the Kingdom of Freedom. A crucial aspect of Moses's class betrayal is the fact that he 'sets out' towards these slaves and *sees* their forced labour (Ex 2:11) (and immediately after he *sees* the murder of a slave by an Egyptian and kills the latter). The story narrates how Moses came to his *brothers*, suggesting that he already knew that he was dealing with his brothers. But how could he have known that these slaves were his brothers? Does it not have to have been this 'seeing' of their misery that moved him?

Does this party also exist? That something in a person that resists is nowhere near organised resistance. It is questionable whether it will ever amount to a resistance movement. The 'organic intellectual' is not infrequently a crier in the desert. Often, he does not encounter any movement and more likely feels called to found, or at least to argue in favour of, such a movement. In any case, a certain loneliness is part of theological existence.

---

9 'Every social group, coming into existence on the original terrain of an essential function in the world of economic production, creates together with itself, organically, one or more strata of intellectuals which give it homogeneity and an awareness of its own function not only in the economic but also in the social and political fields' (Gramsci, 1971, p. 5).

This loneliness can grow into narcissistic self-pity. Hopefully, somebody will then be present to point this out: You are not as alone as all that, seven thousand more are left who did not bow before Baal (1 Kgs 19:18).

The God of the Bible

The Bible not only obliges, it also points to a factor that means that we are not entirely alone. This factor is called 'YHWH', he is God.[10] He is not a common god, who drums the futility of resistance into the people, but a God who accommodates this resistance. He is a God who delivers from slavery a people who do not know where to turn in their yearning for liberation. He is a God who awakens these people to rise, who turns them into his people, who then embody the freedom he has been given. In this respect, the biblical narrative really does 'found' a resistance movement and the theologian does not have to shamefacedly conceal the fact that he has reasons for being 'edifying'. That is his profession, her calling.

God. This word says too little for it to be used without much thought. It can mean everything or nothing. Generally speaking, it indicates a superior power that forces humanity to its knees: a power that oppresses people, presses down on them. In this specific case of the biblical God, however, it is a power that leads the oppressed on to a path towards a world in which life is simply good. This power, according to the Bible, is God; nobody else deserves this name. But what do we mean by *name* here? God is not a name, but a function: that which functions as the 'highest Being'. The decisive question is hence *who* or *what* performs this function? According to the Bible, it is the power that liberates, and this power is not anonymous but has a name, a name which says: 'I will be there, as he who I will be there' (Ex 3:14),[11] that is as the deliverer from slavery. Through this name, this self-designation, this God can be addressed, and he can be taken at his word.

---

10 In Hebrew, YHWH form the four letters of the name of God (the so-called tetragrammaton = the four-lettered). This name is never articulated, but circumscribed with the word 'adonaj' ('Lord') (sometimes capitalised in translations to signify that what is meant is the name of God). In order to avoid the all too imperious resonances of 'Lord', I use the tetragrammaton itself, YHWH, in my text. Another possibility is to use the capitalised word NAME.

11 A play on words with the letters Y,H,W,H.

Does this God of whom the Bible speaks not really fall from heaven? Yes, that is how it is, literally – according to the words of the Bible. Here, however, 'from heaven' signifies the opposite of a flight into the world of ideas. This *from* is the beginning of a movement 'from above' which is continued in a movement 'from below'. The spirit of these letters is turned into a material force within a particular history that writes history within general history.

Theology is both factually and in principle contextual. It is factually contextual in as much as it is determined in every respect by the reality in which it finds itself. It is contextual in principle because this special factor God commands that it take on the purpose of the commanded possibility to overcome the hitherto existing order in which one person lives at the cost of another.

Theology knows that reality is endlessly complex. This is why it will be wary of falling for the dangerous illusion that we will ever gain complete control over reality. We will notice when the time has come when everything is truly in order, when the exploitation of humans by humans and the exploitation of the environment have ended. Then we will realise that this order has nothing to do with an order of the *Übermensch* who has overcome the limitations of the *condition humaine*. Nietzsche's *Übermensch*, who declared, 'The human is something that shall be overcome', is the exact opposite of the new human we hope for.[12] Precisely the limitation of the human – the fact that he cannot do everything, is not a god – will then emerge as 'all right'.

Analysis offers insights and escapes, no more. Resistance creates space, and that means, it leaves space. The God who liberates us also liberates us from the fatal thought of 'wanting to be like God' (Gn 3:5). The fact that we can only exist in context, is in principle and ultimately *very good*, as announced in the story of creation (Gn 1:31). And the theologian who has been distracted from the fatal thoughts that suggest the opposite, repeats it. In doing so, nothing human is strange to him. This is why theology is often quite a miserable affair. And yet: *nothing* human is strange to him! This also means: 'something' within him resists the notion that theology's misery should be all there is. This something holds on to him, renders him sensitive to the word which delivers from this misery. Theology is claimed by this word.

---

12   'I teach you the Overhuman [*Übermensch*]. The human is something that shall be overcome' (Nietzsche 2005, p. 11). There is another way of reading Nietzsche, though: the *Übermensch* is the still unknown, not yet arrived humanity which 'overcomes' the inhumanity of the real human (as Bonhoeffer read him: 'Indeed, Nietzsche's *übermensch* is not, as he imagined, the opposite of the Christian, without realizing it, Nietzsche imbued the *übermensch* with many of the features of the free Christian as described and conceived by both Paul and Luther') (Bonhoeffer 2008, p. 367).

The Field of Ideology

The Bible brings about people's belief: belief in the possibility that the world will turn into a 'kingdom' in which freedom and justice kiss each other'(Ps 85:11), belief in their own power to contribute to the institution of freedom and justice. The Bible achieves this by telling stories intended to be believed.

This means that the Bible is part of the field of *ideology*. One could also say it is part of the field of 'images': the word ideology is rooted in the Greek word *eidos*, which means image. It is the world of images, imaginations, and symbols without which humans cannot exist. We may owe the fact of our existence to nature, but we owe the fact of our humanity to images that are held up to or are even impressed upon us. Our inheritance from those who raise us is the images they hand down; in school, at work and at church we are taught images. Images that show us the world, the human and society, what is proper and how we should be. We cannot, or can only poorly, defend ourselves against these images because they take effect before we are even conscious of it. We already have an image of our mother and our father – and thus of the relation between man and woman – before we even had the chance to gain critical distance. Hence we turn into the person we subsequently have to be from the very beginning. The child of parents who are themselves their parents' child, children who have to foot the bill already presented to them by the dominant order, whether they like it or not – though something remains that resists the fact that the children must always shoulder this bill.

The world of images is also the world of *fantasy*. We begin to fantasise about how things might be different, we dream of happiness, we sing songs of yearning.[13] Dreams, songs, stories: there are images that accommodate this longing, images that offer a perspective on a happy life, a vision of a new world.

Fantasies are not necessarily innocent. The oppressed can dream of it one day being their turn to teach their oppressors mores, to inflict the same harm on them that they have suffered at their hands. The oppressed can dream of his oppressors' torment, of his cries for mercy. Will it ever be possible to overcome this fatal cycle of domination-subjugation-domination? Looking at what happens when the oppressed gain power could lead to despair.

---

13   Not all yearnings are justified, though: 'God is not the autonomous object of a yearning ... He who is worth yearning for refers to him who is not worth yearning for – therein resides his holiness' (De Boer 2001, p. 29).

We not only find the images that reproduce the dominant order in the field of ideology, an order that then seems to be 'the end of history', a 'natural' order that corresponds with human nature, an order that represents the best of all worlds. The dominant images may generally be the images of the rulers, but they are not alone in the field. Counter-ideologies exist, fantastic stories that contradict those of the dominant order and that offer to the people ideas distinct from the dominant ones.

This is why there is a *struggle* in the field of ideology: it is a struggle for power, either to keep hearts and minds on track with the dominant order or to lead them onto a path of radical change. Ideology is not an analysis of reality; it precedes such an analysis. It motivates the affirmation 'yes, that is how it is' or the refusal 'no, that cannot be true'. Ideology is thus the basis of everything that we do or do not do: those who faithfully accept the dominant order let it do as it likes, those who do not believe in it resist. In the field of ideology we find 'belief against belief' (Miskotte).[14]

What is special about biblical ideology is the radicalness of its opposition against that which can be *seen*. Biblical narratives demand being *heard*. Our eyes cannot believe what these narratives say. We cannot see that freedom and justice will kiss each other, often we cannot even see that we are moving towards that moment. There may be traces, people who do justice to each other, who live together in peace, who grant each other freedom, who are loyal and love each other. These are only traces, though, they are traces that pass and vanish in the sand. Who says that this will not always be the case?

The Bible says it. It says it despite all evidence to the contrary. The faith that the Bible calls forth emerges from what has been *heard* (Rom 10:17). We *hear* that there is a God who delivers from slavery; we do not see it. We *hear* this God say: I am YHWH, your God – we do not see it. We *hear* of a Promised Land and that there we will be free; we do not see it. We will see it, yes. But we *hear* the fact that we will see it.

Israel and the Peoples

But do *we* hear it? We are not being addressed when it explicitly resounds for the first time, Israel is: *Hear*, this God, who delivers from slavery, is *one* (i.e. there

---

14   Miskotte 1983, p. 11. He is trying to say that the 'ultimate reason' for a fundamental yes or no is 'objectively' without reason, is an issue of faith. But faith has its own reason: a fantastic story, a 'myth'. And this myth is a motivating reason, a motive for action.

is none other like him). Not all people, then, not all humanity in general, much less without distinction between individuals, but one people specifically:

> Hear, Israel,
> YHWH, our God,
> YHWH is one!
> > Dt 6:4

YHWH: from the start this God is not a general God, is not a term devoid of any particularity. He has a name, calls himself YHWH – a name that he himself interprets in terms both reserved and promising.

> I will be there, as he who I will be there
> > Ex 3:14

What is special about this name, in any case, is that it is bound up with the people of Israel. 'I will be there as he who I will be there' does not refer to a hitherto empty future, in which it remains to be seen who this God really is, whether his name signifies salvation or disaster. The specialness of his name indicates the story that he started with the people of Israel,[15] it points to him as the God who led this people out of slavery, it indicates the bond into which he has entered with Israel, it indicates Israel as his ally, as the people called upon to serve this Liberator-God, to safeguard his liberating commandments.

It is pointless to speculate what the four-letter-word YHWH might mean before and beyond the self-definition in Ex 3:14 ('I will be there, as he who I will be there'). There is no going back from this self-definition, only a keeping track of how the name reveals itself. The question then remains, though, how to translate this self-definition, *ehjeh asher ehjeh* (from the verb *haja*). The Greek translation of the Hebrew Bible renders it as: 'I am he who *is being*' (Greek: *ho oon* from *einai* = to be). Hebrew, however, does not have the word 'to be' in the sense of a signifier of connection between two terms (a *is* b), nor in the sense of 'this *is* how it is and not otherwise', so an essential determination. The word *haja*, which the self-definition plays on, means 'to happen', 'to take place', 'being' as 'being *present*'. Philosophically speaking, Hebrew does not have the distinction between *essentia* (being) and *existentia* (the concrete being present,

---

15   Of this 'nameless name', Miskotte writes: 'First and foremost, its point is that Israel's God thus *withdraws from all invocation* ... But more precisely ... Israel is directed to the *events* that originate with YHWH, to what he does: the path he takes with Israel from Egypt to the Promised Land and further into exile and diaspora ...' (1966, pp. 128 f.).

Dasein) so fundamental to Greek thought. The essence of the name YHWH, then, is the 'happening' of this name in the materiality of its *Dasein*. If we now asked, *how* he 'is present', then the answer is in the history of his deeds, beginning with the exodus of his people of Israel from slavery and subsequently in the spirit of this exodus in the deeds of liberation that he began with this people and which he promised not to relinquish (Ps 138:8). This is why the self-definition is full of promise: 'I will be there' – that is, in the impending exodus and in the future that begins with the exodus that is the path to the Promised Land.[16] I will be there *'as he who I* will be there', though. The self-definition does not leave the question open whether he will be there, but in precisely what way he – or is he a she? – will be there. His paths of liberation are full of surprises and extend much further than we can imagine.

Why specifically this people? What is so special about them? What distinguishes this people from other peoples? A possible answer might be: according to the biblical narrative, this people is special because it is a slave people, that has no life in the world of master and servant, that has no place where it can rest its head in peace. But it shares this fate with numerous other peoples. It is the fate of masses of humans, always has been and looks to remain so forever. Once again: what is special about it?

There is only one answer: this people is special because it and no other hears of a God who says:

> I have called you by name,
> You are mine.
>> Is 43:1

A God who, bypassing all other peoples, chooses this people so as to show that he is *one* – singular, wholly different from the other gods: the deliverer from slavery. The reason for this election is not this people in and of itself. In and of itself it is only a pile of misery, destined to perish under the force of the peoples. But the fact that God says, 'You are my people, I am your God', that makes this people into what it is and henceforth can be: Israel, this God's people. In the 'hear, Israel' it hears and professes its *raison d'être*: YHWH, *our* God, YHWH *one*.[17]

---

16   'that the sign EI [from the Greek *einai*] was carved above the gate of the temple of Apollo at Delphi ... means [according to Plutarch] grammatically and metaphysically the same, namely Thou art, in the sense of timelessly unchangeable existence of God. *Eh'je asher eh'je*, on the other hand, places even at the threshold of the Yahweh phenomenon a god of the end of days, with futurum as an attribute of Being' (Bloch 1986b, p. 1237).

17   In his Pentateuch Commentary, the Jewish scholar Rashi (1040–1105) also reads the *one*

And it professes this to the present day. The continuing repetition of the *Sch'ma'Jisrael* (the 'hear, Israel') – as the profession through which this people stands or falls – in the synagogue ensures the continuity of biblical Israel and Judaism. This 'fact' prevents those of us who also say this *Sch'ma'* from turning 'Israel' into a metaphor that can be used arbitrarily.[18] Israel remains specifically 'this people' (Leo Baeck).[19] No matter how diverse and estranged Jews are amongst themselves, how difficult to define, by calling themselves Jews they remind us that the biblical Israel has not simply dissolved into universality, but faces us in this particular guise. 'Israel' cannot be reduced to a singular term in order to be available to our thought processes. With its Jewish continuation it is a hard, often objectionable, vexing factor. Being aligned with the term 'Israel' is simple, being aligned with the real Jews far more difficult. Without this alignment even the best biblical theology would be essentially cheap.

So we are not directly addressed. The question is whether Israel's God is also our God. And this is not simply a rhetorical question, which would allow the answer: of course he is our God. To be sure, the Bible opens with a creation story that narrates the creation of Adam, the human (Gn 1), but in the immediately subsequent story – the story of the human being becoming truly human (Gn 2–4) – this Adam is portrayed as a human with exceptionally Israelite features. Adam is taken to the Garden of Eden to 'serve on' (Hebrew: *abad*) and to preserve it' (Hebrew: *shamar*) (Gn 2:15). This *abad* already rings with the *ebed* (slave) that is Israel and the slavery from which it will be delivered. And in the conjunction of *abad* ('to serve') and 'to preserve' we can hear the constitution of this people's identity: to serve its God and 'keep' (*shamar*) his commandments.

(Hebrew *èchad*) eschatologically, directed towards the eschatological delivery: 'The eternal one, who is now *our* God and not the God of the peoples, will one day be the only one'. (With reference to Zec 14:9: 'And YHWH will be King over all the earth. On that day YHWH will be the only one and his name the only one').

18   Buber is even more drastic in his wording: '"Israel" is not an entity of which we merely possess biblical report, an entity which we Jews feel bound to through the power of this report and historical awareness. Israel exists: it is unique, singular, there is none other of its kind ... Israel is that which even today is concealed as its own in this Judaism, beneath the manifold distortion, degeneracy, blurring, that which lives within it as a concealed reality' (Buber 1993, p. 544).

19   To Baeck, the phrase 'this people' above all means the mercy of the vocation, it means to do what is commanded: 'This people's constitution is founded in God's commandment ... Israel is not only a people within history, but the people of history. And with the desire to be this, it becomes at the same time the people of humanity. As it cannot and may not think of itself without God, it cannot see itself without all of humanity' (Baeck 1964, p. 10).

You shall follow YHWH, your God, fear her, *keep (shamar)* her commandments, listen to her voice, *serve* her and adhere to her!
> Dt 13:5

And what follows is concerned with the 'becoming of Israel' (Breukelman) in
Adam's lineage.[20] In this context, the peoples pose one problem above all: will
there even be space among them for Israel? What makes God's turn towards
Israel – 'you are my people' (Is 51:16) – singular is that he does what the other
people threaten to prevent: give Israel a place. Israel's 'he is our God' is hence
initially directed *against* the peoples: not your God, our God!

A Bond Impossible to Relinquish

The Bible does not simply blurt out a kind of 'of course we are all children of one
Father'-humanism. This would take things too lightly: we are not to be naïve
with respect to the issue of the one God and the one humanity. The story of the
incarnation cannot avoid telling the story of the 'man and his brother' – a story
of fratricide (Gn 4)! It is the story of how one brother, the stronger Cain, strikes
dead the other brother, the weaker Abel. And it is the story of this singular God,
who *sees* Abel, the weak one, and *misses* Cain, the strong one.

This has nothing to do with inscrutable arbitrariness, as though the one human is
accepted while the other one is rejected without apparent reason. This type of 'godli-
ness' is alien to the God of the Bible. While his preference for the 'weak in the world' is
unheard of in the world of gods (and their earthly representatives), it is fully in line with
his partisanship. It is true that the story goes: 'YHWH heeded Abel and his offering, he
did not heed Cain and his offering' (Gn 4:4–5a). The point of the matter, though, is that
Cain's 'face *fell*' (Gn 4:5b). This means, he refuses to follow YHWH's eye for the weak.
To him, the fact that he is to 'rule' him (Gn 4:7) does not mean that he feels responsible
for his brother, only that he has the power to strike him dead.[21] So law(lessness) of the
jungle.

---

20   Breukelman 1992, p. 5. (Genesis as the book of Israel's becoming in the midst of the
     peoples).

21   'Ruling' is often related to sin: Cain must rule over his tendency to sin. According to Karel
     Deurloo, though, it is unlikely that the desire ('he desires you, you must rule over him')
     refers to sin: the object of desire is male, the Hebrew word for sin is feminine. The narrator
     is creating an analogy with Gn 3:16: the woman's desire for the man. The weak brother
     is directed towards the strong brother just like the woman is directed towards the man
     (Deurloo 1988, p. 109).

The Bible does not simply say 'God and us', it does not immediately say 'God-with-us'. Certainly, it addresses us. We might be being addressed as Cain, though, invited by God to look past ourselves and focus on the other, the weaker brother – and his sister! – as 'the apple of God's eye' (Dt 32:10; Zec 2:12). The question of who this other is, deserving of our solidarity as the weak brother, is not left up to us. This God sees specifics: this one weak brother, this one slave people that cries out in misery not everywhere but in a specific place. When we hear the 'hear, Israel' we hear the name of this one people in particular – this people that attracts God's particular attention and hence demands our particular attention. Through the resounding of the name of this people, Israel, we are no longer free to come up with a weak brother of our choice. And the Bible does not conceal the nature of this people. Unmistakably 'minor and despised' among peoples (Ps 119:141), but also unmistakably shouldered with all the burdens typical of peoples that are kept down: obsessed with the power it does not have itself, with a tendency in its despair to follow the 'gods' who keep it down. A people that betrays the project of liberation that its own God, *nota bene*, started with it. A people that is a caricature of what this God saw in it. By affirming the 'hear, Israel' we profess our bond with this people, from this day on, 'for better or for worse'.

Is this bond limitless? For instance, would it mean, in relation to today's Israeli state: 'right or wrong, my country'? A bond is never without critique. This critique, however, has a boundary, whose transgression would mean dissolving the bond. In any case, this boundary is transgressed when the critique deploys the language of anti-Semitism. We should not conceal the things (and there are many) that speak against the Israeli state's politics. It must then also remain unmistakable, however, that it is not against but for the Jews that we speak – in a great, unbroken bond.

This does not make hearing the biblical pronouncement 'Delivery from slavery' – against all appearances – any less true. And it is no tragic error to know that this God, who shows himself in the fantastic stories of the Bible, is addressing us – if we know we are being addressed. But in that moment when we engage with the good news, we are put in a situation that demands our solidarity from the outset. The *a priori* of biblical ideology is the bond: the strong bond with the weak and the weak bond with each other and are thus strengthened. It is the bond that is the strength of the weak: they can only live on the back of solidarity. It is the bond that finds its *concretissimum* in the bond between YHWH and Israel. This bond precedes. This is the bond we are confronted with.

What Does Israel Hear?

That is what *we* hear. But what does *Israel* hear, when it hears 'hear Israel, YHWH, our God, YHWH is one'? Surely not something entirely different. For the 'one' of this God who Israel can call 'our God' is that he delivers Israel from slavery in order to be a beacon of light for the peoples – to teach the peoples that a world without slavery is possible, that all earth will be filled with the glory of YHWH, the humanity he embodies is universal. So Israel knows that its 'hear Israel' calls upon it to be *pars pro toto*, a 'part' standing in for the 'whole'. And this is where there is a difference to our calling. For while we are called upon to look away from ourselves and to see the other, Israel is commanded to be and to remain precisely itself: the part that through its lifestyle, its social formation, really does stand in for the whole.

'Hear, Israel, the commandments and laws that I say to you today, learn them and keep them, so as to follow them' (Dt 5:1). These 'commandments and laws' constitute Israel's identity: to be holy, as YHWH is holy (Lv 19:2; 20:7.26), the positive embodiment of God's humanity. Giving up this identity would mean giving up the bond that God has entered into with his people. Privileging the other is fundamental to this identity, and without solidarity the other is irretrievably lost. But Israel itself is this other first and foremost! Saved by YHWH's solidarity! It cannot witness this solidarity without witnessing itself.

Israel is that part of the whole which has been chosen by God to demonstrate his solidarity in the world. Israel hears, in the 'hear, Israel', that its God, YHWH, is also the God of the whole – the God who created heaven and earth. He is actually *one*, the one, the only. That is why Israel cannot stop believing, against all appearances, that as a part of the whole it will experience solidarity from the whole. That is how we, who are not Israel, feature in Israel's faith: as those who are expected to be in solidarity with it.

Figures from the world of peoples who render the service of solidarity to Israel, surface again and again in the Bible – one might even say they are structural: the 'King of Righteousness' Melchisedek (Gn 14:18), *erev-rav* (Ex 12:38): the 'rabble' who join Israel in its exodus from slavery, the whore Rahab (Jo 2), the King of the Persians Cyrus (Ezr 1:1). Paul, the Apostle of the 'peoples', holds on to the primacy of Israel among peoples: first the Jew, then the Greek (Rom 2:9). The difference between Jews and Greeks is suspended in the messianic community: within it there is neither Jew nor Greek (Gal 3:28). Nevertheless, the Greek must know that the Jew walks ahead, that he must accompany the Jew.

The synagogue's Judaism, too, is open in principle: any person can convert to Judaism and be a full member of the synagogue. He is even considered a particularly valuable member, for he is willing to shoulder the yoke of the Torah and with it the fate of Israel.[22] It is precisely his becoming a Jew that marks his solidarity. Paul was of a different opinion in this (sore) point.

Creed

The Bible makes us believe. In our bond with Israel we believe in the God who delivers from slavery and who destroys the power of the images that hold us hostage. With Israel we long for the coming of the kingdom of peace and justice. We know we are addressed and we reply: *credo*, I believe! For it is this that the Bible brings about through its ideology: a profession of faith!

This profession of faith is no more abstract and general than the 'hear, Israel'. The 'I' who professes its faith is a very particular 'I': the creed's subject is the 'Christian' (messianic) community, i.e. the community that believes in Jesus Christ (Messiah). And its profession is not a compendium of general truths. The truth is specific: Jesus (is) Messiah. His name figures centrally in the creed: from beginning (creation) to end ('eternal life'), everything revolves around him, the embodiment of humanity as it is intended by the God of Israel.

The classic profession of faith consists of three parts: The first part professes faith in God, the Father, the Creator of heaven and earth. The second part professes faith in Jesus Chris. The third part professes faith in the Holy Spirit. But these three parts are not simply adjacent, nor are they simply sequential. The second part is the core, the essence of the profession: the humanity of the extraordinary Son of Man, Jesus. The Creator is the Father of this Son: the world is created for this humanity. The fruits of the Spirit (the community, the forgiveness of sin, the resurrection of the flesh, eternal life)[23] are inspired by this Son of Man.

---

22   The Talmud (Yevamot 47a) has the following to say on the issue: 'if somebody wants to be a proselyte in these times, he must be asked: what motivates you to become a proselyte, do you not know that the Israelites are tortured, pushed, humiliated and torn in these times and suffer? If he says he does know this, and is not worthy of it, he should be received immediately'. Only during the era of the Messiah may proselytes not be admitted, according to Maimonides (1135–1204). For who could say whether that wasn't motivated by opportunism?

23   All these terms require further elaboration. For what they usually bring to mind – when they are still mindfully engaged with at all – is entirely beside the point most of the time.

So does belief in Jesus Messiah not mean something more or even something entirely different from 'hear, Israel' – a call that is not directed at us anyway? Is *he* not God's word *above* all else? He, who was given the name of all names (Phil 2:9)? Is the community's mission not to profess this name?:

> so that, in the name of Jesus,
> all knees may bend, of the heavenly and the earthly and those below
> and all tongues profess:
> Lord (*adonai / kyrios*) is
> Jesus Messiah
> in honour of God, the Father
>> Phil 2:10

This community must be sure of what it does, however, in its profession of this particular name. It is the name of a Jew (Jesus is the Greek translation of the Hebrew Yehoshuah / Joshua) who explicitly says that he has not come to 'dispel' the word that God spoke to his people, but to 'fulfil' it (Mt 5:17). It is his name that is tied to the word that initiates the story of God and Israel in John's gospel (Jn 1:1: 'In the beginning was the word' refers to Gn 1:1–3: 'In the beginning God created ...' and his first word is: light!): this word is truly embodied in the Jew Jesus ('has become flesh') (Jn 1:14).

The word becomes flesh through a Jew. And the decisive word spoken by this Jew was on the cross when he prayed for his people:

> Father, forgive them,
> For they know not what they do.
>> Lk 23:34

With this word he confirms his bond with his people and invites God to keep the bond with his people. For had Israel *knowingly* betrayed its Messiah to the Romans and so crucified him, that sin would have been unforgivable.

The Bible distinguishes between sins committed unintentionally and sins committed with 'raised hand' (Nm 15:22–31). Those that are committed unintentionally (*shegagah*)

Who still knows that the forgiveness of sins means that the human is not condemned to fail in life but is given the freedom to find the right path? Who still hears the extraordinary promise of a revolution in the rising of the flesh, a revolution that will revolutionise all circumstances in which humans have no life? Who still understands eternal life to mean the life that comes when the 'unliveable' time is *forever* done with?

can be forgiven (though the damage they cause must be amended) (Nm 15:26: 'The whole community of the children of Israel as well as the stranger who is enjoying hospitality amongst them shall be forgiven for it was unintentional'). But he who sins with his arm raised, sins knowingly and with intention: 'this person will be eradicated from their people' (Nm 15:30). This, then, is what Jesus prevents, by praying that God may declare as unintentional what the people are doing to him: they know not what they do.

The Jewish philosopher Hermann Cohen points out that Nm 15:26 'as the Talmud expanded it for the history of Judaism' became 'the motto for the Day of Atonement [Reconciliation]'.[24] And he explains: 'Human wisdom is at a loss in the presence of the possibility of *evil* in man. The Day of Atonement maintains the fiction of the unshakable moral preservation of everything human: all man's sin is *shegagah*. Therefore God can forgive without relinquishing his justice'.[25] He, too, evidently knows of the life-saving function of this fiction. The people sinned in full knowledge of what they were doing. End of story: the people dissolved the bond. The liturgy for the Day of Atonement feigns a situation that enables God to forgive. Without renouncing his righteousness! For the reconciliation between God and his people is not the end of the Torah. The fact remains: only those who do Torah will live! (Lv 18:5). Atonement renders the impossible possible again: a people who do Torah. Jesus prays for this reconciliation and so tries to bring it about.

For the community who professes this Jesus as God's word turned into flesh, this renders the bond with Israel indissoluble.

The fact that this indissoluble bond with Israel is not explicitly professed in the creed is a worrying omission, because it leaves open precisely what Jesus wanted to preclude: that God might abandon the people with whom he has entered into a bond – because they did not (no longer) deserve this bond.[26] Israel is the test case of whether God really does stay true to his bond, even when the partner in the bond fails utterly. For if Israel fails, where does that leave any hope for the success of the delivery from slavery?[27] Is Israel's

24 Cohen 1995, p. 217.
25 Cohen 1995, p. 223.
26 Peter Von der Osten-Sacken articulates this programmatically: 'Ultimately one principle is to be made aware of and rehearsed: the certainty that God holds on to the election of Israel and his devotion to his people, even if they say no to Jesus Christ, is part of Christian faith. This is why this certainty should figure both in the Christian creed and in the Christian catechism' (1994, p. 18).
27 'Do you believe that it lies with us to exclude the Jew from this faithfulness of God? Do you really believe that we can and may deny him this? God's faithfulness in the reality of Israel is in fact the guarantee of His faithfulness to us too, and to all men' (Barth 1959, p. 80).

story not the story of all liberation movements to date: full of promise in the beginning, a severe disappointment in the end?

That is why Israel belongs in the creed: the community believes Jesus Christ, who believed to the end that God would not abandon the work that his hand began with Israel (Ps 138:8). To profess 'Jesus is the Lord' means to believe that Israel has a future, and that the liberation movement has a future! The world's salvation depends on Israel's knowledge: my Saviour lives (Jb 19:25)!

The fact that the majority of Jews do not associate this liberating knowledge with the name of Jesus changes nothing. How might the community profess its faith in Jesus Christ against the Jews? The community knows, after all, that Israel's belief: 'my Saviour lives', is true. And it should meanwhile also know that the Jewish refusal of Jesus as Messiah is very well founded. It was the community itself who made it impossible for the Jews to believe that the time of the Messiah had arrived with Jesus.

The community prays together with the synagogue: God, do not abandon the work of your hands (Ps 138:8). Oddly, though, their creed lacks a reference to his work par excellence: that he delivered the slave people Israel from slavery 'with raised arm' (Ex 14:8). It is the missing link that determines whether the community really knows it is being addressed.

Canon

This book is concerned with *biblical* theology, which is to say, a theology determined by the Bible. But what is 'the' Bible? Is it more than a collection of very different writings: stories, prescriptions, songs and sayings? The only thing that turns the Bible into a single book seems to be the God it constantly speaks of: the *only* God, YHWH, the NAME. Even this is only the case to a certain extent, though: the book Esther never mentions the NAME. Although it does more or less tell a continuous story, with a beginning ('creation') and an end – 'I saw a new heaven and a new earth' (Rv 21:1) –, closer inspection shows that it cannot really be said to be a continuously progressing narrative. It does not tell a linear story, as we would expect from a normal historiography. There are too many duplicate tales: stories are told twice. For instance, the story of the kings of Israel: the books Samuel and Kings tell it very differently from the books of Chronicles. And then there are also the 'miracles', which fill the Bible, and which apparently were unavoidable for the course of history; or more precisely, for the surprising breakthroughs in this story. A historian who studies the Bible will have to ask himself whether it really happened as it says it did (Leopold von Ranke). And he has sufficient reason to fundamentally doubt it. He will search for the facts underpinning the story, for the 'history' at the bottom of this 'story'. Similarly, the literary historian will try to reconstruct the textual history of this piece of literature in order to be able to discover the texts that stand behind this text. In both cases the Bible is questioned as *canon*, the surviving text questioned in its role as 'measure', as 'rule'.[1]

The purpose of the present biblical theology is to follow the canon and to follow it as *regula fidei* ('the rule of faith'), as a guideline for what we can believe with respect to the story, when necessary – and it is often necessary – contradicting the factual course of history. This biblical theology follows the canon and hence proceeds from the Torah, in the sequence of the canon, which is also a hierarchy, the constitution which founds the existence of the Liberator-God's people. The 'story' (re)told by this biblical theology is that of the project 'Israel', which is conceived in the Torah, and the real Israel, called upon to execute this project.

---

1 Originally, the Greek *kanōn* appears to have been the word for 'pipe' or 'rod'. Its meaning then developed into 'straightness' and further into 'guideline', 'rule' – for correct behaviour, for instance.

A-historical History

It can more or less be ruled out that historically the Torah preceded the factual execution of the project (the real Israel, from Joshua to Ezra/Nehemiah). It is far more likely that the Torah is the result of a long pre-history, during which the absence of such a Torah awakened a yearning for it.

The thing that is often forgotten (not least by many Bible scholars) is that the Bible itself is virtually the only source for the exploration of this pre-history. Just as much as it is often forgotten that the age of the texts in the so-called Old Testament does not date any further back than the third century BCE.[2] It is the era of the Hellenistic Empires (Macedonia; the Ptolomaic Kingdom = Egypt, including Damascus; the Seleucid Empire = Persia, up to the Mediterranean Sea), which is hence the real 'life setting' of the biblical writings.

In this case, the Torah is a utopia depicting that which should have been but never really was. Or that only came about as a historical coincidence enabled by the happy coincidence of various factors (a *kairos*): the 'Torah Republic'[3] in the age of Ezra and Nehemiah.

Chance 'would have it' that the Persian king at the time of Ezra and Nehemiah thought that he could better rule his empire with (very!) relatively more autonomous vassal states than rule it centrally, as he had done in the past: 'An autonomous region, loyal to the empire, in the midst of a province that tended towards constant rebellion [Judea], was of sufficient interest to the king for him to entrust a relatively high-ranking functionary [Nehemiah] with its direct administration'.[4] This was 'Nehemiah's small chance':[5] 'This fortuitous constellation of a power vacuum on the one side and the destruction of Babel by Kourosh, the Persian, on the other side, is the material foundation for the experiment of a society without a state that was simultaneously felt to be a completely unexpected and undeserved new beginning'.[6] Thus, chance turned into '*kairos*'!

---

2   Diebner substantiates the 'core hypothesis of [his] position in the field of the OT' (to my mind convincingly) by arguing 'that the Writings of the TaNaK, in the textual shape in which they are available to us, are *passim* literatures of the Hellenic-Roman period, relocated into the (pre-)Christian era: it is literature from the 3rd/2nd century B.C.E. to the 1st century C.E.' (2003, p. 13).

3   This term is taken from Ton Veerkamp (1982, p. 81).

4   Veerkamp 1982, p. 76.

5   Veerkamp 1982, p. 75.

6   Veerkamp 1982, p. 298.

Concerning the Torah itself, one can try to separate its Laws into different 'legislations', each with its own historical context: the 'Book of the Covenant' (Ex 20:22–23: 33), originating in the eighth century BCE, Deuteronomy (Dt 12–26), dated to the end of the monarchy, and the 'Law of Holiness' (Lv 17–26), originating during exile and the return to the Promised Land. This, in any case, explains the contradictions between the legislations, and one legislation can be read as the critical reworking of a previous one.

All this can be done and there is much that speaks for such a procedure. For it is evident that the Torah did not fall from heaven, so to speak, as a whole; just as it is evident that the Torah cannot be attributed to one author, Moses. That is a literary construct: who else but Moses, the charismatic leader, deputy of the NAME – himself an extraordinarily fictive character –, could be the author of the Torah? And even if the Torah is read as the plan for a future society, it is evidently also processing historical experiences. But *the* experience among all these experiences is presumably the failure of all attempts to organise society in a radically different manner. In other words, the Torah is a fantastic story that tells of the possibility of such a different society despite all signs to the contrary: impossible possibility.

We can try to explain all this through historical reconstruction. Bible scholarship that does this is *historical-critical*. It critically investigates the historical content of the texts that have survived as the Bible, as well as the historical context in which the biblical texts were 'produced'.[7] Historical-critical research shows that the world of the Bible has a context without which it cannot be understood at all. Therein also lies its significance for biblical theology: it offers insight into the context in which the surviving text intervenes. With respect to this intervention, though, we have to emphasise the fact that the canon, which determines the logic of the biblical writings, tells its own story.[8]

The canon that this study follows is that of the Hebrew Bible, the so-called Masoretic Canon.[9] This has three 'departments': Torah, Prophets and Writings. The acronym of this division is Tanakh, comprised of the first letters –

---

7 Whilst doing this, though, it must be wary of speculations not grounded in the source material (see above).

8 Ton Veerkamp uses even more radical language: 'The purpose of an interpretation is not to investigate historical facts, particularly since such an endeavour is pointless. Its purpose is to interpret the narrative's internal contexts and to put it into the context of a familiar socio-political contradiction' (2007, p. 87). It is more important to transfer the text into the (all too easily) imaginable social contradictions, than it is to investigate the question, whether things happened as it says they did.

9 The gospels also posit the Masoretic canon: compare e.g. Mt 5:17; Lk 24:44.

T(orah), N(evi'im) and Kh(etuvim). This is why Tanakh is the common appellation of the Bible. The Prophets are subdivided again into the 'first prophets' (Joshua, Judges, 1 and 2 Samuel, 1 and 2 Kings) and the 'second prophets' (Isaiah, Jeremiah, Ezekiel and the Book of the Twelve Prophets). This does not signify a chronology (former and later), but only what is at the beginning and what is at the end of the book – they were all produced roughly around the same time. What is distinct is the verb tense. The 'first prophets' use the past tense: they narrate what happened to the real Israel. The 'second prophets' use the present tense: they proclaim what will happen to the real Israel should it not find its way back to its Liberator-God and his Torah. The future, however, is the time period that leaves past and present open, for both the 'first' and the 'second prophets': it has not yet been decided whether the project 'Israel' has failed entirely. In so far as it is historiography, it is *prophetic* historiography. The Writings are: Psalms, Proverbs, Job, the so-called Five Scrolls (Song of Songs, Ruth, Lamentations, Ecclesiastes, Esther), Daniel, Ezra, Nehemiah, 1 and 2 Chronicles. They are (according to Miskotte)[10] Israel's response to the testimony of the Torah and the Prophets: Torah and Prophets are not fixed truths which he who hears can only silently obey ('like it or lump it').[11] He who listens obeys by being in conversation with the surviving text, by interpreting and commenting on it, if necessary by contradicting it. This is because the text is the word of that God who not only speaks, but who will also listen to reason. The relation to the text hence does not mean simply that the text commands and we obey. The canon itself (including the Writings) recommends taking Torah and Prophets seriously as words that want to be held responsible. They demand, no: they encourage a free subject who follows because of insight, not a subject who does not know any better: an order is an order. The only thing we cannot do to the text is to bring it in line with those texts it specifically wants to contradict.

A different canon is the Septuaginta, the Greek translation of the 'Old Testament'. This is also the canon that structures 'our' Bible. It combines the 'first prophets' with the historical books (Chronicles, Ezra and Nehemiah) to make a historical narrative. In this narrative, Ezra and Nehemiah come after Chronicles, unlike in the Masoretic canon. This is because Chronicles ends with the Persian king Kyros's decree, which is the beginning of the return from exile in the time of Ezra and Nehemiah. This is linear

---

10   'The *'Torah'* is the real basis ... the *prophets* ... call back to the realisation of the bond and the commandment ... the *Writings* ... describe how the community reacts to God's intervention and testimony' (Miskotte 1966, p. 146 f.).

11   Thus Bonhoeffer formulated his critique of what he considered Karl Barth's 'positivist doctrine of revelation, that says, in effect, "Like it or lump it"' (Bonhoeffer 2010, p. 373).

(*Heilsgeschichte*!),[12] not prophetic historiography. The 'second prophets' conclude the sequence, with the Book of Malachi ('my messenger') bringing up the rear. Malachi's final words herald the coming of the Prophet Elijah, the harbinger of the Messiah. The Septuaginta-canon lends itself to a 'Christian' interpretation because of this messianic tendency. This is presumably why the church adopted it. And it is presumably also why the synagogue preferred the Masoretic canon.

In any case, the fact that *Heilsgeschichte* is not portrayed as a continuous progression and that it does not imply that the project 'Israel' has been homogenous, when the reality shows it hasn't, speaks for the Masoretic canon.

The course of this history is wholly 'a-historical'. 'Historically' speaking, the story goes that the yearning for liberation was frustrated again and again by the fact that the dominant order was superior, the utopia the escape of the powerless into a world where the rulers had no place. This 'a-historic' story, on the other hand, relates the unheard-of: that there is a power, a superior power, a God, who accommodates this yearning. This unheard-of tale, that was nevertheless heard, this word-event, is the structural centre of the biblical narratives (prescriptions and wisdom): the liberating intervention of the NAME in the 'historical' story, the escape from the house of bondage. The fact that the cry for deliverance is heard, and does not die away in the endless emptiness of nothingness, moves the *whole* Bible.

By that I mean explicitly the Bible including the apostolic writings. Delivery from slavery is the key topic in these writings, too. The word has become flesh in a man who is executed by the Romans because he is an insubordinate slave. Avowing him – 'Jesus is the Lord (*kyrios*)' – means that the power to rule is attributed to this slave and not to the Roman emperor who is revered as *kyrios*. This is the – very political – good news proclaimed by the apostolic writings. Slavery will end and its end will be that God is all in all.

Even if the God who bears this NAME – it should really be: the NAME bears God – keeps silent, he remains approachable: my God, my God, why have you abandoned me (Ps 22:2). Only those who can at least *hope* for an answer can cry out in despair like that. Crying out into the void is pointless from the start.

---

12   The fact that the Septuaginta 'locate' the Book of Ruth between Judges and 1 Samuel makes sense not only because of the indication that the story of Ruth takes place during the era of Judges, but also in terms of salvation history: a messianic story begins in the pretty despairing era of Judges (with the marvellous birth of Obed, David's grandfather (Ru 4:18–22)).

Even though the project 'Israel' seems to have failed entirely – no, *has* failed entirely – the hope remains that what is cannot be the final word, because the NAME calls that which is not into being (Rom 4:17).

This story is 'a-historic' then: the narrative of the exodus is non-datable. But it fully refers to history as we know it from the history books – and can know from personal experience. Are we not familiar with the house of bondage, even if we know nothing of a historic Egypt where this was actually the case? Are we not familiar with a society, in its various guises, that robs people of their means of production: from the slave-holding society to the capitalist mode of production? Are we not also familiar with the attempts made in the past to break free from this society, to build a new society without domination? Are we not familiar with the liberation movements and their disasters, their perversion, and are we not familiar with the hope for 'perestroika', a radical reconstruction of the corrupted liberation project?

So we can follow the canonical sequence of the biblical books very well without pursuing 'what really happened'. Because yes, that is what happened: a people, for which there was no place in the world of peoples, was condemned to live in slavery. And then came the counter-programme for a new society. This is what the Torah narrates – from the perspective of this people itself, driven by the unheard-of that was nevertheless heard. It is the tale of Israel's liberation from slavery and its pre-history, the 'becoming of Israel amidst the peoples', the foundation of this story of liberation in the '*creatio ex nihilo*', the fundamental liberation from the nihilist nothing, and the 'project Israel' with a view to organising a society without domination. And yes, so it continued: Israel arriving in the land, the real Israel, 'the travail of the plains' (Brecht), the perversion, the defeat. This is the topic of the 'first prophets', who relate what happened without illusion: the failed experiment of a grass-roots democracy and the equally failed story of the kings who were meant to ensure the order of the Torah. The 'first prophets' do this with the courage of despair: despite everything, the story's ending is still open. Though will such a liberation project ever succeed in a land squeezed between the major powers Egypt and Assyria/Babylon? The 'second prophets' doubt it. Their radical critique of the project's ruination coincides with a grandiose expansion of its perspective: the peoples approach Israel as allies; why, Israel will ultimately be all in all, the world revolution (Is 60!). The Writings comment on this, in turn. Ezra and Nehemiah speak of a *kairos* that is certainly not world revolution, but does at least facilitate a Torah Republic. Chronicles retells the story of the kings yet again. They are no less critical in this than the 'first prophets', but they explicitly offer the prospect of the *kairos* which will lead to Ezra's and Nehemiah's Torah Republic. Nevertheless, Chronicles are, quite 'a-historically', positioned at the end of the Writings, after Ezra and Nehemiah. The Torah republic's *kairos* that Ezra and Nehemiah speak of is hence over. Following the logic of the canon, this cannot be the final word, though. The final word is given to the *kairos* itself: the Persian king Cyrus's decree, which ends with the auspicious:

> Those among you from his whole people:
> YHWH your God is with you,
> *you shall ascend!*
> 2 Chr 36:23

Thus the biblical story makes its own, 'a-historic' path through general history – in order to make history within the latter and nowhere else.

Exodus

Exodus is at the core of the biblical narrative: the flight of the slave people, Israel, from Egypt, the 'land of anxiety' (Barnard), the place of oppression, the house of bondage.

The Hebrew word that is translated as 'Egypt' is *Mitsrayim*. This translation is not without its problems because it threatens to reduce the meaning of this country to geography – and, before he knows it, the reader might be led to the conclusion that what is meant here is (also) today's Egypt (including its relations with today's Israeli state). But this would be a terrible misunderstanding with serious consequences. The Hebrew word shares the root *tsarar* (oppress/restrict). This indicates what type of country it is: not where it is located, but how it is constituted. The fact that it once existed in a specific place, the place where Egypt now lies, is only relevant in so far as this 'land of anxiety' actually has a specific location. Incidentally, it is likely that the historical Egypt that the editor or the editors of the biblical narratives had in mind was the Hellenistic Ptolomaic Empire (see Chapter 2). Through this 'a-historic' localisation of the exodus story into Pharaonic Egypt, the name 'Egypt' turns into a kind of metaphor, figurative (ideological) speech: *Mitsrayim* now refers to the whole sequence of empires that succeeded one another in this region and cornered the people of Israel. All of these empires are subsumed under this one house of bondage, from which Israel is delivered.

The God of Israel

The *a priori* of the exodus is constituted by the name – YHWH:

> I am YHWH,
> your God,
> who brought you out of Egypt,
> out of the house of bondage.
>
> Ex 20:2

YHWH is not simply a god. Nor is he the god of the kind of religion that is generally viewed as the highest: monotheism. The fact that he is the only one ('Hear, Israel, YHWH, our God, YHWH is one!') does not lead to a specific affinity with monotheism as the ultimate phase in the evolution of religion from primitive polytheism to God as the one, universal principle of all things. He is 'your God', which means: the God of the slave people Israel. This and only this is how he interprets himself, this and only this is how he determines his identity: I, YHWH, *am* your God. It is his nature to lead this people from the house of servitude. Here, his name – 'I will be there, as he who I will be there' (Ex 3:14) – becomes recognisable as: I am the God of the exodus. The God of *this* exodus, *this* people: the slave people delivered from slavery.

'I am' this: it is determined by his name, because he has determined to be this and no other God. It is his decision from the start, his *pre*destination (*fore*ordination). Israel can henceforth hold him to this decision: that he cannot withdraw from it.

This is why this name is also superordinate to the term 'God'.[1] For 'God' – as already mentioned in Chapter 1 – is a title, an office, a function. It signifies a highest Being, the beginning and end of all wisdom, elevated above all critical doubt.[2] As such, 'God' signifies nothing – except that his power knows no boundaries: he is capable of everything, knows everything, sees everything, is everywhere and always – omnipotent, omniscient, all-seeing, omnipresent, eternal. In general, 'God' is the absolutisation and hence the sanctioning of the earthly power that condemns the majority of people to servitude. As such, 'God' can have a number of faces again – but as it turns out, it is always the face of a bog-standard ruler.

The socio-cultural context of the biblical narratives is a world full of 'God's sons': the Pharaoh, the Babylonian king, the Roman emperor. There are no other sons of God in this world. Here, the son of God is, per definition, a ruler who together with his accomplices rules at the expense of the peoples subject to him. God, then, represents the highest Being of this rule, the heavenly superstructure that mirrors the earthly base. Thus, this earthly base gains heavenly aspects, not least in the eyes of those people who have to believe it. Social being determines consciousness: the subject thinks like a 'subject'.[3] He

---

1 'This is, so to speak, the METHOD OF THE NAME, that is: first this God is our God – and then: this God is the only, the omnipotent, the omnipresent, etc.' (Miskotte 1997, p. 43).

2 'God signifies a point of concentration in the ideological fabric where the different social loyalties meet. This point of concentration can be appealed to antagonistically. It is invoked as the absolute guarantor of dominant conditions, but it can also be appealed to as a legitimating entity for attempts to revoke loyalty' (Veerkamp 2001, p. 917).

3 'All religion, however, is nothing but the fantastic reflection in men's minds of those external forces which control their daily life, a reflection in which the terrestrial forces assume the form of supernatural forces' (Engels 1987, p. 300). Declaring religion 'nothing but' falls short

fails to recognise that this superstructure owes its existence entirely to the base and the 'sons of God' would be lost without the labour of their subjects:

> Who built Thebes of the seven gates?
> In the books you will find the names of kings.
> Did the kings haul up the lumps of rocks?
> (Questions of a worker who reads)[4]

Those who really believe that the kings are sons of God subjugate themselves. The exodus narrative 'plants' disbelief: the only thing that it bids the 'sons of God' to do is to let their subjects go. The message to Pharaoh reads:

> Thus spoke YHWH, the God of Israel, [to Pharaoh]:
> send my people toward freedom!
>> Ex 5:1

LET MY PEOPLE GO!

It is too easy, though, to declare 'God' to be simply a reflection of earthly power relations, as though he were nothing more than a metaphysical pharaoh. Whoever thinks that this declaration is sufficient as a critique of religion does not know what they are talking about. The 'nature' of religion is more the 'feeling' that 'something' exists which exceeds all these human, all-too-human conditions. 'God' is the word for the unspeakable secret of being that is higher than all reason. It is a word that, in a very profound fashion, does not actually articulate anything – and thus articulates precisely everything. Namely it conveys the fact that being is ultimately inconceivable, incomprehensible. This can most definitely lead to lyricism. The language generated by this secret is not infrequently a tender probing of that which withdraws from the dominant order of the conventional word. While this order determines the conditions – it is so and not otherwise – such a language knows that words ultimately fall short. This language arouses a wholesome aversion against all solidity: everything can also always be otherwise.

But the question remains, whether this 'God', who can never finally be put into words, but who also has nothing to say when it matters, will ultimately

---

as a critique of religion. There is also something, albeit 'fantastical', akin to a *protestation* against the powers (Marx 1975b, p. 175).

4 Brecht 1976, p. 252.

be salutary. He – or she, or rather it? – remains silent on the matter. And a person who might approach him about this matter – oh, God, dammit, do not remain silent any longer, say something, say that you love us, or that you want nothing to do with us, so that at least we know where we're at and are no longer frustrated by a religiosity that keeps rescinding what it promises – would be barking up the wrong tree. For that which is unspeakable by nature cannot speak a redemptive word. And where a redemptive word is lacking, fundamentally and for all time, there that which is higher than all human reason threatens to amount to the eternal return of the same thing: a dominant culture and the discontent within it, the perpetual dialectic of master and servant, a struggle between man and woman without reconciliation. The existing order may not encompass everything, there is 'something' that will not be mastered by it, 'something' that resists this order. This can be called 'God', and this God can be linked to the 'something within us' that will not resign itself to what the existing order does to us and to the things we care about. This makes the inevitability of resistance a given: 'God', the highest 'Something', motivates it. Simultaneously, though, this means that the resistance leads to nothing other than a different order that is, again, frustrating. The moral of this story is: we must submit to the inevitable, resistance is futile, and an eternity of 'Civilisation and its Discontents' (Freud) is our fate.[5]

This is the religion that transcends 'civil religion' and its cult of the existing order, 'God beyond God' (Tillich).[6] The concomitant religiosity goes much further than a simple deification of political power. This has little more to offer than the human, the all-too-human image of an *Übermensch*, and is insufficiently unspeakable to really be able to count as a religion. So it seems a little banal to 'politicise' a religiosity, which goes much further than that, to a flat confirmation of the existing order. But is not precisely the 'nature' of its profundity – that being is ultimately unfathomable – the strongest argument of this order? For the unfathomable always carries the threat of disorder, anarchy, chaos within itself. We must master this chaos, which is why we need masters who create order. And it is true: religious experience cannot be fully contained in any

---

5 '[T]he intention that man should be "happy" is not included in the plan of "Creation". What we call happiness in the strictest sense comes from the (preferably sudden) satisfaction of needs which have been damned up to a high degree, and it is from its nature only possible as an episodic phenomenon' (Freud 1991, pp. 263 f.).

6 'It [the God beyond God] cannot be described in the way the God of all forms of theism can be described. It cannot be described in mystical terms either. It transcends both mysticism and personal encounter' (Tillich 1952, pp. 185 f.). Thank god, the latter cannot be said of the God of Israel. He personally encounters his people to the highest degree!

order. Being *is* unfathomable; it cannot withdraw from the dependence on powers that are beyond our control.[7] The modern notion that this might well be possible ('to become like God') turned out to be a dangerous illusion. But without the redeeming word, '[YHWH] did not create [the earth] as chaos' (Is 45:18), this *condition humaine* is eternal, and it will forever and ever push for an order that battles chaos, reins in anarchy.

The Bible is familiar with the Baals and the Astartes who represent more than the superiority of the masters who are in charge. They also embody the superiority of nature: its potency, its fertility. Hence they are the precondition for every culture. But unpredictable as they are, they are also its biggest threat. This is why following these gods is hopeless; they offer no perspective on delivery from slavery. On the contrary, they perpetuate slavery.

So has the last word on religion been spoken? Marx's lucid insight that religion can also be 'the *protest* against real distress',[8] might then be inspired by the subversive core of the Jewish and the Christian religion, it can also help to discover the same core in other religions. For those who, with the Bible, hope for the 'end of religion' (when 'God will be all in all', 1 Cor 15:28), this does not mean they have to despise the potential for resistance it bears.

The Gods of the Dominant Orders and the God who Liberates to Enable Life

The fact that we can speak of an exodus at all is entirely owing to the mercy of the primacy of the Name. The exodus begins with people hearing a voice that says: I am YHWH, your God. With this word the Name steps into the circle of gods, as a liberator. It takes the place they have commandeered for themselves. It breaks the power they have over the people. By identifying

---

7 Marxist religious critique refused to believe that being is unfathomable. The idea of the existence of (natural) powers that are alien and unfathomable to humans, which was fatal in Marxist opinion, is dated: 'When therefore man no longer merely proposes, but also disposes – only then will the last alien force which is still reflected in religion vanish; and with it will also vanish the religious reflection itself, for the simple reason that then there will be nothing to reflect' (Engels 1987, p. 302). In its overly enlightened state, it overlooked the fact that the unfathomable, sombre side of being challenges humans to the end. Even though it also resounds with the hope that we may still see 'through a mirror in the riddle', but then 'will recognise, how we are recognised' (1 Cor 13:12).

8 'Religious distress is at the same time the *expression* of real distress and also the *protest* against real distress. It is the sigh of the oppressed creature' (Marx 1975b, p. 175; cf. Rom 8:22: 'For we know: creation, too, sighs and has pains even to this day').

itself as the God of the exodus, this Name renders everything that the gods (re)present a lie. The name is the great atheist. Now, that which they have concealed in their unfathomability is brought to light: the secret of being is the delivery from slavery. It means the end of religion that humans had to come up with themselves based on their experience of reality. This experience directed them to the superiority of the political order to which they were subjected, as well as – ultimately – the superiority of a speechless nature, which bested it again and again with muteness. The Name opposes this experience. To serve this Name as the only God ('hear, Israel, YHWH, our God, YHWH is one!') means following his opposition. Those who follow him, reject 'natural theology' where the human is 'naturally' a 'debased, enslaved, forsaken, despicable being' (Marx) and overthrow all conditions that condemn the human to this fate.[9] The Name dictates the observance of the qualitatively endless difference between reverence for the sublime nature, which shapes the world of the gods, and the 'fear of YHWH', who puts nature into the perspective of its deliverance – for nature, too, is not good in and of itself; it, too, is thoroughly in need of deliverance.

The 'fear' that befits this God is not at the expense of the human. On the contrary, ordinary people especially are called upon constantly to keep in sight the enormity of the 'project' that this God has started with them – that he leads out of the house of bondage with a strong hand (Ex 13:3). No longer are they to let themselves be bullied by everything that purports to engender fear. For Israel to hear the following is liberating:

> The beginning of wisdom
> is the fear of YHWH,
> an insight that is good for all who follow it
> Ps 111:10

For it presupposes what immediately precedes it:

> Deliverance it sent to its people,
> tied the bond forever.
> Holy and fearful
> Is its name
> Ps 111:9

---

9 'The criticism of religion ends with the teaching that man is the highest being for man, hence with the categorical imperative to overthrow all relations in which man is a debased, enslaved, forsaken, despicable being' (Marx 1975b, p. 71).

This is the 'principle' that Israel must respect ('fear') for its own salvation!

This is an exodus that actually leads somewhere, the beginning of a long path that actually arrives somewhere, too. The exodus from the house of bondage does not mean an eternity on the road – without ever really arriving. This may seem fascinating for someone who is already sufficiently established to deem a permanent world trip a fabulous adventure. But those who are condemned to abandon the place where they are at home – because there is no life there – know better. And demand more. They are not driven by the globetrotter's *Wanderlust,* but by the 'homesickness' of the homeless: for once to arrive in a place where finally they can just *live,* without fear and need. The last book of the Bible ends with the possibility of such a homecoming. It offers the prospect of a city where this God and his people are united, without the possibility of anything ever coming between them:

> The city needs neither son nor moon
> To light it,
> For the glory of God
> illuminates it
>> Rv 21:23

The door is wide open unto a paradise where the 'tree of life' stands in the middle of the road and offers healing:

> In the middle of the road
> On this side of the river and its far side:
> Tree of life
> ...
> And the tree's leaves
> [serve] the healing of the peoples.
>> Rv 22:2

The journey is over, the time has passed when we could long for fulfilment. Utopia (Greek for: no place) finds its 'topos', its place.

Cultivating a longing that is never fulfilled is essentially a luxury that only those who have already found a place under the sun can allow themselves. But for those who have 'no place' in which to rest their head (Lk 9:58), the realisation that their longing will remain unsatisfied is tragic: their 'discontent in civilisation' is condemned to remain a part of this civilisation, their demand for delivery remains unrequited. All that is left is being-for-death. Then, too, the journey is at an end, but what awaits us is only a grave rather than the tree of life.

The fact that the Bible goes further than this and promises fulfilment is no luxury. For the people concerned here it is a matter of life and death. Utopian thought that fails to recognise this – that there are people who really have 'no place anywhere', who may even be denied a grave – demonstrates a light-heartedness bordering on decadence. Utopian thought that takes itself seriously has not finished until it has reason to say 'homeland'. This, then, is also the final word in the 'opus magnum' of the utopian thinker par excellence, Ernst Bloch, the 'principle of hope': homeland [*Heimat*]![10]

So the name represents a *project* that starts with an exodus and ends – finds its completion – in the Promised Land. He has come in order to

> deliver [the slave people] from the clutches of Egypt,
> to bring it out of that land
> into a good and open land
> where milk and honey flow
>> Ex 3:8

This project concerns this particular people, which is why it primarily points towards that which this people is given by God: *land*, which gives *this* people space, space to live, in abundance. Those who find this too limited and who would like immediately to speak of all humanity, quickly resort to common-places. The connection to people of flesh and blood, who start to work towards their freedom at a specific time and in a specific place and under specific con-ditions, is then swiftly lost sight of. The Kingdom of Freedom is turned into an 'idea', the whole world an abstraction, humanity a nice thought. Viewed from this idealist perspective, the real people, who strike out on the arduous path towards freedom, can only disappoint. No objection can be made against the sincerity of this idealism, or against the authenticity of the yearning for a better world which underwrites this idealism. But in this shape the idealism comes at the expense of solidarity with precisely those people, who are left no choice by

---

10   '*True genesis is not at the beginning but at the end*, and it starts to begin only when society and existence become radical, i.e. grasp their roots. But the root of history is the working, creating human being who reshape and overhauls the given facts. Once he has grasped himself and established what his is, without expropriation and alienation, in real democracy, there arises in the world something which shines into the childhood of all and in which no one has yet been: homeland' (Bloch 1986b, pp. 1375 f.).

their hunger for justice but to walk this arduous, human, all-too-human path (often to the bitter end). The project, to which this God ties his Name, is *this* path – of this people, in this land: I am YHWH, *your* God, who brought you out of Egypt.

No path leads past this special project: the generality that all people will arrive in the Kingdom of Freedom, that the whole world will be a space for living, and that abundance will be all-encompassing, is in line with *this* project. The distinctly biblical language, Hebrew, moves along this line: the word *erez* signifies both this special land and more generally: earth.

'In the beginning' *erez* means earth: 'In the beginning God created heaven and earth' (Gen 1:1). Does this mean that the general has primacy after all? But if we, together with Israel, hear this God's concern – this people's exodus from slavery – how can we not also hear the meaning 'land'? This narrative of the beginning is not as general as it seems. Rather, it is trying to articulate the special in its own way: earth is made for this land, for this project! It already aims at the project of the delivery from slavery. That is the aim of creation. This narrative's stubbornness in relation to this project will be discussed in the chapter 'Creation'.

The 'Project' Israel Points Beyond Itself

This liberation story's core is very farsighted, then:[11] the exodus from the enslaving Egyptian order has a universal meaning. The people that is brought into being by this exodus will be the 'light of the peoples' (Is 42:6; 49:6): The 'Torah Republic' (Veerkamp),[12] which it will found, will let the light of the Kingdom of Freedom, Equality and Solidarity shine for all. The revolution that takes place here and now – and not everywhere and nowhere – is intent on world revolution. It will only be over – completed, successful – once 'God [this God, whose name means the exodus] is all in all' (1 Cor 15:28).

---

11   Miskotte often used this phrase – 'The core is farsighted' – which he borrowed from the Dutch philosopher Van Senden, in order to emphasise the universality of a particular story: it tends towards cosmopolitanism, not small-mindedness.

12   'The time is the late fifth or early fourth century B.C.E. Here [in the Torah Republic at the time of Ezra and Nehemiah] a bit of freedom was instituted, without the pathos of the Athenians, who deemed their city state the paradise of freedom in contrast to the slave state of the barbarians (Persians). Unlike Athens's freedom, which relied on slave labour, the Torah Republic was intended to develop into a "free association of agricultural producers"' (Veerkamp 1992, p. 85).

In these terms this liberation movement's universality, its all-encompassing, holistic character is, very specifically: So long as not all – truly *all* – tears have been wiped dry (Rv 21:4), blithe talk of freedom, equality and solidarity remains terribly abstract. And whoever contends that this all-encompassing universality is 'totalitarian' and desirous of the *'übermenschlich'*, must face the question whether they do not take the things that make the world inhumane too lightly – in order to come to terms with that inhumane world. If 'totalitarian' is viewed as a peculiarity of ideologies such as fascism or communism, that work with all their might to exclude the 'other' in the name of a racist or humanist idea, then the question still remains whether there might not be yet another, wholly different but no less effective exclusion: the exclusion of this specific universality.

This is also the openness that is determined by the Name: I will be there, as he who I will be there. The core of this self-designation is: I am YHWH, your God. The continuation of the narrative illustrates that God does not withdraw from this: he is loyal. But the continuation of the narrative also illustrates that he can stay loyal to the project he started with Israel that far exceeds Israel's interpretation of that project. He – or is it she? – shatters the patriarchal frame in which the *sons* of Israel had enclosed the story of their liberation. Then we hear 'women's history' that tells of women's forceful interventions in men's history.

This intervention happens in the small yet significant Book of Ruth. It is a critical remark on 'Israel's becoming' as narrated in the Genesis. This story is handed from father to son: women bear a son to a man and the man then 'calls' his son's name. In the Book of Ruth, things are quite different. Here, Ruth is bearing a son not to her husband Boas, but to her mother-in-law Naomi – who has lost her two sons and with them her own future. And it is not the man, either, who calls out the son's name:

> The female neighbours called a name, they spoke:
> 'Naomi has had a son!',
> they called his name: Obed, – *he who serves.*
> He [who will serve Naomi!] is the father of Isaiah, the father of David.
> Ru 4:17

We can hope that the patriarchy will be pretty astonished at this![13]

---

13 Klara Butting made me aware of this 'intra-biblical critique' with her meaningfully entitled study *Die Buchstaben werden sich noch wundern* [*The letters will be surprised yet*]: 'The

He can also radically cross the boundary between his chosen people of Israel and the 'peoples'.

There are two Hebrew words for 'people': *Am* and *Goyim* (always plural). *Am* usually refers to the people of Israel, *Goyim* commonly refers to the peoples in whose midst Israel must try to realise its 'project'. As such, the peoples are the – very powerful and frequently also antagonistic – representatives of the social order Israel has broken with. The Goy (also in the singular) then becomes the non-Jew in Jewish parlance: the negation of Jewish existence, which for the Jews always means the temptation to assimilate in order to be rid of the yoke of the Torah. The word is usually left untranslated so that the link between *Goyim*, in the sense of the peoples opposing Israel, and the Goy as the non-Jew, who exemplifies these peoples in his entire way of life, is given full expression.

And he does this under such radical conditions that Israel more often than not cannot follow him – understandably so, given what it has itself understood of him. Surprisingly, as it turns out then, the God of Israel can call the community of Jews and Goy that avows Jesus as the Messiah 'his people', people who from Israel's perspective cannot possibly be his people because Israel itself is the 'only people'. This really is an absolute novelty from the point of view of Israel:

> Whom he also called,
> namely us, not only from the Jews, but also from the Goy.
> As he says in Hosea, too:
> Not-my-people I will call: My-people
>> Rom 9:24–25, quoting Hos 2:25

This is at the heart of the harsh conflict between the Jew Paul, who avows Jesus as the Messiah, and the great majority of his Jewish brothers and sisters: does this novelty even conform to the spirit of the Torah? Even within the community who avowed Jesus as Messiah some people took for granted that a Goy, who wanted to join the community, had to become a Jew, that is, had to be circumcised and uphold the Torah (Acts 15:5).

Book of Ruth renders this explosive power visible in the confrontation between a woman's story and a story of conception. And it assists in tracing the hope for the abandonment of patriarchal power relations within the tradition of the story of conception as it has survived, as well as in reading and revising this tradition while holding on to this hope' (Butting 1994, p. 48).

How else, after all, can a Goy demonstrate that he sides unconditionally with the Jews? Paul's enthused project of a community that showed in practice that the 'fence' of animosity between Jews and Goy had been 'torn down' (Eph 2:14) – the reason for Paul's vehement insistence on the fact that it should not be demanded of the Goy to allow themselves to be circumcised, because such a demand would undo the novelty – was pure reverie to their mind. How could he interpret Hosea's words so loosely that they no longer referred to Israel (which was certainly the case for Hosea), but to the creation of a new people? The God of the Bible cannot be as open as that.

Church history, incidentally, proved Judaism, which rejected this novelty from the bottom of its heart, right: the Goy animosity against the Jews quickly gained the upper hand in theory and practice of the church – with all its consequences. Paul's strong repudiation of the terrible misunderstanding of his message, that the novelty was the fact that God had cast out his people (Rom 11:1: impossible!), could not avoid this. (For a detailed discussion see Postscript 1).

The God of Israel takes the liberty to be the God of all people in 'being present' as he then really 'is present': the free-thinking, broadminded, open God. So open that Israel cannot believe its eyes.

And neither, one hopes, can we, because this openness is far from 'obvious'. Obviously, God is the God of all people, that goes without saying. Just as much as it then goes without saying that the universal God's standing, because he is above all particularity, is higher than that god's, who has taken one tribe of people to heart above others. That is our 'obvious' (natural) theology: the specific is subordinate to the general. But for a 'subordinated' people such as Israel this means: the general is a reality in which there is no place for a people like Israel – except in the house of bondage. What the Bible refers to as God shatters precisely this general frame: he is the God of *Israel*. The fact that this God wants to be 'all in all' by no means goes without saying; we have to hear him say it to us. What we will never hear him say, though, is that Israel should subordinate itself again!

A God Who Can Be Moved

Without this God's word of deliverance, the people who wander in darkness (Is 9:1; Mt 4:16) are irredeemably lost. And we, too, who see the light through this people, would be at a complete loss without this word of deliverance. The exodus begins with the revelation of the NAME: I will be there, as he who I will be there. But there is something that moves this NAME to lead this people forth from the house of bondage. It is a sigh beneath the slavery, the people's cry

for help, their outcry: 'Who will save me from the body of this death?' (Rom
7:24)[14]

> In those many days it happened:
> the King of Egypt died.
> But the children of Israel sighed – from slavery
> they cried out,
> their cry for help ascended to God from slavery.
>> Ex 2:23

This cry, which finds no sympathetic ear on earth, has no way out but upwards:
Where will my help come from (Ps 121:1)?[15] Well, definitely not from above.
After all, what is above merely reflects the order down here: what else do the
gods represent but magnified earthly rulers? Those who suffer from the earthly
rulers can expect nothing from above. The higher up they search for it, the
slimmer are the chances of a possible escape route. 'Heaven' is probably the
last place that salvation will come from.

The fact that this cry is not left unanswered, that help actually arrives, is
hence utterly surprising:

> But God heard their moans
>> Ex 2:24a

Those who wish to understand what is being said here must not insist in advance
that God hears ('obviously' he hears). We must bring to mind the context of this text's
intervention. In this (religious, ideological) context, it is out of the question that God
hears in this way. The gods of a natural theology hear – when they hear at all – such
moaning as rebellion against the order they have established. Their answer – if they
answer – is: Subordinate yourselves.

---

14 The Marxist John Holloway, who lives in Mexico, opens his book with such a cry: 'In the
    beginning is the scream. We scream. When we write or when we read, it is easy to forget
    that the beginning is not the word, but the scream. Faced with the mutilation of human
    lives by capitalism, a scream of sadness, a scream of horror, a scream of anger, a scream of
    refusal: NO' (Holloway 2002, p. 1).

15 'It is not said that people prayed to God. They groaned, they cried out. Maybe their cry was
    a curse, or a shout of protest' (Wielenga 1981, p. 49).

What is surprising – absolutely surprising – is that this God is a god who is moved by the cry for help. He wants to be a god who apparently cannot be thought otherwise than as a god who is moved by people who cry out their misery. A god who himself experiences the suffering of these people – as an unbearable suffering that forces him into motion.

We cannot logically derive this God from this people's experience of suffering. As such, this experience represents nothing more than the experience itself, and this cry is left hanging. But ever since this 'God heard their moans' the experience has been inextricably interwoven with the revelation of the Name.

The revelation of the Name, then, means that this experience matters – that the 'something' within humans, which resists oppression, is granted theological status. Their discontent in civilisation is shared – by God himself! And this in such a way that makes their cries constitutive of his revelation: they cry out, he hears. We could speculate at great length as to whether he could have acted otherwise, speaking of his freedom as a divine freedom, that must be thought as absolute freedom by definition in any other way. But then we are the ones again who are contemplating God. Then we are still occupied with that which the name's revelation sought to render finally impossible. Then we again are thinking like people who have not yet heard this God's 'logos' – the Word – and revert to the 'logic' of a natural theology: 'obviously' God could always act otherwise, 'obviously' he is at liberty to do as he pleases. And 'obviously' we cannot depend upon him – only on the fact that what we do witness points to the fact that he is not particularly interested in human suffering. The great philosopher Aristotle is right: God sets everything in motion, but he himself is not moved by anything – for how can a god who is dependent on something other than himself be God? He is the 'mover' who remains unmoved and immovable, obviously.

Nothing else in classical Greek philosophy is as self-evident as the idea that the principle of our moving reality cannot itself be moved. For if 'everything flows' (*pantha rhei*), then nothing is certain, everything is built on sand. Where does that leave the dominant order, whose final truth philosophy purports to be? The extent to which the dominant order really is reflected is made evident by the fact that 'apathy' (not-being-able-to-suffer) is the 'divine' characteristic par excellence: not 'being moved' by anything or anyone is – obviously! – the mark of a god.

The God of the Bible is quite distinct from this. He subscribes to his own, counter-natural logic. No, different even from that: he is moved by a cry from below:

But God heard their moans,
and God remembered his bond with Abraham, with Isaac and with
    Jacob,
and God saw the Children of Israel,
and God recognised.
>   Ex 2:24–25

'God remembered his bond'. So there is something that precedes this hearing of Israel's groans after all. Something has already happened: the bond that God tied with Abraham, Isaac and Jacob. He with them! He first:

YHWH spoke to Abraham:
You go forth from your land,
from your kin,
from your father's house
>   Gn 12:1

Here already then, the NAME is mentioned, YHWH. Here it already reveals itself as the God of the exodus, the Exodus-God: *from* your land,[16] *from* your kin, *from* your father's house. And he does this without heeding an appeal on the part of Abraham. But here, at the beginning of the story of the exodus from Egypt, the exodus in the strictest sense, we are meant to forget that. Because Israel has forgotten it. It is not the people, after all, who remember the bond that God tied with Abraham, Isaac and Jacob. The people cry out with misery, that is all. *God* remembers. And if we follow the narrative: he is moved to remember by the people's outcry. This is the point of the exodus narrative where the name reveals itself, commits itself to being God in that way and none other. Namely that God who hears the outcry of an oppressed people and then decides to 'descend' from heaven and actively intervene on earth:

I have seen, seen the oppression of my people,
which is in Egypt,
I have heard how they cry out at the hands of their tormentors,
I have recognised their suffering.

---

16   Abraham must leave two cities in this land: Ur (still in the company of his father Terah's kin) and Haran. Both are in the Babylonian Empire, both are sacred places (of the moon god Shin). Abraham's 'exodus' alludes to Israel's return from exile, from the realm of the gods who tempt it again and again to assimilate to the dominant order.

So I descended,
in order to save it from the grasp of Egypt
> Ex 3:7–8a

Something entirely new is happening here, something never seen before:

I am YHWH.
I appeared to Abraham, Isaac and Jacob
as the terrible God,
but they never knew my name, YHWH.
> Ex 6:2–3

A Radical New Beginning

The revelation of the Name is an intervention in the dominant order. First, it is an intervention in the order of the gods, in the field of *ideology*. Those who are addressed by the story of the exodus are liberated from the fatal thought that the powers placed above them have been ordered there by God ('It is God's wish').[17] They no longer believe that their state of subjugation is divinely established fate. Said in other, secular, terms – in a non-religious world that has lost the word 'God' – they are liberated from the fatal thought that the orders to date, in which one person exists at the cost of another, represent the be all and end all of historical truth. They no longer believe in the inevitability of giving in to this order, of collaborating with it, of resting in it. Because this is – obviously! – just the way it is. This fatal thought is permanently suggested by the dominant order – and heavily propagated by its media so that the order is elevated above all critical doubt. And in the language of religion this means: elevated to be God.[18]

But the revelation of the name also intervenes in the field of *politics*. For the ideology that it explicitly attacks has a political tagline. It attacks the political system that drives Israel into a corner. The crucial confrontation in the story of the exodus is the confrontation between the NAME and Pharaoh:

---

17   This is the reasoning Napoleon, at this point very understanding, gives for his concordance with the Pope: 'No society can endure without religion. How can a person, who is starving to death beside a glutton, accept this discrepancy unless an authority tells him: it is God's will. Poor and rich must both exist, but one day, in eternity, it will be different'.

18   Thus Margaret Thatcher made a god of that fatality 'there is no alternative' (TINA). Unfortunately, she was not without success.

But then you will speak to Pharaoh:
thus spoke YHWH:
my first-born son is Israel,
I speak to you:
release my son into freedom, so he may serve me,
and should you refuse to release him into freedom,
I will kill your first-born son.
> Ex 4:22–23

Just as according to the dominant ideology Pharaoh – obviously! – is the 'son of God', so the continuance of the Pharaonic system, legitimated 'from above', is embodied 'down below' by Pharaoh's 'first-born son'. Pharaoh's politics are reproduced through this 'first-born son'. By introducing Israel as *his* 'first-born son', YHWH not only shatters the legitimisation of the Pharaonic system 'from above' – not Pharaoh but Israel is the 'son of God' – but also disrupts the reproduction of the system 'down below'. He opposes his 'first-born son' Israel to Pharaoh's 'first-born son'. The crucial question is: Which one has a future, the Pharaonic system or the 'project' Israel? There can be no compromise between them: if a politics in the manner of Israel's is to have a future, then the future of a politics in the manner of Pharaoh must be forbidden. And the fact that there really can be no compromise is emphasised by the words immediately preceding the ones quoted above:

But I will harden his [Pharaoh's] heart,
should he not release the people into freedom.
> Ex 4:21

The fact that it is YHWH himself who 'hardens' Pharaoh's heart suggests that he is the one who renders a compromise between the two systems impossible. He begrudges Pharaoh the freedom to choose a different path, so to speak. But does he not then affirm what has always been the case, anyway, throughout world history: a dominant order that refuses to be brought to its senses? Or is it precisely the fact that the NAME 'plays a part', promises that the final word has not been spoken with this destructive delusion? Ultimately, it is the Liberator-God who determines that a different world is possible!

The exodus represents not only the emergence of the slave from the ideology of the oppression that renders him dependent. The exodus is also and ultimately the beginning of a liberation movement in which political questions play a crucial part. The pros and cons of the monarchy, and a monarchy that explicitly distances itself from what the 'other peoples' mean by it, will be at issue. A monarchy that is not 'of this world order' (Jn 18:36)[19] will be made imaginable, a monarchy without subjects, a society without ruler-ship, a cooperative of 'friends'.

Thus Jesus speaks to his disciples: 'No longer do I call you slaves ... I have called you friends' (Jn 15:15). This circle of friends (which, we may hope, also includes women) is the community. But the community is the beginning of a new world order, the principle of a humanity that still lies ahead for humanity.

'Israel's story' is also primarily a political story. It takes place amidst the great empires of the world at the time: Egypt, Assyria, Babylon, Persia. There is no escape. At most, an – often quite relative – independence can be achieved.

The 'historical' books, which the Hebrew canon includes in the 'first prophets', because they are written from the prophetic perspective where the kingdom has not yet come, all have political titles: Joshua (the charismatic leader of the moving in), Judges (a political function), Samuel (a judge), Kings.

Similarly, exile, which appears to signify the final loss of independence, the end of Israel as a political project, remains a political issue. The end of exile, which is hoped for, will be the return to the Promised Land: the recovery of political independence.

The prophetic books, according to the Hebrew canon the 'second prophets', are actually named after prophets – unlike the 'first prophets'. None of them is a political figure in the way that Judges and Kings are. They are more akin to dissidents, who will not cooperate in the shaping of politics. But their dissidence is political: their critique is directed at the political leadership in the first place, their focus is on a new exodus.

The third category of Bible books known to the Hebrew canon – the Writings (alongside Torah and Prophets) – also contains two books that speak of the recovery of political independence in the shape of a real Torah Republic: Ezra and Nehemiah. In these books, politics is not a thing of utopian thought, but is in every respect a question of 'Realpolitik'. They do not conceal the precariousness of this Torah Republic's status under the present (dreadful!) circumstances. They even defend the necessity of a radical dissociation from the rest of the world, including a 'wall' (Neh 2:17)!

---

19 In relation to the Greek *kosmos*, which is translated as 'world order', Ton Veerkamp remarks the following: 'The word means what rabbis call *'olam ha-se'*, 'this world era'. It is a political category: the dominant world order, [for John] the Roman Empire' (Veerkamp 2005, p. 14).

A Just Order as the Prerequisite of Freedom

Ultimately, though, the revelation of the NAME is primarily an intervention in the field of *economics*: the production and distribution of the things humans need in order to live. And more, much more than that: what is revealed is the prospect of a land of abundance,[20] a world filled with more than anybody needs, a society in which nobody is lacking anything anymore (Ps 23:1):

> So I descended,
> to deliver [Israel] from the clutches of Egypt,
> to bring it out of that land
> into a good and open land
> where milk and honey flow
>   Ex 3:8

Led forth from the house of bondage of a subjugating ideology and the oppressive pharaonic state legitimated by this ideology, the path leads towards the Promised Land. The 'ideology' of the NAME points towards it, the politics of Judges and Kings is oriented towards it, it is the purpose of prophetic dissidence: the Promised Land. It will be the land where everyone shares everything (Acts 2:44), where, in the first instance, everyone has the land in common:

> The land may not be sold irrevocably,
> for the land belongs to me [YHWH]
>   Lv 25:23

The land is the means of nourishment, the means of production par excellence. Without land, no life, or at best a life dependent on those who own the land. The relation to the land determines the way of life, determines how life can be lived, why, it determines whether life can be lived at all. And the relation to the land is an economic question: who controls production; who distributes food? Property relations are crucial: who owns the land?

The revolutionary meaning of the phrase 'the land belongs to me [YHWH]' is that it belongs to no one else, no person has the right to say: this or that land belongs to me.

---

20   As Volker Braun puts it in his 'Song of Communism': Sometime, and this will be soon | The rivers will flow uphill | And no one will be cold anymore | and the sun will rise in the winter. | The table will nearly set itself then – | brothers, what a pleasure! | Our life will no longer be a trickle | But of the highest measure! (Braun 1976, p. 94).

The land is not for sale, under no circumstances may it be 'privatised' (lat. *privare* = to rob).

Land is the material basis of all social riches. This is why a society which is social is one in which the land has been socialised. Different social relations are first and foremost different property relations. So long as the means of production are private property, society remains an a-social affair, despite all good intentions. Delivery from slavery specifically means: arrival in the Promised *Land*.

The fact that following this arrival a long arduous path awaits ('the travails of the plains') is another story – one told in the books of the 'first prophets'. It is the story of the real Israel. Here it is crucial to understand why the delivery from slavery consists in solving the 'land question' – a solution that is impossible without posing the question of property. This is the point where there is an extraordinary affinity between biblical theology and Marxist theory: 'the theory of the communists may be summed up in this single sentence: Abolition of private property.'[21]

---

21   Marx and Engels 1976b, p. 498. In 1935, Bertolt Brecht spoke to similar effect at the International Writers' Congress in Defense of Culture in Paris (against National Socialism): 'Comrades, let us talk about the conditions of property ownership' (2003, p. 162). For a change in property relations is the necessary (even if not the sufficient) condition for the effective combatting of barbarism.

Covenant

The singularity of the God of Israel – his 'unicity' ('Hear, Israel, YHWH, our God, YHWH is one') – is due to the fact that he really wants to be the God of *Israel*. First and foremost this means that he hears the cry of this people, lost in the Egyptian darkness, and decides to let them ascend to a land of abundance where justice reigns – justice for *all*, to the last person, who will come first there. Here, in this movement from on high to far below, he is 'entirely different' from the 'gods'.

The 'language of the message' (Buber) conveys this, down to its grammar. For biblically speaking, the God of Israel is never the subject of the so-called hifil form of the verb *abad*: to make a slave of. On the contrary, in the relationship to his people he is the subject of the hifil form of *alah*: to let ascend. And when he himself stands up, then it is not in order to elevate himself to the status of a highest Being, but in order to 'descend':

> So I descended,
> to deliver it from the clutches of Egypt
> > Ex 3:8a

The Reality of Liberation Struggles

The God of Israel is in conflict with the 'gods'. Unlike the God of metaphysics, he is neither too great nor too absolute to repair to the thick of the battle and actually fight out this conflict: the battle over who wields power in heaven and on earth.[1] He disrupts the peace on Mount Olympus, where the gods revel in their blissfulness. The world of the gods is turned into a battleground, and their earthly representatives are not spared either:

> YHWH of the hosts,
> the God of Israel, has spoken:

---

1 'God is great, but not "absolute" … God, the eternal and true God, humbles himself to become "a" god in the assembly of gods and to appear within the sphere of influence of the powers' (Miskotte 1967, p. 225).

Here I am
to call Amon of Thebes to account,
Pharaoh and Egypt,
his gods and his kings,
the Pharaoh and those who seek shelter with him
      Jer 46:25

This is the same message that God gives to Moses concerning the question of whether Pharaoh will let the people issue forth into freedom: it will be a fight to the death. The word that he commands this 'son of God' to speak is extremely militant:

But I know
that the king of Egypt will not let you go
– except by the force of a strong hand.
I will reach out my hand,
I will strike Egypt with all the marvels
I will perform in its midst –
only then will he send you forth into freedom!
      Ex 3:19–20

These are words of command and the 'marvels' that are announced are acts of violence: the 'strikes' to be inflicted on Egypt are real and relentless. The realism of the oppressed, who know that the oppressor will never voluntarily cede power in his lifetime, is shared by the God of the oppressed ('I know …'). Those who feel superior to this realism – and even consider it the moral high ground (of the Sermon on the Mount, for instance) – have to ask themselves whether it is not only on account of their privileged position that they can afford this feeling of superiority.

Whether the Sermon on the Mount (Mt 5–8) intends to offer a moral high ground, by the way, is questionable. The phrase 'turn the other cheek' when struck on the right cheek (Mt 5:39) can easily be read as not moralist: it is the only way for the powerless victim of violence to maintain their dignity. The victim, after all, does not have the power to strike back.[2] What they can do very well, though, is to say: 'Go ahead, strike me, you will not break me'. Equally, the command to offer your coat to the person who

---

2   In his piece on the ethics of the Sermon on the Mount, Rochus Zuurmond says: 'Under the circumstances of total oppression the only way to resist power is to render it objectless. Verse 39 ff. shows one way of achieving this … You remain in charge … This prevents you from letting yourself go – succumb to a full-blown depression from which there is no escape any more, where all hope for liberation is lost' (Zuurmond 1983, p. 90).

has robbed you of your shirt and who is stronger than you (Mt 5:40) can be read as follows: 'Have the rest of my clothing, but do not think for a moment that I, too, am now your property'. If we can speak of morality here, then it is the morality of the weak, who does not concede the triumph of violence to the strong. It is the strength of the weak to 'defeat' the evil done to them 'with the good' (Rom 12:21). Perhaps this makes the strong reflect, and breaks the fatal cycle of violence and counter-violence. But this cannot readily be made into a 'moral high ground' that is valid everywhere, always and for everyone.[3] It is a different thing altogether that the messianic community is indeed commanded to break this fatal cycle – not by prescribing the ethos of the Sermon on the Mount to others, but by *not* repaying evil with evil in its own practice.[4] For thus it avows, through its actions, that God's word, as it 'became flesh' through Jesus, is not violence but solidarity to the end.

The God of Israel is hence 'entirely different' from the gods who make humans their subjects: he lets them ascend. This is not to say that only God acts and the people simply passively let what happens happen. This people are not clockwork that proceeds according to the mechanism the 'great clock maker' devised for them.[5] The living God lets a *people* ascend, not a thing, but an assembly of humans, who go along with this ascension in their entirely human fashion. They are committed – with 'all their heart, all their soul, all their power' (Dt 6:5: *'Sch'ma'* Israel'). Set in motion, they now also start to move. To ascend means: head held high to consider what serves the purpose of liberation, and heart held high in order to take courage to keep going. For this people knows: above, in heaven, rules none other than their God,

> Who has his seat on high,
> who looks down below – on heaven and on earth,
> erects the small man from the dust,
> raises the poor man from the dirt
>> Ps 113:5–7

---

3 'We can ask ourselves, whether this entwining of strategy and ethics, which is very circumstantial, even retains any value beyond the context of humiliation and oppression. The answer will have to be that an ethos born from oppression, where love and solidarity have to be learned under great pressure, can hail a new era of possibilities for peace among men after that oppression' (Zuurmond 1983, p. 91).

4 But Paul also says: 'If possible – in as much as it is up to you' (Rom 12:18).

5 'Clock maker' was a popular metaphor during the Enlightenment that intended to express the following: 'God' may have created the world, but now it simply runs like clockwork, rendering interventions on his part impossible. This is comforting for those who see a reactionary monster in God, fatal for all those, who have no life in this world.

The 'moral' of this God's story is anything but 'God is everything, humans are nothing'. He is also a 'singular' God in as much as he does not single-handedly wage war against the gods and their earthly representatives. He includes his people in this battle.

Admittedly, it is he who takes the initiative, and he is prepared to take it again and again. He does not abandon his people, either; he stays involved in this battle.[6] This is his name, too: YHWH, I will be there! Which is why the people have the courage to profess:

> Be furious, you peoples –
> and be shattered!
> Listen, all you far-away lands:
> arm yourselves – and be shattered,
> arm yourselves – and be shattered,
> make a plan, it will be thwarted,
> speak a word, it will not come to pass,
> because *immanuel*, – God is with us!
>   Is 8:9–10

But he does everything in conjunction with his people, in a bond[7] that he keeps from beginning to end. His unique 'I will be there, as he who I will be there' reveals itself to be a *'Being*-in-bond'. Admittedly, *immanuel* (God is with us) initially signifies God's liberating presence among his people:

> but you,
> Israel, my servant,
> Jacob, whom I have chosen,
> descendant of Abraham, whom I love!

---

6 According to Frank Crüsemann, the radicalness of this involvement is already evident in the making of the Covenant in Gn 15:17: 'metaphorically and partly veiled the story is told of how God himself undergoes a *berith* [bonding] ceremony, which is usually performed by the human partner ... means that God can leave [this covenant] only on the condition of his own death. This God would no longer be God should his pledge lapse. God without Israel would be a different God from the one the Bible speaks of' (Crüsemann 2003, pp. 285 f.).

7 [Translator's note: The German words 'Bund' and 'Verbundenheit' clearly share the same root, a link which is lost in the English translation for which I have chosen the words 'covenant' and 'bond'. The link is important, though, and bears noting].

...
be never fearful,
for I am with you [*imacha ani*: with you I],
never look around,
for I am your God [*elohim*];
I strengthen you,
yes, I help you,
yes, I hold onto you
with the right hand of my righteousness
> Is 41:8–10

But the name Immanuel is given to a human being:

there, that young woman will become pregnant
and bear a son.
She shall shout out his name:
Immanuel, God is with us!
> Is 7:14

God's Presence in the Liberated Human

God does not want to be a God-with-us without this son, who embodies the 'with us'. The fact that a human child bears this name shows in what way God wants to be 'with us': it is a human who, with his name, is allowed to attest to the humanity of the NAME.

The community that avows Jesus as Messiah is moving along the line of this correlation intended by God himself: the human not without God, but God not without the human either. The 'fulfilment' of God's word is the occurrence of this word spoken by Isaiah (Mt 1:23). Whether Jesus is really the Messiah is the big question that divides this community from the synagogue. But they should be able to come together in the belief that the 'Being-in-bond' cannot exist without being fulfilled – by God *and* by humanity. The church should then cease to suggest, though, that it worships Jesus as though he were God.

God begins:

I am YHWH,
your God,

who brought you
out of Egypt, out of the house of bondage.
> Ex 20:2

But in the same breath he goes on to address the responsibilities of this 'you'. What follows are imperatives, commands, instructions. Now you must do what you are commanded to do: really be the 'you' who ascends to the Promised Land with this 'I am YHWH'. You are to be a free person, who will henceforth refuse to follow the gods, who will only lead you into slavery:

next to me
you shall have
no other gods
> Ex 20:3

A liberated person, who no longer deifies any earthly power, and who will never again fall to your knees before these 'gods', whom you can look in the eye with head held high:

make no likeness of God for yourself,
nor an idol
of anything in heaven on high, on earth below or in the water under the
   earth.
> Ex 20:4

A liberated person, who does not speak the name of your God in such a way that it becomes an empty phrase, which can then refer to all manner of things that contradict this Name:

Do not abuse
the name YHWH, your God's,
for nothing
> Ex 20:7

A liberated person, who knows you are beholden to the social programme of the liberation of work(ers), and is decided in this Name:

Remember
the Sabbath Day
– keep it holy

...
no work is to be done
by you, your son, your daughter,
your male slave, your female slave, your animal,
and the stranger who stays in your house.
> Ex 20:8–10

A liberated person, who champions a solidary society which is not determined by the law of the jungle:

do not commit murder.
> Ex 20:13

A solidary society, where women are not the objects of sexual exploitation:

do not commit adultery.[8]
> Ex 20:14

A solidary society, where fellow humans are no longer snatched up to be sold into slavery:

do not steal.[9]
> Ex 20:15

And falsehoods do not rule:

Make no statement against your neighbour
in order to slander him.
> Ex 20:16

A solidary society, where each leaves the other sufficient space to live, and does not begrudge them what is theirs:

do not desire
your neighbour's house,

---

8 The social context of these commandments is a patriarchal culture. It is the man who is addressed. He should not treat the other's wife as though she were his own. It does also mean, however: not treating her as an object to be handled at will.

9 The 'stealing' refers to kidnapping: people were abducted in order to be sold into slavery.

> do not desire your neighbour's wife,
> his male slave, his female slave, his oxen, his donkey,
> or anything else that belongs to your neighbour.
>> Ex 20:17

These are all quotations from the so-called Decalogue ('ten words').[10] These 'ten words' concisely capture the entire structure of the alliance 'God-with-us'. The 'I' who speaks here (YHWH) gives the floor to a 'you', who thus also becomes responsible for the purpose of the covenant: a society without domination. The punchline is a socio-economic programme: the phrase 'do not desire' '*anything* that belongs to your neighbour' precludes any kind of private property, where people steal what they need from each other (*privare* means to steal, after all) – house, woman (the programme is patriarchal), male and female slave (but theirs, too, is the outlook of delivery *from* slavery: the jubilee, the great liberation announced by Lv 25:8–24), the means of production (*work* animals: oxen and donkey). This presupposes a society in which everyone is still the owner of their means of production. The prohibition to dispossess these is, in a society based on the premise 'property as robbery', the commandment to dispossess the dispossessors.[11] The perspective is communist: everyone will have everything *in common* (Acts 4:32).

The structure of this alliance 'God-with-us' is most appositely expressed in the phrase:

> I take you as my people,
> I become your God
>> Ex 6:7

You to me, I to you – this is the alliance brought to a point. The variations of this phrase showcase the extent to which this really concerns a true bond in which both God and his people are present: for each other, and hence together. One variant puts it this way:

---

10   So-called in Ex 34:28 because these are not, after all, ten *commandments* (as we tend to call them), but the word of liberation ('I am YHWH, your God, who brought you out of Egypt, out of the house of bondage'), and the subsequent words are intended to lead to a liberating practice.

11   In the *Communist Manifesto*, too, the first measure after the proletarian revolution is: 'Abolition of property in land' (Marx and Engels 1976a, p. 504).

> listen to my voice,
> then I will be your God
> and you will be my people!
>> Jer 7:23

Here, it is God's voice that first announces that he wants to be the God of this people, and that this people can hence be present as this God's people. This people would have never existed without this voice, would never have been a people. But the people's own responsibility can already be heard in the 'listen to my voice' of deliverance. For only by listening to this voice are the people truly turned into this God's people. Should the people move beyond the realm of this 'hearing' – should they be disobedient – they will turn back into a non-people and God says:

> Call out his name *Lo-Ammi,*
> 'Not-my-people',
> for *you are not my people,*
> *and I, I am not there for you.*
>> Hos 1:9

A different variant of the phrase articulates this quite explicitly:

> listen to my voice,
> do everything
> that I command,
> *then you will be my people,*
> *and I will be your God!*
>> Jer 11:4

Here, acting in accordance with the commandment takes precedence. The people have to be there for God first, and then God will, in turn, be there for the people. The bond cannot proceed only from him. The 'I will be your God' is inextricably bound up with the 'you will be my people'.

This correlation between God and his people is part of the 'essence of Judaism'. God and his people need each other: 'As Rabbi Elazar haKafar said (so that God speaks, as it were): "My Torah is in your hand and the end is in mine, and we both need each other. As you need me to bring the end, so I need you to guard my Torah"' (Pesikta Rabbati 31). And the Midrash to Is 43:12 ('You are my witnesses, says YHWH, and I am God') is quoted again and again: 'That is, when ye are My witnesses, I am God, and when ye are not My witnesses, I am, as it were, not God'.[12] As it were! There remains a slight asymmetry that may perhaps be significant: even when the people fully abandon their role as witnesses, the covenant has not been lost entirely. This is because God 'is there', even then. And what if he is not there, as was the case for many Jews in Auschwitz? Then everything can depend on the Jews keeping their faith with their God. Keeping faith in him means doing Torah.[13] For even when God abandons his people, they still have the Torah. And there is a Midrash that says that for God himself, too, doing Torah is more important than that the people honour him: 'If they abandon me, I will come to terms with it, so long as they do not abandon my Torah' (Chagiga, Halacha 7).

The Covenant under Threat and God's Loyalty

And if God has anything to do with it, they will stay bound to it! Where experience suggests that the people do not want to be his people, he does not settle for that. Experience – it is what it is – does not have the final say. Despite all that has gone awry between God and his people, there will come a time when they find each other: he *will be* their God, they *will be* his people!

This is what the people hear the prophets say – those persistent witnesses to the principle of hope against all hope. To them, it is unimaginable that the covenant might have no future, that the people might no longer have hope, that their world might forever be a valley of tears. Visionaries that they are they see: a different world is possible! They believe in the coming of a *kairos*, an extraordinary moment when suddenly, unexpectedly, surprisingly everything is different. They declare God's word, which promises:

> I give them a unified heart,
> and I give a new spirit into them,
> I remove the stony heart from their flesh

---

12   Fackenheim 1987, p. 286.

13   'A midrash asks why the Divine covenant with Abraham was required. "This", is the answer, "may be compared to a house on fire. People ask, does the house have no owner? Through the children of Abraham God says: "I am the owner of the house". A Jew today still willing to convey this message has a question of its own: If the house has an owner, why does He not put the fire out? Perhaps He can and yet will. Perhaps He cannot or will not. But if he cannot or will not, a Jew today must do what he can to put the fire out himself. A cabbalistic saying is to the effect that the effort from below calls forth a response from above' (Fackenheim 1987, p. 292).

and give them a heart of flesh:
so that they follow my commandments,
keep my statutes
and practice them.
They will be my people
and I will be their God.

      Ez 11:19–20

What we hear is the fantastic protest against the fatal thought that the coin-ciding of a liberating God and a people who also let themselves be moved by the consequent freedom is doomed to fail. But this protest does not pursue the obvious solution into a religion of deliverance where God does everything because humanity has marginalised itself through its sinfulness. God does not take the place of the human, but creates the new human, the one he had envisioned from the start: the human in his own image. And this new human is not the deputy of the real people either, a people who have so hope-lessly lost their way. The new human *is* this people, but this people animated by a 'new spirit' who whole-heartedly follow the path shown by God in the Torah (his 'commandments' and 'laws'). The commandment remains: Act in his spirit!

The alliance structure of the 'God-with-us' is hence not revoked, but radically renewed:

And look
The days will come,
– thus YHWH's word –
when I will enter
into a *new covenant*
with the House of Israel and the House of Judea.
Not like the bond
I entered into with their fathers
on the day I took their hand
and brought them forth from Israel:
this my bond they could break.
...
For this is the bond
that I will enter into with the house of Israel
...
I will give my Torah into them,
will inscribe it on their heart,

thus I will be their God,
and they will be my people.
> Jer 31:31–33

Israelite religion is no escape into heavenly spheres where everything is set aright. This people's service to God is listening to the commandment to be a liberation movement in practice. Serving this God does not mean to subject oneself to all manner of religious rituals, all of which amount to the human having to walk through dust on behalf of some higher power. This is a God who 'raises the poor from the dirt' (Ps 113:7). Serving him hence means abiding by his bond with the poor, being a follower of his partisan preference for the oppressed. Biblically speaking, 'true religion' is to serve 'your neighbour', the 'comrade' as Buber translates, who like you depends on solidarity, who like you is helped by a liberation movement.

This is why the commandment 'love your neighbour, (he is) like you'[14] is *equal* to the commandment 'love YHWH, your God, with all your heart and all your life and all your reason' (Mt 22:37–40). The fact that the commandment to love God is called 'the great and first commandment' (Mt 22:38) does not contradict this. On the contrary, this commandment takes precedence because this God leads the way with his great initiative to bring the slave people forth from slavery!

The usual translation of this commandment as 'love your neighbour *as yourself*' is ambiguous. It has nothing to do with love of the self as the condition for the possibility of loving somebody else – as true as it may be that those who have never experienced love themselves (victims of sexual violence or parental neglect) are often not able to love others. The 'neighbour' is, specifically, whoever is closest to Israel, the slave people. It designates a social position: those who, 'like Israel', are at the bottom of society. And *'loving'* in this context does not mean the kind of love that exists between lovers – and that is celebrated in all its lustful glory in the Song of Songs. This love cannot be commanded, either. Loving your neighbour means: acting in solidarity, standing alongside the other, who cannot save him or herself without you – as you cannot save yourself without them.

Remembrance and Celebration

But even a liberation movement needs its rituals: rituals that visually represent the liberation and thus bear witness to the flight from oppression. The labour movement is unimaginable without the May Day marches with their flags,

---

14   The Hebrew *kemocha* literally translates into: (he is) like you.

slogans and songs. The women's movement is equally unthinkable without International Women's Day and its slogans and songs. The gay movement has its Pink Saturday and celebrates this by taking a stand in a colourful parade. The anti-imperialist movement in Latin America has a liturgy that symbolises the fact that the *compañeras* and *compañeros* who have died in battle also walk amongst their ranks: the living shout 'presente' when the names of the dead are called out. These are all rituals that serve to express the uprising and the dejection, the expectant joy and the angry sadness, the hope and the despair that the movement experiences throughout its struggle. It is due to these rituals that the movement keeps going – or, forced to stand still, nevertheless remains standing in order to better fight its fight when the *kairos* has arrived.

At the moment, these rituals have become rare. They are now just as exotic as the movements that demonstrated through these rituals their belief in the delivery from slavery, the liberation of woman, the end of heterosexual domination, the emancipation of the Third World. But thank God: there are always people who rise up, who cannot help themselves and who demonstrate that a different world is possible. And now and again we still come across communities that cannot stop singing of justice, celebrating a meal of communion regardless of a person's standing, dancing about with the Torah (climax of the celebration of Shabbat in the synagogue). They are only signs. But they are signs of a rebellious life!

Rituals are essential because the struggle is also, and often in the first instance, an ideological struggle. It is the struggle against the dominant imagination ('power to the imagination' is usually the fantasy of power). Above all, though, this struggle has the characteristics of iconoclasm:

> Make no image of God,
> nor of any idol
> ...
> do not bow before them,
> do not enslave yourself to them
>> Ex 20:4–5

'Do not make an image' – of the powers that oppress you. It is iconoclasm in the name of a God who does not want there to be an image of himself. Because he is the living God who 'will be there, as he who will be there': incessantly breaking the static images into which the liberation movement solidifies – so that this movement safeguards access to the path of liberation in his image, open-hearted and generous.

The only thing that can be compared to this God is the human, whom he created (Gen 1:26). A human who is called upon to 'be there' in the same way that this God is there: open-hearted and generous, safeguarding the path to liberation. Ultimately, the only image of this God deserving of the name (his name!) is this humanity. This is why the messianic community dares to sing of Jesus, the human who did Torah, as he who was given 'the NAME above all names' by God (Phil 2:9).

But the liberation movement knows it is sustained by what is itself visual fantasy: the Bible's fantastical narratives that keep the belief in this free and liberating God going. And these narratives, in turn, generate rituals that 'make them present'.

Thus the narrative of the exodus is inextricably entwined with the ritual that celebrates this exodus. It narrates at great length how YHWH gives Moses and Aaron instructions for a ritual which the people must carry out as a symbol of what will happen:

> It is Pesach [from *pesach* = pass (by)], a rite of passage, for YHWH.
> I want to stride through the Land of Egypt on this night
> and strike down all first-borns in the Land of Egypt, be they human or animal,
> I will bring judgment to all of Egypt's gods
>
> Ex 12:11–12

And immediately afterwards, YHWH commands to make this ritual a permanent part of Israel's liberation movement liturgy:

> May this day be a day of remembrance,
> celebrate it as a feast for YHWH,
> celebrate it always, as a commandment for your generations
>
> Ex 12:14

A liberation movement cannot subsist without rituals, without a liturgy. But it must be a liturgy that breathes liberation: a Pesach meal that 'remembers' the exodus from Egypt, a Eucharist that celebrates the endless solidarity of the Messiah – embodied in the death of Jesus on the cross – 'until he comes' (1 Cor 11: 26). *Simchath Torah* ('joy at the Torah') is celebrated – the festival of a 'law' of freedom, equality and solidarity – Pentecost is celebrated – the festival of the Holy Spirit, that animates and awakens the abject and the underdog. The path to the 'holy place', the temple, is an ascent in the spirit of this God, who lets his people ascend into a Kingdom of Freedom for everyone, the last ones first of all.

But is there not also sacrifice in this temple? Is the human, who worships like this, not also the victim of a highest Being? Are people not taught mores here, too – the mores of the dominant order? Would Christian religion have ever become the dominant ideology of the West had it been otherwise? Because it offered the sacrificial rite that this order needed? Did it not, in the name of Jesus Christ, turn the necessity of sacrifice into the virtue of a willingness to make sacrifices? What sacrifice is 'remembered' in the Eucharist and the Communion?

Concerning sacrifice, the Bible is incredibly guarded. God's commandment does not simply demand: Sacrifice. Leviticus, the book in which the sacrificial rites are described, explicitly uses the conditional mode when speaking of sacrifice: '*if* a person sacrifices' (Lv 1:2).[15] Apparently the people must learn above all that sacrifice – and the worship of God in general – is a highly problematic issue. Before they know it, it goes awry and they have subjugated themselves by sacrificing to the powers from which God has liberated them. Church history provides the living, the fatal illustration of this.

Not Subjects, but Allies

The story of sacrifice in the Bible is that of the sacrifice of Isaac (Gn 22). But it is precisely in this story that God reveals himself as a God who does *not* want human sacrifices:

> Never reach for the boy,
> and never harm him in the least way!
>> Gn 22: 12

That is the message of YHWH's messenger, the good news, the Gospel: the only one who is God does not want any human sacrifice, does not send humans to their death, but gives them life. A god who demands human sacrifice – for the fatherland of the bosses and the patriarchs, for example – is a false god.

---

15   The theologian Thomas Naastepad pointed this out to me: 'The entirety of the book of Leviticus, for instance, is characterised by such a reservation from the beginning. The first rule already states: *if* you sacrifice ... So it does not say: you have to sacrifice, but *if* you do, then do it in such and such a way ... It is latent paganism that wants to sacralise life as much as possible, as if we could not trust the fact that the Lord descended into our midst – that is why we ascend towards him, through our sacrifices. But have we still not understood that those who sacralise life simultaneously demonise it? Today's "sacre" bears tomorrow's "mas-sacre" within itself' (Naastepad 1999).

But this is not the whole story. It starts with 'God *tested* Abraham' (Gn 22:1). And he does this by saying:

> Take your son, your only one, whom you love, Isaac,
> and go to the Land of Moria, the land *of sight*,[16]
> and there let him ascend as a sacrifice by fire on one of the mountain
>   tops,
> which I will show you.
>
>   Gn 22:2

God says this. But is this word of God YHWH's voice?[17] Or is this God speaking like the gods who demand everything of humans, so that these are reminded once more of the fact that they are nothing? The commandment 'go' can only be found in one other place in the Book of Genesis. This is at the beginning of the twelfth chapter, where it is clearly YHWH who says:

> *You go* forth from the land, from your kin, from your father's house
> to the land that I will let you *see*.
> I want to make of you a great people
> and want to bless you,
> want to make a great name of your name.
>
>   Gn 12:1–2

The story of Abraham, which starts with this word, is the prototypical exodus from an existing order which determines Israel's identity. Abraham precedes the people, he turns into the father of the faith that drives this people. He does this by following YHWH's call and setting out towards the Promised Land. And he does it again when he places his future in this God's hands and forfeits his life for the work YHWH commenced through him. His future, his life, is Isaac, the son that Abraham and Sara should not have been able to have according to the dominant (biological) order, but who is purely a gift from YHWH, from that God who makes the impossible possible. In a second prototypical exodus, Abraham has to return this promised son to the giver – God. God? No, YHWH!

---

16   The name Moria includes the word *raah*, to see.

17   In Jewish readings of the Bible, the distinction between the word 'God' (Hebrew: *elohim*, which can also mean 'gods' in the plural) and the name YHWH is always the occasion for particular attention, even where it seems to be obvious that 'God' refers to YHWH: is God really YHWH?

He is returned to that singular 'God' who falls entirely outside the order of the gods, who did not want to be on his own from the start – creating a world in the context of self-fulfilment – but exclusively and only 'with us' – creating us humans 'in his image and his likeness'. As it turns out, this is the God who 'tests Abraham', tests whether he really obeys. He wants to know whether Abraham does indeed want to be his ally, with heart and soul. He wants his son, but not so as to send him to his death. He wants Abraham to be like him by 'loving' the world – the world of humans – so much so (showing unconditional solidarity with this world) that he forfeits his only son to keep the world from being lost, instead to be delivered from slavery (Jn 3:16–17).[18]

Having faith in this, trusting in it, is a real test. It is not perfectly clear from the outset that the God demanding this sacrifice really is YHWH and that Abraham, who so radically positions himself outside of the existing order, really has a future.[19] Why, it is questionable whether YHWH could have even been YHWH if Abraham had not been prepared to take the risk of the path to the Promised Land leading into nothingness, thus rendering his son's sacrifice futile. Everything appears to depend on Abraham's willingness to actually run this risk. Only when it has been made clear that he is prepared to do this can YHWH speak the words of deliverance:

> because you have done the word,
> because you did not spare your son, your only one,
> I bless, yes, I bless you,
> I want to make your descendants numerous, yes as numerous
> as the stars in heaven and the sand on the shore of the ocean,
> your descendants shall inherit the gates of their enemies,

---

18   Judaism identified less with the father and more with the son: 'Israel, meanwhile, knows – from its shifting and mostly tragic history – that the *bloody* 'binding of Isaac' [as Jews call this story], the sacrificial death, the martyrdom in God's name, has been put into practice millions of times. Jewish literature calls the faith sacrifice, which is willing to forfeit its own life, *'aqeda* [bond] – "For the sake of the sacralisation of the divine name" (*'al qidusch Haschem)'* (Gradwohl 1995, p. 86).

19   Is the journalist Herman Schulte Nordholt not right when he writes in his open letter to the archbishop Romero '25 Years Later' (broadcast April 2005): 'Shortly before your death in 1980 you surely knew that all these deaths and all this pain had not been in vain: "this blood that has been shed will bear fruits in the shape of daring, urgent and radical structural reforms, of which our mother country is in such dire need". I am sorry to now have to write that you were proven mistaken'?

all peoples of the earth shall bless each other with reference to your
  descendants,
because you obeyed my voice!
  Gn 22:16–18

The God of Abraham – and of Isaac, for this is no God of the dead, but of
the living (Mt 22:32)! – demands no other sacrifice of his humans than betting
everything on humanity's card. Biblically speaking, serving God means serving
humanity.[20] As God renders humanity the service of delivering them from
slavery, so humans are called upon by God to render each other the service of
forming a liberation movement, for and with each other. Their life is service, but
this service is their free choice, and the aim of their service is a society without
a ruling power. Their worship serves the covenant, mutual solidarity of one for
the other, with the other.

That is the meaning of *abad*: service liberated from the subjugating con-
jugation that makes a slave of the subject (the hifil form of *abad*). It is the
pinnacle of the injunction to 'love your neighbour (who is) like you': the bond
between humans who find themselves in the same situation. It is the messianic
community's programme encapsulated in its great theoretician Paul's words as
follows: 'owe nothing to anybody – except to love one another' (Rom 13:8). For
this is what the community owes the world: proof that it is possible 'to love one
another', which means: to be a community based on solidarity.

The Making of the Covenant

Led forth from the house of slavery, the people initially end up in the desert,
this unhomely place, faced with the frightening question: Will we ever arrive in
the Promised Land? Here everything depends on solidarity. This is why YHWH
chooses the desert as the place to reveal to this poor, lost people the fact that
the beginning and the end of all wisdom is the bond. This is where the story of
the making of the covenant takes place (Ex 19–40).

The story starts with YHWH's commandment to Moses to remind the people
of what they have *seen*: 'what I did to Egypt' (Ex 19:4). This seeing, however,
should not turn into mere contemplation ('oh the things God has done for us'),

---

20   Whether this is the case, however, must always be queried: 'Clever enough is the paradox
      that the service of God is or must become the service of man; but that is not the same as
      saying that our precipitate service of man, even when it is undertaken in the name of pure
      love, becomes by that happy fact the service of God' (Barth 1957, p. 276).

now the people must also hear what they are commanded to do: 'when you listen to my voice and keep my covenant' (Ex 19:5a). For it is then that 'you will be a kingdom of priests for me' (Ex 19:6), that is a people without a king and without priests, a society without rulers. This is followed by the Decalogue (Ex 20:1–17), which constitutes the 'constitution' of all 'regulations' that govern every detail of social life (Ex 21–23). The first one immediately clarifies what kind of society is concerned: whoever buys a Hebrew man as a slave is required to release him after six years (Ex 21:2).[21]

The actual making of the covenant (Ex 24:3–8) takes place when Moses tells the people 'all YHWH's words and statutes' and 'the people, with one voice, reply: All words that YHWH has spoken, we will practice them.' Sacrifices are made – *peace* feasts'! Blood is shed, blood on the altar and blood on the people. But it is the 'blood of the *covenant*', the blood that is shed in the name of solidarity. For this ritual of blood and sacrifice revolves around the bond. At its centre (between v. 6: blood on the altar, and v. 8: blood on the people) it says that Moses takes 'the book of the covenant' and reads it aloud to the people, who in turn affirm once more: 'everything that YHWH has said, we will do it, we hear it!' (Ex 24:7) Here, doing even precedes hearing! That is how important it is to hear what needs to be *done*, when we hear!

The covenant then 'materialises' in the task put to the people to build a holy place for YHWH so that he can truly live in their midst (Ex 25:8). The key is not to produce a holy place that distorts YHWH into a false god. This is also where the priests' task lies: they stand between the people and YHWH in order to prevent the people from approaching YHWH too closely. They have to make sure that nothing 'alien' finds its way into the liturgy. How quickly that can happen is made immediately apparent: the people make a (golden bull) image of YHWH and the high priest is their accomplice (Ex 32:1–6). The covenant has failed. YHWH decides to start anew with Moses, but without the people (Ex 32:9–10). And then a miracle happens, not through YHWH but through Moses. He refuses to leave the people behind and convinces YHWH to remain the people's ally. Here, above all, the fact is made evident that YHWH does not want to – cannot – be a god if not at least one human stays loyal to him – when he threatens to be disloyal to himself! YHWH even finds himself urged by Moses to be more precise about his name, 'I will be there, as he who I will be there':

---

21   Apparently, this is a patriarchal society, where the delivery from slavery is the delivery of a society of men.

I want to shout out
the name YHWH
in your [Moses'] presence:
that I *pardon* whom I pardon,
that I *have mercy*, for those I have mercy for.
Ex 33:19

The covenant is renewed: YHWH writes down his words once more, once more YHWH turns to the people:

here I am,
I am making a covenant.
Ex 34:10

Now the time has come to execute the project 'holy place', too: the covenant continues – despite everything!

In a very concentrated fashion the story of the making of the covenant explains and brings to a point what must be taken into consideration throughout the entire story, from the exodus to the arrival of the Kingdom of Freedom: liberated from slavery, to remain with this liberation, not to pervert it into a new oppression, but to realise it in a society based on a 'constitution' that commands to provide the means required to live for everyone, without exception, in view of a world imbued with the spirit of an all-encompassing solidarity.

The delivery from the house of slavery that is Egypt is hence the great *a priori* that Israel can take for granted. God addresses the people as allies with responsibility only after they have experienced liberation first-hand:

you have seen for yourselves what I did to Egypt,
I carried you on eagle's wings and let you come to me.
And now, if you listen to my voice and keep the covenant,
you will be
precious to me
above all peoples.
Ex 19:3–5

The people have seen that it is possible. They have seen that the dominant order, with all its pomp and circumstance, with all its ideological wealth, does not have the final say for all eternity. They have seen that those who always end up having to foot the bill are empowered – and take power! – to follow their own path, to dare the exodus, to attempt a different society. Once they have seen this, the moment has come to translate this vision of liberation into practice as well as is possible, rather than merely holding on to it as a theory of hope. Those who hear this God's voice hear a tale of liberation and a tale of the covenant. But now they also hear what they are commanded to do within this covenant, in the Gospel they hear of God's bond, the 'law', which must be abided. Whether the momentum from the exodus is maintained, whether the liberation will lead to liberation, whether the people will be free enough to really be solidary, now also depends – now also entirely depends – on them: '*if* you listen to my voice', *if* you 'keep the covenant'!

'Seeing is believing' is hence not as unbiblical as one might think. The story of the making of the covenant, in particular, emphasises that this liberation could be seen. The exodus is announced with the words: 'Now you will *see*' (Ex 6:1). The people have *seen* that YHWH spoke to them (Ex 20:22). And when Moses asks God what he should say if the people do not believe him, because this YHWH, who will liberate, would not be seen by the people, YHWH promises no less than to give three signs 'so that they trust in the idea that YHWH, the God of their fathers ... has let himself be *seen* by you' (Ex 4:4–9).

It is quite possible to lose sight of the liberation so that it is nothing more than a memory: once it could be seen, but now we no longer can. This is the case when we remain standing 'through faith alone', where only the following is true: 'Faith means: foundation for hope, proof of realities that one *cannot see*' (Heb 11:1). The fantastical stories that keep the hope for liberation alive, originate especially in hopeless situations. The story of the exodus, too, is one such fantastical story. For the Bible is a book written by people in diaspora who live in occupied territory: near and far, nothing is to be seen but the supremacy of a subjugating culture. But the story remembers: the liberation movements which did become visible, the 'times and circumstances' (*chronoi* and *kairoi*) (Acts 1:7) which awakened the abject of the world: the exodus from Egypt, the 'Peasants' War' of 1525, the October Revolution of 1917, the revolutions in Cuba, Nicaragua, the *kairos* in South Africa when apartheid was abolished. They remind us of the spirit of the bond that reigned at the time, of the people's determination to build a society without domination. The story hence points us towards a tradition that tries again and again to oust the dominant order. It wants to make sure this tradition is preserved. It wants to move its listeners to hear the word, to act in its spirit. It wants to reveal to them: Now it depends on you, whether the voice of liberation remains heard, whether the covenant remains kept![22]

---

22   Walter Benjamin speaks of 'a secret agreement between past generations and the present one' ... 'Then our coming was expected on earth. Then, like every generation that preceded

The Great Perversion

Now that the people have taken responsibility for the covenant ('Everything that YHWH has said, we will do it, we hear it!'), it is possible for the impossible to happen: perverting liberation into its opposite. It is precisely this perversion that is terrible: the language of liberation is not simply discarded, but distorted. It is no longer a language that keeps the liberation movement in line with its outlook, and serves as the medium for self-criticism. The necessary distance between the Kingdom of Freedom, towards which the liberation movement is headed, and the kingdom of necessity, in which it operates, is missing. That which is wrong is made to sound good, what is unjust is justified. Instead of abiding by the law of the covenant, the liberation movement takes charge of the covenant itself: God or the laws of history are with us, hence justice is, by definition, on our side. The good news that God – this special God – wants to be close to his people is abused in order to approach him too closely.

The issue is not that circumstances force the liberation movement to 'adapt' its politics, though the circumstances are generally awful. It could not do anything else, and the Bible is realistic in this respect. For instance, it is realistic with regards to the kingdom (the biblical word for 'state'). This institution, which is so problematic for a liberation movement – state and revolution have a very tense relation – is basically conceded to the people by God (Dt 17:14–20 the Torah of the kingdom; 1Sm 8:7). But the Bible does not conceal how questionable this institution is, and critically reminds us of the qualitative difference between earthly kingdoms and the Kingdom of God (1Sam 8:11–18). Earthly kingdoms – even the best: the revolutionary state – are repressive. Their purpose is to ensure, 'under the threat and exertion of violence', that justice is done.[23] God's kingship or kingdom (they are the same words in Hebrew), on the other hand, is the sublation of all dominion: God wants to be 'all in all' (1Cor 15:28). The moment when this qualitative difference is lost from sight, things go wrong, and the status quo of the liberation movement is presented as the end of all historical wisdom: the kingdom of necessity as the Kingdom of Freedom, real socialism as the realisation of the communist programme.

---

us, we have been endowed with a *weak* messianic power on which the past has a claim. Such a claim cannot be settled cheaply' (Benjamin 2003, p. 390).

23   In the words of the Confessing Church, who opposed the Nazi deification of the state: 'Scripture tells us that, in the as yet unredeemed world in which the Church also exists, the State has by divine appointment the task of providing for justice and peace. It fulfils this task by means of the threat and exercise of force, according to the measure of human judgment and human ability' (Theological Declaration of Barmen, May 1934).

The story of the making of the covenant, where God binds himself to his people with such intensity, also creates distance. God equips himself with the insignia of a grim and terrible deity: 'thunder, lightning, a heavy cloud' (Ex 19:16). Here, he reveals himself as the hidden one. His 'descent' is accompanied by the explicit injunction to the people to 'climb the mountain' (Ex 19:11–12). He threatens 'anyone who touches the mountain' (Ex 19:12) with death. Moses alone may 'ascend' the mountain onto which God 'descends'. Even the priests – even Aaron, the high priest – who 'approach YHWH' (Ex 19:22) and thus move between the people and God, can only do this up to a certain point. For while Moses has to take a delegation of priests and representatives of the people with him when he 'ascends' ('Aaron, Nadab and Abihu and seventy of the elder of Israel'), when it comes to it, God says:

> Moses alone may approach YHWH,
> they must not approach,
> And the people, they should not ascend with him.
>   Ex 24:2

So is God here revealing himself ultimately as terribly far away and unapproachable, an endlessly ambivalent entity whose creations are never simply 'good', but always and for ever 'good *and* bad' so that we can never know what to expect? Is the God of Israel, in the end, only a variant of God-in-general, after all? But what the people hear, distant as they are, turns out to be definitively good:

> God speaks all these words,
> he said:
> I am YHWH
> your God,
> who brought you out of Egypt,
> out of the house of bondage.
>   Ex 20:2

The phrase 'all these words' breathes salvation, proclaims the law of liberation, constitutes the content of the merciful covenant.

The distance that the people must keep for and following 'all these words', serves the sole purpose of protecting the covenant, which does only good for the people, from perversion. It creates the distance which permanently distinguishes the God of the covenant from the gods and their earthly helpmates. It thus offers his people the space to remain a truly human liberation movement – by keeping it at a distance from the inhuman desire to be 'like God'.

But the impossible happens: together with their high priest the people lock the Liberator-God into an image, transform the open ending of the Kingdom of Freedom into an ideology that determines the shape of fantasy as a symbol of strength and power: the 'bull calf' (Ex 32:1–6)! The story of the making of the covenant not only entertains the thought that the people *could* lose their way, it makes it clear from the start that they will actually lose their way. We cannot, the story wants to say, remember the origin of the liberation movement without also commemorating its perversion. The point of this is not to totally destroy the hope for the success of the liberation movement: 'Look, has it not always gone wrong, have we ever experienced a liberation movement that did not turn into new oppression, or at least was assimilated into the dominant order?' The only option left, then, is the fatal conclusion that humans are simply not suited to freedom in the shape of a bond. Then all we can say is that humans are simply bad 'by nature', communism by definition Stalinism. And so on – evermore.

The story of the so-called 'golden calf' can be read as follows:[24] Moses, the charismatic leader, no longer exists (he 'hesitated to descend from the mountain') and the revolution returns to normality ('make us gods'). For the revolution cannot survive without 'gods': Lenin is inevitably followed by Stalin, so Moses is followed by a 'bull calf' – divine personification of the power relinquished by the people. Reading along these lines, one can also relish the details: how the 'bull calf' is intended to represent 'the god who let you ascend from the Land of Egypt': the relapse into the '*ancien régime*', masked as revolutionary ideology, and how the people subjugate themselves of their own free will and full of enthusiasm: they give everything ('their gold earrings') so as to have a god above them once more. The whole episode demonstrates yet again that the masses do not measure up to their own freedom, and revolutions are always betrayed.

This, however, is an outsider's reading, and surely not an impartial one. Theirs is the *Schadenfreude* of someone who does not have to consider the fact that a liberation movement might well be successful. They remark with relief that revolutions are apparently doomed to fail. And they are pleased that people who are impertinent enough to think they can change the world are also entirely 'normally' 'inclined towards all things bad'.[25] Thank God, humans are not good, and it should stay that way forever.

The story of the 'bull calf', however, is an insider's story, written by someone who is completely devoted to the liberation movement. It is a story from the Bible, so a book that serves the purpose of strengthening the belief in the coming rather than the

---

24   The bull calf may be made of gold, but it is above all a symbol of potency (bull!).

25   Thus says the Heidelberg Catechism, though full of hope it also adds: 'unless we are born again, by the Spirit of God'.

ceasing of the Kingdom of Freedom. This story is not determined by a triumphant 'I always knew it', but by horror and anger: this cannot be true. God asks Moses to give him space for his wrath towards the people to flare high. Moses, once he catches sight of the catastrophe, is himself enraged and destroys the 'plates of the covenant'. God's and Moses's 'no' is not in response to the revolution, though, but in response to its betrayal.

A Real, not just an Ideal, Bond

The story continues, though. The betrayal of the revolution is not accepted as a *fait accompli*, with which the last word has been spoken. The exciting question now is: What to do? This liberation movement failed – does not the real covenant with this people now have to be revoked in order to save the idea of the covenant?

Of course, the people who wrote the Bible knew that liberation movements failed time and again. They knew: never did a liberation movement stick with the liberation, it always trampled the 'law' of the covenant underfoot. The people who wrote the Bible also knew that this experience immediately suggested the fatal conclusion that this failure would be true 'for all time'. This experience is not repressed in the Bible, either. On the contrary, it relates that the perversion was there right from the start: the story of the 'bull calf' is part of the story of the making of the covenant. This makes it impossible to turn the covenant into an abstract principle that is immune against the reality of its corruption: not flight into the realm of ideas, but a theory that proves its truth through practice. The issue of the real liberation movement impeding the idea of its own success exists from the beginning. This is why this problem has to be discussed right at the start.

YHWH plays a key part in this story. He is the surprising answer to the cry for liberation that finds no way out. He makes the impossible possible: delivery from slavery. But now what should have been impossible, precisely because of this, becomes reality: the covenant he made with the people is broken by the people. Is it not obvious, then, that God will break the covenant in turn, will henceforth go his own way and leave the people to their fate? Or even worse: that he will destroy the people, who disgrace his covenant with the oppressed, a covenant unheard of among gods, and attach his intention to liberate the poor to another people?[26]

---

26   Then God would have acted in the way that Brecht recommended to the GDR government in the wake of the uprising of 17 June 1953, on the occasion of a remark made by the

This is indeed the thought the story inspires in God's mind. For he says to Moses:

> I see this people,
> yes, it is a stubborn people.
> Now,
> leave me be,
> so that my wrath rages against them
> and destroys them –
> but you I make into a great people!
>> Ex 32:9–10

By God's hand, the covenant would then really have turned into an idea that could no longer be struck by the reality of the concrete liberation movement. God remarks that the practice of the real Israel no longer corresponds with the idea of the project 'Israel', and imagines a new people, who will not disgrace the idea of the covenant. But will this new people not disgrace the idea all over again? And will this not lead to the fatal conclusion that the idea will always be disgraced, and the thought of liberation should hence be abandoned?[27] This, in any case, is Moses's argument: if God evaporates his covenant with Israel into an idea, then his enemies – who never cared much for the revolution anyway – will be retrospectively justified: all that is to be expected from revolution is disaster.

> Why,
> YHWH,
> should your wrath rage
> against your people,
> who you brought forth from the Land of Egypt
> with great power, and strong hand!
> Why
> should the Egyptians be allowed to speak, speak:
> he brought them forth with ill intent
>> Ex 32:11–12a

---

secretary of the writers' association, 'stating that the people had forfeited the confidence of the government': 'Would it not be easier / In that case for the government / To dissolve the people and / Elect another?' (Brecht 1979, p. 440).

27   Marx and Engels remained hopeful that the 'idea' was only disgraced so long as it was not yet tied to a concrete 'interest' (Marx and Engels 1975c, p. 81). But the history of liberation movements shows that the idea can be fully disgraced even when it is led by an interest.

And then the unimaginable happens one more time – that which is unthinkable in the thought process of dominant thought. God, who answered the cry for deliverance and formed a bond with the lowest of the low, is actually swayed and stays true to this covenant:

> Then YHWH regretted the evil
> he had spoken of afflicting on his people.
>> Ex 32:14

He remains aligned with society's underbelly, even though the covenant has been wholly betrayed. The story of the making of the covenant does not spare the liberation movement the embarrassing memory that it failed right from the beginning. But this does not happen without recalling that God did not take this as reason enough to withdraw from the project. The breaking of the covenant is 'integrated' into the making of the covenant: God does not let go of the work his hand has started.

The story does not conceal the fact that Moses, once YHWH has avowed his people, organises a mighty cleansing – in YHWH's name (Ex 32:26–28)! The Levites, the only ones who side with him, are given the task 'each to kill his brother, his friend and neighbour'. And what follows is a massacre that costs the lives of 3,000 humans. Now it has to be observed that no liberation movement to date has managed to avoid such bloody cleansings. But is that reason enough to resign oneself to their purported inevitability? Even the fact that Moses, contrary to his own assertion, is not acting on behalf of God directly, fails to appease me. For I am not entirely convinced that YHWH might not issue such an order. I am equally unable to consign the whole matter to metaphor, though.[28] I can only hope that even when the necessity of a cleansing imposes itself, one liberation movement will succeed in desisting. Perhaps it could proceed in similar fashion to the chairman of the people's tribunal in Bertolucci's film *1900*: rightfully condemn the squire to death in order to then call out: The squire is dead, long live the human (followed by the squire's name)! This could be called mercy before justice. Or the justice of mercy?

---

28   Tom Naastepad warns against reading this story as 'historicisation': 'This night in Egypt [when all firstborns were killed – except for YHWH's firstborn, Israel] was no more a bloody St Bartholomew's Day massacre, than we should think of this [story] as a massacre. Naturally, this sword is a rhetorical figure for a far more forceful, albeit invisible reality: that a worldly myth is brought to an end, the myth of survival of the fittest' (Naastepad 2003, p. 338).

Note: he does not let go of the *covenant*! Whether the project continues is now dependent on God – the liberation movement no longer offers hope – he does not confirm the covenant without including his ally. God gives Moses time to think by telling him what he intends to do:

> So leave me be
> that my wrath rage against them
>> Ex 32:10a

And Moses makes use of this space by not leaving God. He has the courage to remind him of the order of the covenant:

> Turn back
> From the incensing of your wrath,
> Regret the evil
> That you [intended] for your people!
>> Ex 32:12

The 'singularity' of this God is that he lets himself be called to order! He does not want to be present in anything but mutuality. He makes himself dependent on people like Moses.[29] People who will not settle for the idea that this 'fantastical tale' of the liberation from slavery should have been told for nought; people who do not give up the hope that the hitherto impossible could become reality: that the real liberation movement will not betray the revolution, but bring it to a good end; people, who are not unfamiliar with despair, but who, even in the midst of despair, do not cease to cry out: my god, my god, why have you abandoned us?

Here, the path for any theology that somehow thinks God in separation from this bond is thoroughly obstructed. Because concerning God, the issue is final: you my people, I your God. It is not beneath him to keep bothering with this 'stubborn' and hard-of-hearing people who constantly lose their way.

---

29 There is a lovely Midrash about this: 'And the Lord said to Moses: Go, descend. What does this mean: go, descend? Rabbi Eleazar said: the Holy One, hallowed be his name, spoke to Moses: Moses, descend from your dignity! Did I not bestow dignity upon you only for the sake of Israel? Now that Israel has sinned, what use have I for you? Moses's power slackened immediately and he had no strength for speech. But when He spoke: "So let me be, I want to destroy them!" Moses said: so it depends on me! Immediately he rose, fortified himself with a prayer and cried for mercy' (Berachot 32a).

One can even ask whether the word 'God' is not too misleading with respect to this 'being' that is so dependent on others. The history of theology – the theory of God – also shows how YHWH was elevated above this scandalous dependency again and again, and then inevitably gained the features of whatever one generally wished to understand as divine. But even if we drop the word 'God' – and there is much that speaks in favour of this – it is salutary to follow the Bible where it makes an eternal qualitative distinction between YHWH and humans, the difference between heaven and earth:

> Heaven, heaven is for YHWH,
> to the children of men he gave the earth.[30]
>> Ps 115:16

It is YHWH, after all, who creates an opening in the decisive moment, for a new beginning, a continuation of that which appears to have come to a final standstill. When everything appears to have been in vain, there is still his *creatio ex nihilo* – his creation *out of* nothingness. Demanding such a *creatio ex nihilo* of humans would be inhumane. The almightiness that it requires can only lead them – us – to ruin. An almighty liberation movement is an oxymoron.[31] The freedom that exists in the bond is, by definition, relative. It is freedom-in-the-relation, shared power, society without rulers. Biblical humanism knows only one action and hence only one action word that is reserved exclusively for God: *bara* (creating in the absolute sense: out of nothing). This 'creating' out of nothing is the absolutely necessary condition for every liberation movement. It is the condition of its humanity – the humanity of the covenant.

---

30   Rabbi Alexander says the following on this matter: 'God takes care of making heaven heavenly. Our worry is that the earth, too, be heavenly' (Siach Sarfe Kodesh, I, 99).

31   Which is why Lenin's hypothesis, 'The Marxist doctrine is omnipotent because it is true' (Lenin 1960, p. 23), must be discarded. Such an almighty claim to truth damages the humanity of the movement that lays claim to it.

CHAPTER 5

Creation

The liberation movement, brought out of the house of bondage, sets out for the Kingdom of Freedom. But does this path really lead any*where*? Will the exodus ever turn into an entry? The fact this journeying really does lead somewhere is based in the happy knowledge that the liberating God is also the creator of the world in which the project of liberation takes place. When everything seems to have been futile, Israel remembers the story of the 'beginning':

> In the beginning God created heaven and earth.
> Gn 1:1

This story is the response to the anxious query whether the liberation movement really does have good reason. Is it not, rather, a washout? Have not all previous liberation movements stumbled over power relations and internal failure? How can one possibly overcome the fatal notion that delivery from slavery is obviously an impossible enterprise?

Humans Lost in Indifferent Nature?

This is 'obvious' not least because nature frustrates it by definition. Imagine: nature in the sense of outer space, that endless space. No origin – except for possibly a 'big bang' – and no goal apart from dissolving into itself. How can we think that humans and their movements could be anything more than an unremarkable ripple in this outer space, condemned to disappear without a trace, a brief sigh that is unheard. The human, 'a breadcrumb on the skirt of the universe', to be neglected absolutely.[1]

In his theses 'On the Concept of History', Walter Benjamin cites a biologist: 'In relation to the history of all organic life on earth the paltry fifty-millennia history of homo

---

1 The Dutch poet Lucebert (1924–94) summarises the experience of the destruction of the aesthetic by reality: 'In this age what people used to call | beauty beauty her face has burnt | she comforts mankind no longer | she comforts the larvae the reptiles the rats | but she startles mankind | and strikes him with the sense | of being a breadcrumb on the skirt of the universe' (Lucebert 2013, p. 181).

sapiens equates to something like two seconds at the close of a twenty-four-hour day. On this scale, the history of civilized mankind would take up one-fifth of the last second of the last hour'.[2] Eternity that voids any liberated humanity's hope for 'eternal life'.

Thinking about the 'nature' of humanity, however, is even more frustrating. Though it is a microcosm, it is no less immeasurable, unfathomable and capable of anything. True, the 'ego' surfaces as the centre of a conscious and mature agency – as civilisation surfaces from barbarism.[3] But this civilisation in particular, which set out on the exodus from immaturity to the Kingdom of true Freedom, erected monuments to barbarism.[4] Its ruling consciousness, that the ego would let itself be led by reason, turned out to be the consciousness of the rulers that was not able to leave behind its own 'ego'.

> Miserable person that I am! Who will save me from the belly of this
> death?
>
> Rom 7:24

Paul cries forth because he experiences it first-hand:

> For I do not do what I want to do: good,
> but that which I do not want to do: evil, that is what I do
>
> Rom 7:19

Does this cry for help, uttered by the 'unhappy consciousness' of a tragic contradiction, not pierce the core of our so self-conscious ego-age?

The experience of being 'somewhere' in this endless space, and the consciousness that it is all over for me before my 'ego', is part of the *condition humaine*. We owe our existence to a predetermined reality, we cannot 'found' ourselves because the foundation has already been laid elsewhere – before the question about the reason for our existence even crossed our minds. Posing this question, hence, must mean to look at what reality itself has to offer, to listen to

---

2 Benjamin 2003, p. 396.

3 As Freud puts it: 'Where id was, there ego shall be' (1991, p. 112). But he learned the error of his ways eventually. The ego, like the id, is (in part) subconscious, formed before I am aware of it.

4 As Walter Benjamin writes: 'There is no document of culture which is not at the same time a document of barbarism' (2003, p. 392).

what can be heard in this reality. We live by enquiring of reality what possibilities it offers. And in this we depend on the records of those who went before us. This is the truth of 'materialism': being precedes consciousness.

'Historical materialism' brings this truth about human existence in reality to a head: to be situated within a *history*. Humans make history, but not under circumstances of their own choosing.[5] This does not yet mean that this history is meaningful: the history of humankind progresses, but whether this is synonymous with progress is questionable, that it moves towards anything at all remains (at best) an open question.[6] Somehow to make history, however, is inevitable.

And this truth is articulated by the Bible. It starts with the story of the creation of heaven and earth. When humans arrive on earth, everything is already there – the given, on which they can rely and to which they can respond.

This may not be what the creation story is primarily intent on expressing. That would be the announcement of the great *a priori* of all reality: it is not left to 'something', but is *created* out of nothing. This good news, though, is directed at humans who know that they are 'material beings', dependent and vulnerable. It has nothing to say to 'spiritual beings'.

This truth, however, is the liberation movement's problem: nothing in reality suggests that it has a purpose, is justified, leads to the Kingdom where freedom and justice will be two sides of the same shalom. What, after all, do we see throughout this history but the eternal repetition of ups and downs? What else can we hear from it but the narrative of growth, flowering and decay? Essentially, what are the successful revolutions but transitions of power?

Certainly, liberation movements do – or at least did – exist; revolutions do – or at least did – take place. It cannot be precluded that the Book of Exodus contains a historical core. The problem is not that they are absent, either, but that they fail. They most certainly have a foundation – in the yoke that enslaved peoples, organising themselves into a liberation movement, discard – but they cannot find a reason in the reality of an indifferent 'universe' and human nature that is capable of every inhumanity. So it may be inevitable that humans revolt

---

5   'Men make their own history, but they do not make it as they please; they do not make it under self-selected circumstances, but under circumstances existing already, given and transmitted from the past' (Marx 1979, p. 103). The point of this thesis is revolutionary: 'If man is shaped by environment, his environment must be made human' (Marx and Engels 1975c, 130 f.).

6   'The concept of progress must be grounded in the idea of catastrophe. That things are "status quo" *is* the catastrophe' (Benjamin 2003b, p. 283).

against that to which they are subjected. But the question remains as to what good it does.

Philosophical Intermezzo

Idealism is seen as the great opposing force to materialism. Idealism, in its classical form (Plato), however, is not simply the inversion of the materialist hypothesis that being precedes consciousness. For it is not consciousness, but the 'being' of ideas that precedes being (in the sense of a perceptible reality) – and is by far superior to it: it is *true being*. In practice, though, it is indeed opposed to materialism: humanity's destiny is to transcend the reality in which it finds itself and to 'behold' true being (the world of ideas) – rather than changing this reality. The culmination of this Idealism is theory, the 'theoria' (Greek: contemplation) of the idea. Nor is Idealism in its modern form (from Kant to Hegel, for example) simply the hypothesis opposed to materialism, that consciousness precedes being. It does not deny that conscious being, so the human, succeeds being (of the material) and it finds their 'material' for thought in it. Instead, Idealism proposes that humans have the capacity to overcome the status of being an object of circumstance, to command reality as a sovereign subject, to actually emerge from their immaturity. The culmination of this modern Idealism is practice, the realisation of the realm of ideas. Its pathos, that consciousness *makes* being, that humans make history, does not fall from the skies, but is the product of the 'modern' experience that the space in which humans find themselves is in actuality infinite, incalculable, immeasurable: not an ordered cosmos in which humans have a designated place (and know where that is!), but chaos which humans themselves must first bring to order. The knowledge that this order is given from the start is no longer available to them, they must – whether they want to or not – create their world themselves.

This 'modern experience' is not only a consequence of modern natural science. It also – perhaps even primarily – has a social cause: the experience of the capitalist mode of production with its distinctive 'eternal' uncertainty about what lies ahead. Does the subject of modern Idealism not exhibit the traits of the free entrepreneur who must find their way through this uncertainty – and who trusts in finding it? It is also possible, though, that this uncertainty is less fascinating – as a challenge to actively prove maturity – than it is terrifying.[7] According to the *Zeitgeist* at the time (only at

---

7   'The eternal silence of these infinite spaces terrifies me' (Pascal 1966, fragment 206).

that time?), however, suffering under this uncertainty is for 'modernity's losers', those who are not strong enough to withstand the challenges of a 'risk society'.

The Subjects of Idealist Thought

Both classical and modern Idealism have a certain similarity to biblical thought. Classical Idealism's declaration: 'It is not down here, on earth – true being is elsewhere', shares something of the attitude towards life that the biblical narrative articulates: down here, things really are not as they should be, salvation must be sought elsewhere. But there is also an essential distinction. The humans that the Bible is concerned with cannot afford the luxury of transcending reality in order to behold true being from the height of the world of ideas. Their salvation – if they can believe in it at all – has to be a response to that which aggrieves them, the cessation of the conditions that oppress them. True being, which they look out for, is 'a new heaven and a new *earth*' (Is 65:17) – 'where justice resides' (2 Pt 3:13)! Classical Idealism, on the other hand, is the flight of ideas of people who have the time and the leisure to float among the clouds. How did Plato actually earn a living?

Even when the damned of this earth see no way out, they are more likely to 'flee' into the world of religion, where 'elsewhere' is associated with food and drink, where poor Lazarus truly finds solace, not in the idea, but in Abraham's lap (Lk 16:22–23). There is truth to Nietzsche's description of Christianity as 'Platonism for "the people"'.[8] It is, so to speak, 'impure' Platonism, still tainted by the materiality without which the people will not imagine their deliverance.

Modern Idealism can be called 'biblical' to an even greater extent. The definition of the Enlightenment as the 'emergence from immaturity' and the designation of its vision as 'eternal peace' (Kant) show just how intentional this affinity was.[9] According to their own understanding, this was Idealism in the spirit of biblical imagination (Hegel).

---

8 Nietzsche polemicises against 'Plato's invention of pure spirit and the good in itself' and writes: 'Christianity is Platonism for "the people"' (1990, p. 32).

9 'In this way nature guarantees perpetual peace through the mechanism of human inclination itself. To be sure, it does this with a certainty that is not sufficient to foretell the future of this peace (theoretically), but which is adequate from a practical perspective and makes it a duty, to work toward this (not simply chimerical) goal' (Kant 2006, p. 92). Kant has especially high expectations of 'the *Spirit of Trade*, which cannot exist with war' (ibid.). Unfortunately, we know better.

According to Hegel, religion is the 'imaginary' reconciliation of all contradictions in the shape of a lack: 'The Spirit of the community is thus in its immediate consciousness divided from its religious consciousness, which declares, it is true, that *in themselves* they are not divided, but this merely *implicit* unity is not realized, or has not yet become an equally absolute being-for-self'.[10] The aim of (his!) philosophy is 'absolute knowledge' in which reconciliation has been made real (this is what is meant by 'being-for-self'). Not being able to let go of the expectation of a true reconciliation is, indeed, the 'spirit' that drives the community, but 'absolute knowledge' is not at its disposal.

The emphasis is shifted from God's actions to humanity's actions. They must act, and they can act. But is that not also the fulfilment of the biblical promise that God would pour out his spirit over *all* flesh (Jl 3:1, quoted in Acts 2:17)? But even still there is an essential difference. Modern Idealism is, one might say, the project of an emergence that is not carried by the happy knowledge that the world was *created* with a view to this emergence. It presupposes a human who is lord and master: the delivery from slavery is a self-delivery. This is tied to 'modern experience': humans cannot count on anything during the process of their emergence; they have to rely wholly and entirely on themselves. From where, though, does modern Idealism derive the notion that humans will actually succeed in creating such a Kingdom of Freedom? Looking at the human masses, who laboriously try to keep their head above water from day to day, this thought is far from obvious. But the human of modern Idealism is not this human mass, Idealism envisions a human who has the ability 'to use [his reason] without guidance from another' (Kant)[11] in order to get a hold on the world. This human surely is not simply an idea. It is the real human type of the wealthy, the owners of the means of production, who are able to let others work for them. They are the subject in whom modern Idealism basically founds its trust that humanity will succeed[12] – even though this surely invokes an abstract notion of the wealth required for humans to survive. The human of modern Idealism is led by reason (the epitome of everything true, good and beautiful), not by capital. This human is an abstraction: the ideal subject, free of the deficiencies of the concrete human being. Essentially, an *Übermensch*,

---

10   Hegel 1977, p. 478.

11   Kant 2009, p. 1.

12   'The system's principles are those of self-preservation. Immaturity amounts to the inability
        to survive. The bourgeois in the successive forms of the slave-owner, the free entrepreneur
        and the administrator is the logical subject of enlightenment' (Horkheimer and Adorno
        2002, p. 65).

the product of pure fantasy, imagined by people who, deep down, are 'like God' because they cannot think their emergence from slavery and the entry into the Kingdom of Freedom in any other way.

The highest possible degree of pride? The courage of despair? In any case, tragic: How can the idea be spared the humiliation of being confronted with reality? Is it purely coincidence that the extremely 'objective' Idealism of Hegel, who dared measure himself against 'absolute knowledge', which encompassed everything – all contradictions 'sublimated', universal reconciliation turned into reality – progressed no further than *conceptualising* 'reality'?

Biblically speaking, this *Übermensch*, who wants to be 'like God', is a caricature, a non-human (according to Gn 3 'wanting to be like God' is precisely humanity's *fall*). The people of whom the Bible speaks know how precarious their existence is, they are unfamiliar with the feeling of being lord and master, their 'courage to be' does not suppress their despair.[13] Their emergence cannot be explained rationally, it is a miracle. For such people it is good to know themselves to be carried by a *creation* story: the existence of the reality (well!) created by YHWH determines their consciousness!

In the Beginning: A Fantastical Story

The fact that reality as it is given is suitable for a liberation movement cannot be seen in that reality. For reality *per se* does not say anything.

This is not entirely true. Reality certainly says something: it offers the opportunity for the discovery of physical laws and historical tendencies. The natural sciences as well as historical studies would be unthinkable were this not the case. And inversely, science proves in practice how meaningful reality is – and the many ways in which one can put it to use! Anything, really. But knowing this can also be a terrible knowledge. If reality says one thing, then it is that anything is possible, everything is ambivalent, everything is a question of 'good *and* evil'. Thus, it ultimately says: nothing(ness).

But the Bible tells us:

---

13   The phrase was coined by the theologian Paul Tillich, who saw it as a given for humanity: 'there are acts of courage in which we affirm the power of being, whether we know it or not' (Tillich 1952, p. 181).

In the beginning God created heaven and earth.
> Gn 1:1

It is the beginning of a story that culminates in the unequivocal:

And see, it is very good.
> Gn 1:3

The earth under heaven is good, very good – and the latter is said once the human has appeared on earth. The reality – *given* to us, by definition – is good, yes, it is very good, because it offers so much space for humanity. On earth, human life is really possible. In this narrative, in light of the promise, the human-all-too-human is allowed to be good.

The fact alone that the story speaks of a 'beginning' is a salutary contradiction to the fatal thought that reality is infinite, infinite in the fatal sense of the word: all the physical laws and historical tendencies that we might think we recognise, ultimately lose themselves in the immeasurable universe. There is no beginning there, no qualified beginning, and hence no ending: no ending in the sense of a destiny that we humans could seek – at most, our destiny is the fall into nothingness. Emergence remains, without entry; liberation does not extend to liberty; homesickness is not quenched because a 'home' is not on the cards for us. Reality is uncanny, forever and always.

In this story, though, there is a qualified beginning:

In the beginning God *created*

Our reality begins by being created by God. Hopeless uncanniness is hence excluded from the beginning, cannot play a part. God has made a beginning, which we can no longer precede – thank God, no longer have to precede. This qualified beginning enables us to really call the rays of hope we do see in this reality 'good' – without the thought at the back of our mind that everything will always also have something bad about it. Yes, it is down to this qualified beginning that that which first comes to light is light itself:

God said: Let there be light! And there was light.
God saw the light: yes, it was good.
> Gn 1:3

We see the light in this light (Ps 36:10): that earth and oceans, plants and trees, the sun, the moon and the stars, the fish and the birds, the land animals are really simply good

(Gn 1:9–25). But after God creates the human, he can say: Very good (Gn 1:31). And the human is very good – in this light, well understood! For in this light we see the light that God himself lets shine through his creation. It is the light that is the beginning of all wisdom, the *a priori* of all theory and practice, the presupposed: a fantastical narrative.

Reality Fore-told

This narrative tells us what reality itself cannot tell us. It says:

> God *said*
>> Gn 1:3 and subsequently nine times in the creation story

This is what salutarily distinguishes this God from all other gods. These may also speak from time to time, but when it really counts, they are silent.[14] That is why every time Rabbi Zusuya's teacher, the great Maggid, read the Scripture and he heard the words 'And God said' or 'And God spoke' he was so enraptured that 'he cried out and moved around [so wildly] that the company at table was disturbed and he had to be taken outside. And there he'd stand, in the hall or in the wood store, banging the walls and crying: "And God said!"'. Rabbi Israel of Ruzhyn remarked the following in this context: 'If one speaks the truth and another absorbs in truth, then *one* word is enough – the world can be elevated with *one* word, the world can be redeemed with *one* word'.[15] We can only add to this: Amen, 'so be it'.

This holds true only if God really speaks, though. As a rhetorical device, the 'God said' refers to 'something' *beyond* our reality – to *somebody* beyond our reality. Moved by this story, people oppressed by the weight of reality stand up in the hope that 'somebody' exists who corresponds with this 'God said'. The

---

14   As Miskotte writes: 'Whether there were always gods, we do not know; but that they never spoke is certain' (1967, p. 9). This silence constitutes their nature: 'When the gods are dumb, when the "godhead" is silent, this is ultimately not so much because they have been put to silence, but rather because their eternal silence has been exposed as their most essential, their "mystical" characteristic'. This is why '[i]n its first and purest form atheism is the reverse side of Israel's faith. It is a happy thing, a liberation forever … The "hallowing of the Name" commanded to the People of God, always begins with a profession of this "atheism"' (Miskotte 1967, p. 11).

15   According to Martin Buber (1956, pp. 236 f.). [Translator's note: translation slightly changed].

story refers beyond itself, and it cannot defend itself if it dares to imagine a 'beyond' that puts the reality in which humanity finds itself into perspective. This 'beyond' is not 'something' (but you do not know what) that reproduces once again the ambivalent character of reality, let alone a 'nothingness' that destroys any perspective. Instead, it is someone who has the power and the will to create reality in such a way that a liberation movement can take its course – thus, a God, but one who deserves this name, no, who serves the NAME and makes reality into an earth under heaven in this NAME ('I will be there, as he who I will be there').

The fact that it is this God who speaks and not a generic god who only bears the traits of a 'something' is made evident by the effect his speech has: a world in which everything that humans need is provided, a world in which humans are no longer out of place.

This 'beyond' is not merely beyond our reality. A movement that makes this reality 'good' proceeds from there. The story is beside itself, lifts the hearts of its audience to new heights, but hears God's word, who says: Down here is where it will happen. Thus the story carries its audience – from heaven to earth, from the idea to materiality, from religion that searches for its salvation in the beyond to politics that is set on finding it in the here and now.[16] Following this story – especially in this pointer to the 'God said' – means allowing the protest against a world that is amiss, that has been projected into the beyond, to return to the world. There and only there can God's word be heard, the word wants to take us there and only there. For it is his world – in the strictest sense: his world, *created* out of nothingness by him. It is due to this *a priori* of reality that it can be said with good reason that we humans live *thanks* (a positive aspect!) to the given reality. Because it has been created by God, made 'well' and 'given' to us as such, it is a reality that is custom-made for our needs, is tailored for human beings becoming-human, more than equipped for an extensive and enriching material exchange between humans and nature.

The materialist position is not only inevitable – simply because we depend on matter – but also salutary: In reality, such as it *is*, reside the possibilities for a reality such as the people, who suffer under it, hope it *will* be. And the optimism that materialism

---

16   'Thus the criticism of heaven turns into the criticism of the earth, the *criticism of religion* into the *criticism of law* and the *criticism of theology* into the *criticism of politics*' (Marx 1975b, p. 176).

historically associated with it – the conditions in which the liberation movement makes history side with that movement – is true: Tomorrow, the Internationale will rule the earth (thus the Dutch version of the Internationale puts it).

The fact that reality is created means that it is solely the work of God. Humans, with all their inventiveness, cannot bring about a reality that is first and foremost good. Their creativity has to take the available matter and the possibilities that arise from it as its starting point. No matter how far these possibilities take them, the active radius of this creativity remains located *in* reality. Humans cannot do everything.

What we can very well do is destroy everything: total destruction. Caught up in the delusion of being divine ourselves, we can accomplish no more than a caricature of what God does: create *out of* nothing. Instead of following his liberation movement, we definitively reverse it.

The Word Against the Power of Chaos

To create is God's distinctive action word: the word with which he calls what is nothing into being, the act that first creates reality.

The Hebrew word *bara*, which is translated as 'to create', is a word that appears exclusively in conjunction with God as the subject, while our language also speaks of the creative artist. It could be said that *bara* refers to God's unique act: having created reality out of nothingness. The verb 'to create', meanwhile, refers to that which links God and humans: humans, too, can create – in his image and in his likeness.

It is the exclusivity of this work of creation that constitutes the core of the salvation determined by it. It rules out the fatal thought that there might be other forces and powers – contradicting this God – that are in charge.[17] God has – thank God! – the first and final say, and only the (heartfelt) repetition by and participation of humans, who are given voice through his word, are in line with this.

---

17   This is what the Theological Declaration of Barmen stated in opposition to the Nazi Führer cult: 'We reject the false doctrine, as though the church could and would have to acknowledge as a source of its proclamation, apart from and besides this one Word of God, still other events and powers, figures and truths, as God's revelation'.

Solely through his word! The fact that God addresses a collective ('let *us* make humans, in our image and in our likeness' (Gn 1:26–27)) precisely when speaking of the creation of humans does not contradict this. From the beginning God does nothing without involving others in his unique work. The Talmud also associates this 'us' with conversations between God and his angels about the question of whether God would do well to make humans.[18] And in light of the fact that the bond between God and humans is woven through the biblical testimony like a common thread, it may even be conceivable that God is here already addressing humans, encouraging them to want to be responsible for the project of the human being becoming-human alongside God.[19] Or do we have to go so far as to read this 'we' as pointing to God's 'manifoldness'? As clearly demonstrating from the beginning that he is a 'social being', invested in the bond?[20]

The creation story is a liberation story: the word that God speaks 'in the beginning' intervenes in a world of stories that are trying to convince humans that they are at the mercy of powers and forces to which they can never match up. This is why they should subjugate themselves to rulers who can control these powers and forces. Without these rulers, the stories suggest, chaos will ensue: *Tohuwabohu.* The eternal struggle between chaos and order is invoked in order to hold the people down. They might get ideas about how the earth on which they live is actually not chaotic, but offers everything that humans need to live humanely. The creation story intends to point them precisely towards this liberating thought. In doing so, it by no means negates the *Tohuwabohu.* In fact, it is named explicitly:

---

18   Sanhedrin 38b tells the story of God asking the angels whether they will agree to 'us making a human in our image'. They reply: 'Lord of the World, what will his deeds be?' When he responds that his deeds will be human, all-too human, they cite Psalm 8: What is a human that you think of him, and a human being that you enquire after him? And with this they mean to say that God should not even create the human. God's reaction is to burn the angels! And when, after the Flood and the Tower of Babel, the angels appear who say: but weren't those angels right?, God replies: 'Even to my old age it is I, and even to your gray hair it is I who carries it [the people of Israel]'. He is citing Is 46:4 which ends with 'I will carry and liberate you!'

19   In relation to 'let us make humans', Gerrit de Groot writes: 'Is this a pluralis maiestatis? ... Following Naastepad, I think that this "we" refers to us and the reader ... The "we" comprises God and the human he is addressing. Really, he is always a "we". After all, he does not want to be without the human' (de Groot 1979, p. 27).

20   The Christian doctrine of the Trinity can be understood in this way: God himself is already father, son and Holy Spirit, of one spirit with his son in advance (Jesus, in the first instance Israel, though).

> Then the earth was chaos and desert (*Tohuwabohu*)
>
> Gn 1:2

However, this story only names the *Tohuwabohu* in order to confront it with God's spirit, whose first word was: light.

> God's power of spirit moved in the face of the waters.
> And God said: Let there be light and there was light
>
> Gn 1:2–3

The light makes darkness into a manageable entity – as night beside day it no longer has the chance to extend into absolute darkness, in which humans are at a complete loss. The *Tohuwabohu* is named so that it can be immediately 'superseded'. It no longer plays any part in the creation story and can no longer be used as an argument to scare humans into accepting slavery. Rulers have no place in the creation story; they simply do not exist in it. Only humans are allowed to figure next to God in the story. Humans alone are awarded the honour of representing God on earth: in his image and in his likeness.

The fact that the creation story starts with the words, 'In the beginning God created heaven and earth' does not mean that this is then followed by *Tohuwabohu*, and then the Spirit, and after that God's speech again, and the light that this creates. As though the *Tohuwabohu* were something original after all, something God's Spirit might know what to do with. The creation story's first sentence is a title, a heading, or one could also call it a principle. It articulates in advance that which will subsequently be executed: the beginning of everything that is, is to have been *created*, that is certain. Fundamentally, nothing else can be said about reality. When the first sentence of the narrative itself then speaks of how 'the earth was *Tohuwabohu*', this does not refer to a second principle along the lines that earth may have a creation side and hence is called good, but it also has a chaos side and hence ultimately it must always be called 'good and evil' after all. The fact that earth is a *Tohuwabohu* is a quotation from the narratives that are contradicted by the creation story. These narratives really do speak of origin in chaos that can never be conclusively mastered by any imposition of order. If we want to know what God's Spirit – his inspiring breath[21] – has to do with *Tohuwabohu*, then we cannot stop at the 'moved on the face of the waters'[22] where the Spirit is still above

---

21   The Hebrew word *ruach* encompasses all meanings: 'breath', 'wind', 'storm', 'spirit'. This makes it difficult to construe the 'Spirit' as purely 'spiritual'.

22   The Hebrew word *rachaf* roughly means 'to be in trembling movement'. As the movement of the 'Spirit' it is 'the beginning of speech' (Deurloo 1998, p. 18). The Spirit has not yet spoken, but it is close to doing so.

to the earthly valley of tears (the 'waters'). The creation story is the movement from up above to down below, the word's intervention: Let there be light! And there was light (Gn 1:3).

From this moment onwards it is impossible to argue that the earth is a *Tohuwabohu*. From this moment onwards! The creation story did not always exist, it does not immortalise that which is into something that has always been. On the contrary, it intervenes in already existing narratives that do precisely that. Those narratives that make the existing order absolute: things have always been the way they are now, and that is a good thing – a different world is impossible. The creation story can only be understood if it is read in context: in the context of these narratives, as their rejection.

The creation story is not a theoretical contemplation on the emergence of the world. It takes a side in the ideological battle that is fought in the context of a history that has long been happening. We are 'always already' (Althusser) in a world full of mythology, full of stories that demonstrate what the world should look like in principle, what its purpose is. The ideological battle revolves around the issue of which 'image' – worldview, image of humanity – should rule the hearts and minds of the people. 'In the beginning' does not refer to 'prior to, ever', but means a 'principle':[23] in principle, the world and humans are creation, the creation of a God who has goodness in sight and rejects evil. Worldviews and anthropologies that suggest the opposite are actively killed off, and directly, right from the start of the story of the liberation movement that the Bible begins to tell. Maybe it really happened as the myths claim it did during the emergence of the world: the world in chaos. As long as humans can remember, in any case, it assumed chaotic traits again and again. But in that moment, when the Bible gives God the floor, these speculations about the 'ever' are over.

One of the Midrash asks why the Torah starts with the second letter of the alphabet (bet – ב) and not with the first (aleph – א). Surely the point is what comes first? But, explains the reply, the form of the bet is closed on all sides, open only in the direction of reading (Hebrew is read from right to left), the aleph is not. And this is to say: What is above, beneath or behind the creation story cannot be interrogated, only from that day onwards, when the world was created and beyond, may questions be asked.

Here, a fantasy reaches for power that does not lose itself in the depth of existence but that soars to the fabulous heights of a movement that strikes, in

---

23   The Latin translation of 'In the beginning' is: *in principio*.

liberation, 'perpendicular from above' (Barth) into a world under the influence of chaos.[24]

The creation story begins with the emergence from the ideology that secures humans in their fear that everything is ultimately futile: *Tohuwabohu*, chaos, *nihil*. The creation is not the beginning of the world that *exists*, but the exodus from this world with a view to the world that *is coming*.[25] Reality is constructed in such a way that it is custom-made for liberation movements such as the one emerging from the 'land of fear' that is Egypt. Reality is given a 'structure' which, because itself liberating, represents the basis of all liberation.

It cannot be made clear enough: The creation story is a 'poem', not a (pre)scientific treatise. Does this mean that it has nothing to say about the world that exists in the scientific sense? Not necessarily. The answer to the question about what ultimately lies ahead of us, and hence what we can expect, can humanly only be imagined as a fantasy. But when human beings fantasise, they are absolutely processing their experience of reality. The very real experience that reality is immeasurable is elaborated into the myth of the ur-chaos from which there is no escape.[26] By contrast, the experience of resistance against this, which is no less real though far more contested, leads to such fantastic stories as that of the creation. And the language of the imagination is a language of images that cannot be subdued by science. Whoever thinks the 'light' that 'God said' must somehow be the same light of which the natural sciences speak, has misunderstood something. But whoever thinks that this 'light' sheds no light whatsoever on reality, understands just as little.

First there is the *light*. Disregarding the *Tohuwabohu*, the light constitutes the beginning of all historical wisdom; it constitutes the beginning of what can even be called history. Light's calling is to be 'day':

---

24 'By "movement", to be sure, I do not mean either the socialist movement in religion, or the general, somewhat problematical, movement of so-called Christianity. I mean a move-ment from above, a movement from a third dimension, so to speak, which transcends and yet penetrates all these movements and gives them their inner meaning and motive ... I mean the movement of God in history ... the movement whose power and import are revealed in the resurrection of Jesus Christ from the dead' (Barth 1957, p. 283).

25 Miskotte writes about 'experience' as 'a reminiscence of the golden age': 'In biblical thought, the experience here described is understood not as an afterglow of something past but rather as a foretoken of the future' (1967, p. 367).

26 Miskotte describes the myth as 'a possible view of what the world, according to our experience and *with the exception of the Revelation*, must be', and he states: 'We see this by virtue of the Revelation' (1983, pp. 387 f.).

God called to the light: day!
And to the darkness he called: night!
>   Gn 1:5

Darkness ceases to be immeasurable; its calling is to be 'night', a temporary affair that is not even given the final say. For the story continues as follows:

It turned evening and it turned morning: Day one.
>   Ibid.

We can only speak of a 'day' once morning has broken. Rather than darkness lying ahead of the subsequent days, they are looking forward to the day when night will no longer exist:

Night will be no more,
and they require neither lamplight nor sunlight,
for God, YHWH, will shine on them.
>   Rv 22:5

The temporal structure that is being created here is that of a liberation movement.

The World as Space to Live

And then there is the vault, the rampart that God erects against the evil that, so to speak, 'hangs above our head'. This image adopts the structure of above and below where humans are enclosed below. These humans really do not know what to expect from above. Experience has taught them that it is usually nothing good. The above, over which they have no power, renders the space in which they find themselves sinister. The image of the 'vault' offers a perspective on a structure that knows no other 'above' than 'heaven' from whence humans can expect salvation. For that is the 'vault's' calling:

God created the vault
and it separated the water beneath the vault
from the water above the vault.
...
God called the vault 'heaven'.
>   Gn 1:7–8

Thus, the image of the vault intervenes in what is commonly understood to be its meaning: the location of a 'cosmic ocean' above that expands the real threat of the oceans down here into a boundless, universal catastrophe. The image of the 'cosmic ocean' renders the battle that humans could wage against the things that really oppress them hopeless. Heaven, constructed like a vault, which energetically precludes this catastrophic vision, gives hope for winning this battle.[27]

This imagery is taken from a worldview in which reality is represented as a three-story building: the cosmic ocean on top (the water above the vault), underneath it the earth, and underneath that the underworld (the water beneath the vault). The imagery of the creation story rejects the image of the 'cosmic ocean' – by replacing the image of the cosmic ocean with that of the 'vault' – and has no interest in an underworld. What remains are 'heaven and earth'. This is no longer our worldview – scientifically speaking. But we, too, still live in a world in which we do not know what to expect from above. And as it was back then, this is not only due to nature and its threats. It is also related to the 'nature' of the social order – the opacity of its economy, the (related) unpredictability of its politics. It is impossible to change it without knowing how it (nature, society) works, without science. But the question whether we also *believe* that the world can be changed in that way so that we can really say: it is good, that is a different story. This is the story told by the creation story.

This creates space for a world where living is good. 'Water' knows its place: 'to be collected in one place' (Gn 1:9), underneath heaven. Thus it makes room for the 'dry ground', the place where those people, who escaped the catastrophe from above, can advance towards the good life. The image of 'dry ground' is taken from the exodus of the slave people from Egypt. Right at the start, the people encounter an ocean that threatens to destroy them. But the divine miracle occurs: the ocean is parted and Israel makes it onto 'dry ground' (Ex 14:22). The 'dry ground' is the unique piece of reality that opens the way to a walkable path. And in the creation story, this 'dry ground' is called 'earth':

> God called the dry ground 'earth'.
> Gn 1:10

---

27   This is why Frans Breukelman counts 'the earth beneath the heaven' among the four terms that together comprise the structure of biblical theology: 'name' (the NAME), 'words' (the WORD) and 'days' (the DAY) are the others (Breukelman 1999, p. 195).

So the *earth* is created as a place of liberation right from the start. This story has no interest in earth in general, earth that could be destined for all kinds of things. It is written exclusively for people in the underbelly of society, who can know that they can depend on earth. Spatially, reality is structured like 'earth beneath heaven'.[28] Underneath heaven it is 'the Promised Land', destined to accommodate the hunger and thirst for justice.

'Naturally', this earth is fertile. This cannot really be said of earth in general. This is, after all, naturally, also infertile time and again, a catastrophe for humans and animals. The plant will not grow because no rain has fallen for too long, rivers burst their banks and ruin the harvest, volcanoes erupt and oceans flood: nature is fascinating, but it can also be terrible. But this earth is the creation of an imagination that cannot imagine that reality must remain a world of 'ups and downs' for all eternity. Then it speaks for itself, that earth produces everything that is understood to be good nature:

> God said:
> 'Let the earth sprout greens:
> plants, that sow seeds,
> fruit trees, that produce fruits in their own way,
> in which are their seeds, above the earth.'
> ...
> the earth produced greens,
> plants, that sow seeds in their own way,
> trees that bear fruits
> in which, in their own way, are their seeds.
>
> Gn 1:11–12

Notice that everything is fertility; the word 'fruit' appears three times in two verses.

The fact that this earth does not simply exist, however, also speaks for itself. It only 'exists' in the story that talks of a God who creates a world that is opposed to the existing world. Viewed from the world that is, this earth is utopia:[29] from

---

28   '"Erez" [Hebrew for earth/land] is ... the place God has prepared for his people, where he can be with them, it is the stage for the history of the covenant' (Breukelman 1999, p. 195).

29   'Creation is not by any means that which exists and the things we can deduct from or oppose to it. We can only surmise Creation in our longings, in our analyses, in our art, in our intercessions. And woe befall us should we fail to do this for we are ... made for it. But what precisely Creation is, what the purpose of its liberation is, that we do not know' (Naastepad 1989).

their point of view it is *u-topos*, 'no place'. But it sustains the people who believe this story, who believe that this earth is coming, that utopia will find a place. 'Naturally', this earth is fertile, as God – the God of Israel – created heaven and earth.

Life without Idols

Before the story now continues with life on earth, there follows a 'de-mythologisation' of the 'heavenly vault'. The sun and the moon can no longer figure there as divine beings that humans bow down and pray to because their fate depends on them: earth's fertility on the sun, the course of history on the moon who rules the tides. They are nothing more than *lights*, created by God to serve life on earth:

> God created the two great lights,
> the greater light to manage the day,
> the smaller light to manage the night,
> and with it the stars.
> And God placed them in the heavenly vault,
> to shine on earth,
> to rule the day and the night,
> and to separate light from darkness.
>> Gn 1:16–18

That is their task: they can have no other name beside this. They are plainly and simply a couple of lamps, hung from the 'vault' that wards off chaos.

Now the story can start to celebrate life:

> Let the waters teem with living beings,
> and let birds fly
> above the earth, along the heavenly vault.
>> Gn 1:20

We are not yet on the earth. First come the 'living beings' in 'the waters', this place to which something deadly always adheres (the water underneath the vault). Thus the story emphasises that there is life there, too. Then there are the birds: life above the earth, along the heavenly vault, that area that borders on the sinister distance, where all life threatens to be lost (the water above the vault).

Of primary concern, here, are those parts of reality which drive the mythologising imagination to absolutise that which threatens the good life. Water represents death, which threatens to engulf everything. This is also why the fish are not called fish, but are called that which is essential to their role here: *living* beings. And heaven has to be explicitly called 'vault', too – in order to rule out once more any thought of a 'cosmic ocean'.

In this context the story also lets God create the 'great (sea) monsters' (Gn 1:21), which the mythologising imagination projects into the water. Precisely by making these mythological beings into creatures – apart from in the title and in relation to humans, the word 'create' (*bara!*) appears only here in the creation story – the mythologising imagination is disabled.

Incidentally, elsewhere in the Bible, social entities are called 'great monsters': Pharaoh is one such monster (Ez 29:3; 32:2), as is Nebuchadnezzar (Jer 51:34). It is probably this social monster that YHWH will 'afflict' on Judgment Day (Is 27:1).

Above and underneath the earth: life rules everywhere, a blessed life:

> God blessed them and said:
> 'Be fertile and reproduce'
>> Gn 1:22

Life is not being-towards-death, but is meant to be fertile, to reproduce.
   Finally, life on earth itself is related:

> God said:
> 'Let the earth produce living beings, each in their own way,
> livestock, critters, the fauna of the earth, in their own way.
> ...'
> God made the fauna of the earth, in their own way,
> the livestock, in their own way
> and all the critters in the field in their own way.
>> Gn 1:24–25

In this utopia these living beings can be just as they are: in their own way.

The way in which the story speaks of the animal kingdom shows that it was written with the human world in mind. First comes the livestock, at the end comes the 'field' (Hebrew: *adama*), the ground, destined to be ploughed by the human (Hebrew: *adam*).

But while it might be expected that these living beings, too, will now be blessed by God and hear him say: 'Be fertile and reproduce', this is not the case. So are they lesser than the fish and the birds? That is more than unlikely. Here, too, we hear what we have heard before: God saw, and it was good. Except, concerning life on earth, one living being has not been mentioned yet. This is the human, the only one who can actually hear what is being said. What is the point of narrating that God sees, that his *creatio ex nihilo* is good, if there is no human to agree with him? Why, what else does the story of God's good creation want but to address humans, who, based on this story, say in turn: The world is made well, despite all evidence to the contrary? Humans, who, from this story, derive the courage to object to this world as it is? Human are the creatures who not only exist in this utopia, but who can put it to use – to set off towards the Promised Land. He (and she!) plays a very special part in this story: to represent this God on earth. This is why the human becoming-human is introduced with a particularly special phrase that is used only on this occasion:

> God said: let us make humans, in our image,
> in our likeness!
> ...
> then God created Adam, the human, in his image
> in his image he created him.
>> Gn 1:26

The meaning of this 'us' is uncertain, but what is clear is that the creation of the human – 'making' (2×!) explicitly means 'creating' here, after all – is an event that is qualitatively distinct from everything that has happened up to this point in the creation story.

Speaking in terms of religion, this 'us' most likely refers to the 'council of gods' whom God approaches to take part in this event. But do we not, in light of the bond between God and humans, of which the Bible constantly speaks, have to keep an open mind towards a non-religious interpretation: that God involves the human in the creation of the human right 'in the beginning'?[30]

'Let us make': God's making is directed towards a human who will practice liberation in his likeness. It is opposed to the making with which humans try to elevate themselves above everything and everyone by building a tower, whose

---

30   See footnote 19 in this chapter.

spire reaches into heaven – instead of rejoicing at the earth beneath heaven. Then it sounds like a caricature of the divine 'let us make':

> Thus let us make a name for ourselves
>> Gn 11:4

This is the Tower of Babel, which is the culmination of Babylonian imperialism.[31] But thank God there are also those people who say:

> Everything that YHWH has let us say,
> *we want to do it.*[32]
>> Ex 19:8

Intended as the Image of God

Above all, though, this event is distinct from everything that is said about God and humans in other stories. The fact that there are humans who relish the privilege to represent God on earth, is by no means extraordinary. But these stories speak of a type of human who is far superior to ordinary humans, of kings whom these ordinary humans have to look up to. They speak of people like Pharaoh, who plays such a fatal part in the story of the slave people Israel: in his realm of power he is seen as 'the king, carnal (son of Re) ... image of Re, son of Amun, who trampled the strangers'.[33] These kings are in turn depicted in images that are installed throughout the land in order to hammer home who is lord. In the creation story, on the other hand, the right to be the 'image' of God is given to humans, kings simply do not figure in this piece. Humans, too, are allowed to be the 'likeness' of God. An unbelievable privilege considering how incomparable this God is, in the Bible's language:

---

31   The story of the Tower of Babel is inspired by the ziggurat ('heavenly tower' or 'mountain of the gods') in the centre of Babylon, a gigantic terraced temple in honour of Marduk, the principal Babylonian deity. To the Jews living in Babylonian exile, this tower must have seemed like the symbolic representation of Babylon's power reaching all the way to the heavens.

32   Exodus uses the same Hebrew word that Genesis uses earlier, there translated as 'make'.

33   Jenni and Westermann 1976, p. 561.

Who do you want to compare God to?
What image liken him to?
>   Is 40:18

It is crystal clear: he is incomparable. But this is the word of comfort Israel is given (Is 40 opens with: 'Be comforted, be comforted my people'). God's incomparability takes away the people's fear of the powers that could permanently impede their liberation. Whatever these powers might achieve, they can never be 'like God'. Of the king of Babel, who lifts himself into heaven ('I want to ascend into the heights of the clouds, I want to resemble the highest Being'), the following is proclaimed: 'But you have fallen into the realm of death, deep into the pit. Those that see you, will look upon you, will watch out: is this the one, who let the earth tremble, who shook the kingdoms, levelled the world into a desert, tore down its cities, did not let his prisoners go?' (Is 14:15–17). That is the practical point of this God's incomparability: the rulers lose the right to liken themselves to him. Their self-deification is already destroyed in the creation story: humans and none other may be the 'likeness' of God.

So the human and none other is the image of God, his likeness. That is the nature of humanity: to be free of all domination. The only specification provided in this context is that he is created 'in God's image', 'male and female'. But this refers to his 'gender', whose function is to 'beget' the human who really will represent God on earth: Israel.

The great topic of the Book of Genesis, which starts with this story, is that of 'begetting' (Hebrew: *toledot* – from *jalad* = beget, procreate – a plural which can also be translated as 'history'). We hear it for the first time at the end of the creation story itself:

> This is the begetting of heaven and earth: their having been created.
>   Gn 2:4a, according to Buber

Heaven and earth were not 'begotten' by some grim ancient power, but were created by God: *ex nihilo* (the sinister nihil). This verse is simultaneously the liberating heading of the story that follows: about Adam, the human, erected from dust by God, and who can live from the beginning due to this having been created. The story then continues with the 'begetting' of generations (Gn 5:1: Adam; 6:9: Noah; 10:1: Noah's sons; 11:10: Shem; 11:27: Terah; 25:12 Ishmael; 25:19: Isaac; 39:1.9: Esau) and culminates in the 'begetting' of Jacob (37:2), who is given the name Israel.

'Gendering' as the 'occasion' to identify humans as men or as women is not an issue in the creation story. That is what Genesis 2 is concerned with. It is about biblical anthropology: the human as man and woman (Breukelman).

Humans as the image of God is hence not a given (whether you like it or not you are male or female), but a purpose, the goal of a story: 'The Book of Genesis is the book of Adam, the human's toledot, of the *becoming* of Israel in the midst of the peoples of the earth' (Breukelman).[34]

This human can now be fertile with God's blessing, and (ful)fill the earth. And he is at liberty to 'dominate' the earth and to 'rule over' the animals:

> Be fertile, reproduce,
> fill the earth and dominate it.
> Rule over the fish in the ocean, the birds in heaven
> and all living beings who walk the earth.
> Gn 1:8

This liberty implies an anthropocentric worldview: the human is at liberty ... to do as he pleases with the earth and the life that surrounds him.

The verbs used here are also hard. Both *kabash* ('dominate') and *radah* ('rule') mean as much as to stamp down, to trample. The rule of power referred to here is hence assuredly not idyllic. But was it even possible for the people, who came up with this story, to imagine the utopia of the 'good earth' as idyll? Is the path to the Promised Land not tied to necessary hardship? Does that make it any less the path to the Promised Land?

Reality and Utopia at Once

But the human at the centre of this story is called upon to be the likeness of that God who declares '*everything* he had made' to be 'very good' (Gn 1:31).

---

34   'After the creation story has spoken of "*heaven and earth*", there follow the Toledot of heaven and earth, and after *the human* – 'adam' on the 'adama' ['field'] coram Deo [before God] – has been spoken of in Gn 2:4–4:26 under the heading "These are the Toledot of heaven and earth, when they were created" there follow the Toledot of Adam in *sefer toledot adam* [the book of Adam's, the human's, begettings] from 5:1–50:26 which is concerned with the becoming of Israel in the midst of the peoples. The sequence of topics ... is therefore: heaven and earth → the human → Israel. In order to understand the narrative of the book as an annunciation, however, we have to reverse the order ...: Israel → the human → heaven and earth. For it is due to the existence of Israel coram Deo on the erez [land, but also: earth] that God gave to it that Gn 2:4–4:26 speaks of 'ha-adam' on the 'adama' coram Deo. And it is also due to Israel's existence on the erez that God gave to it that Gn 1:1–2:3 speaks of "creation as divine *land gift*"' (Breukelman 1992, p. 11).

'Domination' and 'rule' do not correspond with the image we are to make for ourselves of this human and the world around him. In what way he 'dominates' the earth (Hebrew: *erez*) can only be seen in his treatment of the land (in Hebrew also: *erez*), which is given to him as the Promised Land. For it is there that he must fulfil the likeness.

There it will transpire that the Sabbath Israel is commanded to 'keep' includes the animals that have been entrusted to them:

> Remember the Sabbath, keep it holy
>
> ...
>
> Nobody should work then,
> not you, nor your son or your daughter,
> nor your male slave or your female slave, nor your *livestock*
>> Ex 20:8–10

And the rest of the Sabbath extends to all the land, too:

> In the seventh year, the Sabbath Year, there shall be a Sabbath for the land of categorical interruption.
>> Lv 25:4

This is the temporary climax of the story: the creation of humans, who can be addressed by God:

> God blessed them, God *spoke to them*
>> Gn 1:28

'To be fertile and to reproduce' is also part of humans' blessedness. For us this has meanwhile become questionable: can the earth still bear the unrestrained growth of humanity – and let us not forget their products! Today it is evident that growth has limits, which we humans cannot transgress unpunished. So it is advisable not to interpret the blessing, of which the creation story speaks, in a fundamentalist or literal way (then the letter kills, as Paul says in 2 Cor 3:6). If we want to 'protect' creation as the promise of a good earth, then we must learn to relinquish an economy that cannot function without permanent growth.

This was the point of the whole story: God *and* human and no other (higher!) being that comes between them. Now God sees 'everything he has made':

And see, it is *very good*.[35]
>   Gn 1:31

Now the exodus from the world of *Tohuwabohu* is complete, God has done his liberating work:

> The heaven and the earth were *completed*, and all their hosts.
> On the seventh day God had *completed* his work that he did.
>   Gn 2:1–2a

Now the great entry can start, the liberation can be 'celebrated'. The last day, the Sabbath, the day which God takes off and the humans are free – 'free at last':

> God blessed the seventh day, and made it holy,
> For on it he rested (*sabat*) from all his work that God had created while
>   making it.
>   Gn 2:3

Sabat means not only 'to rest' but also 'to celebrate'. It is like our Sunday, both a day of rest and a day of celebration. Contrary to our Sunday, the Sabbath is the end, but this also means it is the purpose of the working week: the liberation from work.[36] Then, work itself can turn into a liberating practice: work as pleasure. Without Sabbath, though, without the view to leisure time (which, in turn, is itself the product of work: liberation through work), work is hopeless hardship, mere 'drudgery'. This 'drudgery' will have an end (Rv 21:4).

For God's Sabbath and the Sabbath he commands his people to keep are inextricably linked. It is unthinkable that he would not grant the rest that he granted himself to the human who is at the centre of the creation story.

The fantastical story of the creation out of nothing is not a worldview but stirs belief in a world to come – in the shape of a forceful no to the chaos-ideology:

---

35   Karel Deurloo comments: 'This is astonishingly different from what the human sees in 'nature' ... The human does not have knowledge of what is being told here on account of any "*seeing* is believing"; it has to be *heard*' (1998, p. 35).

36   As is sung in the Dutch labour movement: We must liberate our labour / Delivery from slavery.

He did not create it [the earth] as chaos (*tohu*),
but to be lived in.

> Is 45:18

And the prophet who speaks this cannot imagine anything else but a 'new *creation*', even if the credibility of this story has been plunged into deep crisis by the unbelief of the people. He lets God speak:

see, I *create* a new heaven and a new earth!

> Is 65:17

CHAPTER 6

Anthropology (Gn 2–4)

Brought forth out of nothing: the human is called upon to be the image, the likeness of God. 'The' human? The becoming of Israel in the midst of the peoples is in question here, Israel becoming-human. When the Bible speaks of 'the' human it is referring to this Israelite human from the start. Biblically speaking, the *condition humaine* is the 'condition' of that human who like Israel is nowhere ... if he is not raised from his misery by the Liberator-God. Biblical anthropology does not comply with the logic of the human in general, but brings this one human into focus, this special 'Adam' (Hebrew for 'human'), who would be hopelessly lost within general history without the delivering intervention of this special God. As such, this human is 'dust from the field' (Hebrew: *adam-a*) (Gn 2:7): drifting sand on the edge of the field of humans, 'when the wind blows, [he] is gone' (Ps 103:16), he is no longer anywhere. But God 'forms'[1] this 'breadcrumb on the Universe's apron' (Lucebert) into a human deserving of the name. He 'breathes' life into him, it is because of this 'breath' of the NAME that this 'nobody' is turned into a '*living* being'.

Humans and animals have their 'living being' in common. And animals are also explicitly called this in Gn 1 (Gn 1:20–24). Humans are not called this because that passage is concerned with the qualitative distinction between humans and animals: the human as the image and the likeness of God. Here, in Gn 2, the emphasis is laid precisely on the precarious status of the human, which approximates him to animals: just like them, he is an ordinary 'living being'. In other words, he is no God who reigns sovereign over and administers the world, but a human, who can be human because of the God who grants him life. Because of this God he does not need to be 'like God', either.

YHWH places this human, raised from the dirt (Ps 113:7), in a garden – by the name of Eden, 'pleasure garden' – to "serve" (Hebrew: *abad*) and preserve it' (Gn 2:15). He is an *ebed*, a 'servant', but not as an inferior, as slave (even though

---

1 The Hebrew word *jatsar*, which is here translated as 'form' actually refers to the potter's 'kneading' and is primarily used for the 'kneading' of idols. Tom Naastepad has the following to say about *jatsar* in Gn 2:7: 'There the irony and the polemic is crystal clear: serving the idols and the exercise of power have reduced the human to "dust" that can be trampled. They have kneaded him into a marionette and a yay-sayer. God, on the other hand, "kneaded" him from the dust, made of him a living being' (Naastepad 1979).

the Hebrew word means that, too). He is a free human: the service he renders is not imposed. There is only the human (*adam*) and the field (*adama*) he 'works on' (*abad* also means 'to work on'). A master-slave relation is nowhere in sight.

The wordplay with *abad* alludes to the protagonist from the narrative of the exodus, the *ebed*, the slave, who is liberated from the *bet abodim*, the house of bondage. This wordplay is essential; biblical anthropology cannot be understood at all without it. Without it we no longer understand that it is not the human in general who is at issue here, but the special human: the *ebed*, liberated by YHWH.

This human is shown that he is destined to live in a world without privilege, a world where everyone shares everything. Here, the garden is not the king's exclusive property, as was the case, for instance, with the legendary Babylonian 'Gardens of Semiramis'.[2]

The narrative of Gn 2 (and 3) presupposes a reader who is familiar with these 'Gardens of Semiramis' – in the first instance, 'Israel', the reader who has experienced the Babylonian exile first-hand, as it were. This reader is surprised by the good news that in the Bible everything is different. The 'royal garden' is, as it were, repossessed and turned into a people's garden.

Here, humans no longer have to look on from afar and with a desirous gaze upon the magnificent trees that adorn this garden which is forbidden ground for them. Here the world is the domain of a God who makes the trees that he lets 'sprout' ('charming to behold and good to eat', Gn 2:9) 'from the *adama*', the *adam*'s habitat, available to all humans. He also, and not least, releases the 'Tree of Life', which the gods had specifically withheld from humans according to Babylonian mythology.

This anthropology does not predetermine human ('dust from the field') misery, but offers him a view of this democratised garden, where life is 'prince-ly' – a Promised Land.

Here, already, the Promised Land is anticipated, where the people of Israel will find 'peace' and will no longer have to fear tomorrow, fear the enemy who might attack at any moment, fear the omnipresent threat of hunger, the omnipresent threat of poverty.

---

2 The Babylonian 'Hanging Gardens of Semiramis' were considered one of the Seven Wonders of the World. Whether they really existed is uncertain. What is certain is that like all royal gardens at the time, they were inaccessible to the common people.

For the story says that YHWH takes the *adam* and 'lets him *rest*' (Gn 2:15) in the garden. The common translation is 'to place', but the Hebrew word *nawach* also means 'rest'.[3] It alludes to the 'rest' (the same Hebrew stem *nawach*) that YHWH gives the people of Israel in the land that he lets them 'inherit' (Dt 3:20; 12:9–10; 25:19; Is 14:1–3).

Knowledge – of What?

This is the great offer made to the human in this 'Doctrine of the Human': to set up this garden in such a way that it remains preserved as a garden for all humans. And this is why the commandment is to keep to this doctrine now, not to believe the narratives about humans that suggest the opposite. It is a commandment full of mercy:

> YHWH, God, commanded the human and said:
> You may eat from all the trees in the garden, you may eat from them.
> Gn 2:16

In other words: Human, remember that all trees are available to you, *gratia gratis data*, a gift, complimentary and free of charge. *All* trees, including the Tree of Life that stands in the middle of the garden, that is hence its centre, the tree around which everything revolves:

> YHWH, God, let all sorts of trees sprout from the field,
> charming to behold and good to eat,
> and the Tree of Life in the middle of the garden
> Gn 2:9

Do not let anyone take this knowledge away from you, do not let anyone tell you that the real knowledge is the knowledge of 'good and evil', the knowledge of eternal ambivalence: you know that things will never be good because that would simply contradict the 'nature' of reality as well as human 'nature'. This is the mythological wisdom against which biblical anthropology goes to war:

---

3   In his interpretation of the name Noach (Hebrew stem: *nawach*), Barnard writes: 'Nawach is an important word. It is so important *that it points towards the purpose of the human*! Gn 2:15 already says: [...] and he took the humans with him, and *gave them rest* – namely in the pleasure garden that is the symbol of the good earth' (1987, p. 48).

> But from the Tree of Knowledge of good and evil –
> from that you should not eat.[4]
>> Gn 2:17

For this tree has no place in this garden. It only has to be mentioned in passing in order to make plain that it really has no place there, because this knowledge would be fatal for the human.

This is why it is also fatal when the translation overlooks the odd syntax, which is odd in Hebrew, too ('the Tree of Life in the middle of the garden, and the Tree of Knowledge of good and evil'), and simply transplants the Tree of Knowledge of good and evil into the middle of the garden – and thus equates it with the Tree of Life. Whoever translates it like that has already been seduced by the snake, which will appear later and then will tempt him into this thought (Gn 3:2).[5]

This is the knowledge that the Babylonian Gilgamesh epic pronounces as the end of all mythological wisdom. This epic tells the tale of Gilgamesh's odyssey in search of 'eternal life', life without death. While this odyssey brings him close to the 'plant of life', it ultimately fails. Though he finds this life-promising flower (in the underworld! As though wrested from death), when he goes to take a bath in a spring of fresh water (of life?), a snake appears from the depths and takes the plant from him. Thus the snake – that profound animal that so often also appears as a counsellor in mythology – robs Gilgamesh of the possibility of life without fear of death. And the moral of the story is: 'You will never find the life you are searching for! When the gods created the human, they determined he should die, life is firmly controlled by them'.[6] It is the moral of the rulers who command life and death 'like gods'. In their regime, life is a privilege that they reserve for themselves, and death is the fate of their subjects. These rulers are themselves the embodiment of 'good and evil', eternal ambivalence: their rule ensures order – against the omnipresent threat of chaos – but for the majority of people this order means disorder that has little to offer them.

---

4 The second commandment, 'you should not', stands in the service of the first commandment, 'everything is allowed'. As the Jewish commentator Sa'adya Gaon (892–942) writes: 'Everything we need is allowed, except for the things Moses tells us are forbidden'.

5 The 'Good News Bible' goes especially crazy: 'In the middle of the garden stood the tree that gives life and the tree that gives knowledge of what is good and what is bad'. This is precisely not the knowledge that the Tree of Knowledge of good and evil bestows! On the contrary, the knowledge that this tree bestows is snake knowledge!

6 Gilgamesh epic. Old Babylonian version.

Humans, who have been called (and appointed) to freedom by the God of the Bible, should not 'eat' of this 'wisdom'. This wisdom is fatal for them:

> For on the day, when you eat from it, you will die, you will surely die.
> Gn 2:17

For this wisdom subjects them to the regime of those rulers who have death in store for them. There is no escape, no exodus: the exodus narrative drowns in the fatalist thought that Pharaoh's army will catch up with them after all. The narrative of the exodus out of nothingness has then been in vain, the hope that it created, for a reality that is good and hence not 'good and evil' for all eternity, is from now on completely unfounded.

But is it not childish to believe things could ever be any different from what mythology pronounces? Were they ever any different? What is the belief that a different world is possible even founded on?

Biblical anthropology breaks the spell that says things will always continue as they have so far. The 'always', and before you know it the 'forever', is an absolutisation that fixes history as that which has 'not yet' been achieved. This absolutisation ignores the liberations that have nevertheless taken place. If we believe the myth, then we can forget about these liberations, and the myth contributes to this forgetting by suppressing these liberations – or narrating their demise.

Gilgamesh's search for life is in vain. Prometheus, the hero who stole fire from the gods in order to give it to humans, is a tragic figure according to Greek mythology. His courage is *hubris*, presumptuousness, for which he is then eternally punished: forever chained to a mountain, forever beset by an eagle, which forever feeds on his liver. 'Prometheus unbound' is inconceivable in this mythology. The 'adam' of biblical anthropology, however, is just such a liberated Prometheus.

The human envisioned by biblical anthropology is not childish. He has the capacity to 'serve and preserve' the Garden. He hears the commandment and is hence obviously mature enough to obey it. Nothing in the narrative suggests that he remains ignorant and hence has not yet achieved knowledge. He knows what is crucial to his existence in freedom: not to lose faith in the fact that the world is made well, which means that it qualifies for liberation. He experienced first-hand that he owes his existence to God, who raised him from the dust.

The interpretation of Gn 2 and 3 which reads the human's 'paradisiacal state' as the state of his childhood, when he is not yet aware of any evil, and which hence interprets his eating from the Tree of Knowledge of good and evil as his becoming-aware, is a fatal misreading. This interpretation is led astray by general anthropology, which can imagine no other *condition humaine* than that the human, in the moment when he becomes aware of his situation, 'knows': the end of all wisdom is ambivalence. According to this anthropology, the human as a being of reason is a tragic figure, the human becoming-human is by definition a 'fall'. Biblical anthropology, on the other hand, presupposes both the rising (raised from the dust), as well as the exodus (the exodus from nothingness).

Or does the Bible account for something akin to a stage of the human becoming-human, where knowledge of good and evil does not *yet* exist, after all – suggesting that it will be acquired at a later point? In his great farewell sermon, the Book of Deuteronomy, Moses lets YHWH say to the people:

> And your children
> …
> your sons, who do not know 'good and evil' today,
> *they* shall come there [to the Promised Land]
>> Dt 1:39

At play here, though, is the generation that follows the generation who had no faith in God's promise that life in the Promised Land would be simply good, and who wanted to return to Egypt (Nm 14:2–4). This generation was hence not allowed to enter into the land, because they no longer qualified for entry: they had fallen prey to the wisdom that life will always be 'good *and* evil' and hence there is no point in fighting for a good life. This generation is told that only its next generation is to come to the land, *because* (this is how I read the sentence) it is liberated from this fatal 'knowledge of good and evil' today (today! – when you hear my voice!). Only he who has been liberated from the myth of eternal ambivalence is suitable for the society free of domination that is to be established in the land.

Here, knowledge opposes knowledge. The knowledge of 'good and evil' has a crippling effect: what point is there in good actions, when they will not ultimately lead to anything good? But the knowledge of the world having been made well gives purpose to good actions. The logic of biblical anthropology is ethical and founds agency. *Action* lies ahead of the human raised from the dust: to *choose* what is good (the good life). This is what Moses says to his people at the end, before they enter into the Promised Land:

> Look,
> today I have given you

life and what is good,
death and what is evil,
since today I command you,
to love YHWH, your God,
to follow his path,
to keep his commandments, his regulations, his statutes:
then you will live,
then you will reproduce,
then YHWH, your God, will bless you in the land, to which you come,
to inherit it
...
I call upon heaven and earth, today, to witness:
today I have presented you with life and with death,
the blessing and the curse,
choose life
so that you live and your descendants can live, too!

    Dt 30:15–19

Moses points to the space of the good creation, the earth beneath heaven, and calls upon these as witnesses against the people. He introduces heaven and earth as the determining motive for the people to do what they have been chosen to do: to organise the good life in the Promised Land – by loving God, following his path, keeping his commandments. He holds up the good and the evil before them, not to confuse them about 'good and evil', but so that they may *distinguish* between good and evil: to know what is good and be able to consciously choose it.

    This is why Solomon prays to God, when the former asks the latter what he should give to him:

So give your servant an obedient heart,
to judge your people,
to *distinguish* between good and evil[7]

    1 Kgs 3:9

---

7 Thomas Naastepad remarks: 'This "judging" is not meant in purely judicial, nor the "separat-ing good from evil" in purely ethical terms ... It is more closely tied to the Tree of Life than to the Tree of Knowledge of good and evil. He who "knows" good and evil is part of the unholy generalities in which the peoples live, he shares their blindness. But he who asks to "separate" is requesting the special teaching that proceeds from the Torah' (1975, p. 21). For the Tree of Life par excellence is, after all, the Torah.

And this is also why the promised Messiah will 'discard the evil and choose the good' (Is 7:15).

For how else could Solomon 'judge' the people if he did not know what was good and evil, because it is never as easily discernible as that? And how else would he learn to recognise it, but by having God tell him – instead of mandating good and evil at random, himself like a god?

Humans as Social Beings

Within this anthropology, what is definitely *not good* can then also be forcefully articulated:

> YHWH, God said:
> Not good is
> that the human be alone.
> Gn 2:18a

This can surely not be said in general. 'Hell is other people', wrote Sartre, and he will have spoken for many people. Experience has taught them how awful having to live with others can be: their marriage hell, the society they live in hell. The general anthropological fact that humans are social beings *per se* is a hugely ambivalent matter. Social relations are such that people's dependence on each other factually means that one lives at the cost of another. So, if at all possible, gaining independence, not relying on help from others, has to be achieved. But this, in turn, is only possible if one possesses the power or the ability to render others dependent, to force others to do the work – especially the dirty work – or to buy their willingness to help. And so on and so forth, endless 'good and evil'.

Biblical anthropology, however, is directed at those people who have to foot the bill in this (a)social order. They lack the wealth to render themselves independent in this way. For these people it truly is not good to be alone. Then they are hopelessly lost. They are told:

> YHWH, God, said:
> ...
> I want to create a help for him,
> like a counterpart.
> Gn 2:18b

A 'counterpart' is announced to the biblical human, one who will help him be a social being who lives in solidarity and who exists in conditions in which mutual dependence does not mean that one lives at the cost of the other. For this 'help' that God makes for the human is help in the likeness of God himself, in other words it is help that – entirely at liberty, without subjecting itself – liberates rather than enslaving.

The word 'help' which is used here (Hebrew: *ezer*) is usually used exclusively in conjunction with the liberator-God. Like in the 'credo' in Psalm 121:

> Where does my help come from?
> My help comes from YHWH,
> who has made heaven and earth.
>> Ps 121:1–2

This help is complimentary and free of charge. In order to receive it, Israel has to do nothing except avow:

> Our help is in the name of YHWH,
> who has made heaven and earth.
>> Ps 124:8

In biblical anthropology this liberating 'help' is declared the definitive dimension of becoming-human: the human becomes a fellow human, otherwise he becomes non-human.

In this anthropology, this 'help' is concrete: woman as the 'counterpart' to man. Here, the man-woman relation then functions as the image par excellence for fellow humanity as the basic form of biblical humanity. This is not only due to the fact that the author of the narrative of Gn 2 was fascinated with sexual difference and tried to answer the question of its purpose. It is also and above all due to the society that is presupposed here: a society based on tribal kinship and the rules that apply to it. One such rule is *exogamy*, which means that marriage takes place outside one's own tribe. This ensured the reproduction of the tribe: incest threatened that reproduction. The relationship between men and women obviously played an essential part in this reproduction. The concern was not only the reproduction of the species as such ('procreation'), but also the reproduction of a social relation: the relation between men and women.

The Book of Genesis (the name says it all) narrates the 'genesis', the becoming (the 'begetting') of the people of Israel in the shape of *family* histories: Terah's 'begettings' (Hebrew: *toledot*), the father of Abraham (Gn 11:27), those of Isaac (Gn 25:19), and of Jacob (Gn 37:2). Finding a woman outside your own clan plays an important part in this. It seems to be typical for Israel, though, that the woman has to hail from a related clan: Abraham sends his servant 'to his country and to his kin [related tribe] ... to find a wife for his son Isaac' (Gn 24:4), Isaac commands his son Jacob to go to the 'House' of Bethuel, his mother's father, and there 'to take a wife from the daughters of Laban, his mother's brother' (Gn 28:2). This is how Israel 'comes into being': organised as a community of related tribes, the twelve tribes, named for their progenitors.

It makes sense, then, that this anthropology should discuss the social nature of humans based on this social system, of all things. But it does this in its own special way. It liberates the man-woman relation from the ambivalence that generally appertains to it: an inevitable bond, but similarly inevitably entwined in sexism. And the sexism of the time, for which this anthropology is chiefly written, is patriarchy.

The Bible is a predominantly patriarchal book: the people of Israel come into being from father to son, and it is the '*sons* of Israel' who are in charge throughout the history of this people – as a rule; there are (significant) exceptions: the judge Deborah (Jgs 4–5), Naomi's neighbours, who 'call' the name of their daughter-in-law's first-born son (Ru 4:17), Esther, who saves her people from persecution and is the founder of Purim (Est 9:32). Normally, mothers and daughters are *taken* – from their clan so as to pass over into the tribe of the father and his son.

This patriarchy, which can take its course without issue throughout the narratives of Israel, is rectified here in revolutionary manner. When the human 'calls' the name of his 'counterpart', woman (Hebrew: *isha*), for she has been *taken* out of the man (Hebrew: *ish*) (Gn 2:23), then it is not the man who *takes* his woman. On the contrary, this woman is *brought* to him by YHWH (Gn 2:22) – as 'help', yes, but she is a help in the likeness of this God: as the man's liberator. The wordplay of *ish* and *isha* can hence not be taken as an occasion to deduce women's subordination to man. And therefore, in order to substantiate this notion in society:

> A man leaves his father and his mother and follows his wife,
> and they become one flesh
>
> Gn 2:24

Here, the system of relations, organised as patriarchy, is reversed: it is the man who leaves his father and his mother and passes over into his wife's tribe. And this is also where the rule of man finds its happy end: the woman walks ahead on this anti-patriarchal path and the man follows her, like Israel 'follow' their God.

The Hebrew word *dabaq*, when it means 'to follow a person', takes as its 'object' either a woman (here in Gn 2, also in Gn 34:3 and 1 Kgs 11:2) or YHWH. Israel is commanded to 'follow' him:

> Fear YHWH, your God
> serve him,
> *follow* him.
>
> Dt 10:20, see Dt 11:22; 13:5; 30:20; Jo 22:5; 23:8

Paul, the Jew who avows Jesus as the Messiah, goes so far as to parallelise woman's 'subordination' to man – which the anthropology of Gn 2 does not speak of! – with the 'subordination' of the community to the Messiah (Eph 5:23). Woman as the image of the messianic community! That is why men are commanded to 'love' their wives, which means to be solidary with them (Eph 5:28). And it says a lot that Paul emphasises this commandment by quoting Gn 2:24: A man will follow his wife (Eph 5:31) – like the community 'follows' its Messiah!

But even in Gn 2 and 3, the outlook remains patriarchal: they speak of (the) '(*hu*)*man* and his wife' (Gn 2:25; 3:8). The human appears to be male. Or might it also be read as follows: concerning the human and his humanity, 'his wife' above all must be given voice? For without this 'helping counterpart', that male human can only ever be a non-human.

Only once woman has made her appearance and the human has become coupled can this anthropology speak of *one* humankind: removed from patriarchal order, *ish* and *isha* become '*one* flesh'.

In biblical language 'flesh' means: embodiment. 'Flesh' is opposed to 'spirit' – though this means that it owes the fact of its life wholly and entirely to God's Spirit, without which it would be hopelessly lost (Gn 6:3). This is what the human shares with 'all flesh' (Gn 6:19): transient being that can exist purely because God 'remembers' it:

> He [YHWH] remembered they were only flesh,
> a passing breath, never to return.
>
> ...

He brought his people forth as sheep,
like a herd he led them into the desert.
Ps 78:39 and 52

But 'flesh' can also refer to a sense of togetherness among humans, based on the fact that they are of the same 'flesh'. This is the argument Judah invokes in his attempt to stop his brothers from killing their brother Joseph: 'he is our brother, our *flesh*' (Gn 37:27). This sense of togetherness is the point of 'becoming one flesh' (the phrase appears only here, in Gn 2): one 'body' that constitutes humankind, and the culmination of biblical anthropology.

The following comment underlines the fact that the particular humankind at issue here is qualitatively different from what usually constitutes the unity of the human species – its discord:

> The two of them, the human and his woman, were naked and they were not ashamed.
> Gn 2:25

In this anthropology, the human's 'nakedness', the fact that he is defenceless and vulnerable, is not a 'defect' against which he must arm himself. For here the other is your helper, who meets you so as to save you from danger, to raise you from the dust, to love you like her neighbour, because like you, she depends on this love, this solidarity. This is why, even though it bears the potential of your downfall, you do not have to be 'ashamed' of this *condition humaine*. This shame will end for liberated humankind. For the human who seeks to take another's life will be a thing of the past.

Nakedness, shame. This obviously brings the *erotic* to mind – especially as it concerns the relation between man and woman. But, as mentioned above, the man-woman relation primarily concerns the kinship system. In this context, erotics are subordinated (in this system). Erotics are never mentioned explicitly in this narrative, either. The link that is often made to the Song of Songs is associative, not based on concordance, congruent word usage.

Evidently, there is a utopian element to this anthropology. The sense of togetherness, where humans no longer have to be wary of each other, has not yet arrived, the exodus from patriarchy has not yet taken place. The narrative in Gn 2 exceeds the order we encounter in the subsequent narratives, it radically transcends them. But utopia is not suspended in mid-air, it is based on the liberation of the people of Israel from slavery and it radicalises this liberation to its furthest point: the human in the right place in the Garden of Eden, having arrived in the Promised Land, with the Tree of Life at its centre, is no longer alone, but together. In light of this, the commandment is given: not to eat from the Tree of Knowledge of 'good and evil'. For those who do not believe that the history of humankind will find a good end will resign themselves to the evil – will have to resign themselves to it.

Is this anthropology not too naïve to be true, though? Do the people of Israel, in the midst of the 'peoples', not have to be wary? How else can they protect their togetherness from external aggression? We should not forget that biblical anthropology is born from a *fight*: the fight Israel had to fight in order to 'protect' its identity as a liberation movement, in the present and for the future. Israel's anthropology takes part in this fight – by fighting against everything that is said about the *condition humaine* in general around Israel. What Israel is commanded to do specifically in its fight for survival in the real conditions, is outlined in another book (Deuteronomy; see Chapter 7).

The Fall

If we speak of the liberated human, we cannot remain silent regarding his fall. Here we encounter the great problem of the liberation movement: often, all too often, it betrays its own liberation. The human is raised from the dust. He is destined to 'serve' the view of the world that sees it as a great 'Garden of Eden', and to 'preserve' it. This is why he is commanded to keep away from the fatal wisdom that knows the world only as 'good and evil' because wisdom is at the mercy of the despotism of the 'gods' who are so unpredictable.

Is it really as fatal as all that, though, to know the ways of the world? If this wisdom is allowed to speak for itself, it suggests the opposite. Certainly, the 'gods' are in charge and a world without gods is unthinkable. But there is a solution: to become a 'god' yourself.

And biblical anthropology lets this wisdom speak for itself, too. It appears in the shape of a snake, the animal from the depths, in mythological thought the keeper of wisdom, who purports to offer good advice. This snake is given the floor, and the climax of the conversation it has with the human is:

Die, you will not die,
but God [Hebrew: *elohim*] knows:

> on the day when you eat of it [the Tree of the Knowledge of good and
>   evil], your eyes will be opened
> and you will be like God [*elohim*], knowing good and evil
>   Gn 3:5

In conversation the snake proves to be the embodiment of everything that constitutes this wisdom: to be 'good *and* evil'. Its speech is highly ambiguous. The manner in which it plays with the Hebrew word *elohim*, which can mean both God and gods (in the plural), is ingenious. Is it speaking of 'God' and so the God who is given voice in the Bible, or is it speaking of the 'gods' who are in conflict with this God? And the questions it poses – about what God supposedly 'really' said – already suggests a God akin to the 'gods' without explicitly saying so:

> Would God really have said:
> Do not eat from all the trees of the garden?
>   Gn 3:1

This is a flat-out lie. God says exactly the opposite: You may eat from all trees, including and not least from the Tree of Life. But those who know the 'gods' will say: that figures. This is so typical of the 'gods': to begrudge humans life. This is also the part that the snake plays in the myth: the part of the lying animal that speaks the truth, which is, that the 'gods' cannot be trusted. The wisdom offered by the snake is that the 'gods' will lead the human astray at the decisive moment, will make a maze of the garden. That is the moral of the Gilgamesh epic.

In mythology, this lie is the end of all wisdom. The Adapa myth tells the story of Adapa, the Babylonian 'adam' who is offered 'eternal life' by Anu, the god of heaven, in the shape of bread and water. His father, the god Ea, god of the underworld and of wisdom (like the snake), however, has given him the treacherous advice never to accept such a gift on account of this bread and this water being the bread and water of death. This divine betrayal is the end of the story, the *ultima ratio* of Babylonian anthropology: death wisdom. That is just the way it is: the human's longing for the good life will always betray him. But the lie is also telling the truth. It is true: the 'gods' really do begrudge humans life. And this is why humans do well to draw the practical conclusion that they have no other option but to become 'like the gods': to seize (complete) power in order that they may mandate 'good and evil' themselves, autonomously, with sovereignty.

But for the humans at issue in this anthropology, this truth is fatal. The moment they – the woman leading the way, the 'following' husband in pursuit –

let the snake convince them to follow its logic and to eat from the fruit of the Tree of Knowledge of 'good and evil'

> Their eyes are opened
> and they knew ...
> that they were naked.
>   Gn 3:7a

Now they have to know what the Liberator-God had hoped to spare them: If they want to save their naked existence, they have to 'arm' themselves against each other, too:

> they wove fig leaves and made belts
>   Gn 3:7b

The Hebrew word *chagor* means 'belt' – the fact that it is often translated as 'aprons' (KJV) here is most likely due to the inability of the translators to imagine that anything else could be made from fig leaves, *nota bene* in paradise. The belt is an element of a suit of armour (1Sm 18:4; 2Kgs 3:21; Ez 23:15). Here, the practical conclusion of the knowledge of his nakedness is at play for the human: to arm his body, always prepared for battle.

What the snake concealed was that being 'like the gods' was never a real option for humans. The snake's wisdom is the wisdom of rulers in two respects. First, it is only the ruler, the sovereign, who has the power to be autonomous. And second, it is the ruler who benefits if the 'ordinary people' start to believe that they must themselves be sovereign and autonomous, and forget that they then forfeit their only chance of liberation: solidarity with each other, now and in future.

This is also why the communist philosopher Louis Althusser opposed the idea, also popular among Marxists, that 'humans make history'. For 'the' human was nothing other than 'a little lay God ... endowed with the prodigious power ... of "transcending" every situation, of resolving all the difficulties which history presents, and of going forward towards the golden future of the human, socialist revolution'.[8] This god-human is a dangerous illusion which the oppressed would do better not to fall prey to, for they can only make history as a '*mass* movement', together, as a collective. This is why

---

8   Althusser 1984, p. 75.

Althusser opposes the idea that 'humans make history' with the idea: the masses make history.[9]

Why is the snake given the floor at all, though? After all, it does not fit into this paradisiacal state in any way. Is biblical anthropology itself not ambiguous in this respect? Before you know it, the narrative of Gn 2 is read again as the fantastic narrative of a blissful original state, when the human is still completely innocent. The snake's destruction of this *dolce far niente* can then hardly be interpreted in any other way but that God himself allows evil and hence reveals himself as 'good and evil'. But like the creation story, this anthropology is an intervention in the world of myth. It does not speculate about an original state that precedes the (hi)story as we know it. This narrative takes sides in an ideological battle: 'faith stands against faith' (Miskotte).[10] It does not spare those humans who believe that what they have been told is the truth in Gn 2, the confrontation with this other belief: the disbelief that denies the possibility of a different world from the one that exists. The myth is not besieged, but fought against. This is why biblical anthropology 'invents' the Tree of Knowledge of 'good and evil' (the myth has never heard of such a tree) as the symbol of 'knowledge' that the liberator-God explicitly refuses! And that is why the snake is given the floor, so that it can do what the myth says it should: thoroughly question this God's word.

The narrative is not intent on luring the human into a trap. He knows everything he needs to know in order to rebuff the snake as it deserves to be rebuffed: that the true God has granted him the space to live in and has commanded him to exclude the Tree of Knowledge of 'good and evil' (it is not even in the middle of the garden, anyway). *Status confessionis* is commanded to the human: to avow, in opposition to the snake, that the liberator-God is the 'only' God and to reject completely the suggestion that things might be different (more complicated, more nuanced) after all. But what the human does is communicate with the snake. The snake's question – whether it really is the case that God has said: 'Do not eat from all trees of the garden' – is not met with indignant refusal: 'No, absolutely not', on the contrary, we may eat from all the trees, including the Tree of Life. Then the conversation would have ended immediately. The snake's suggestion is denied, but this denial includes an important concession to the snake: The tree from which the human may not

---

9   Ibid.

10 Miskotte is speaking of the irreconcilable opposition between Edda (the Germanic myth) and Torah. The issue here is an opposition that is ultimately a question of (dis)belief (Miskotte 1983, p. 11).

eat, because this would be fatal for him, replaces the Tree of Life in the middle of the garden. Or worse still: now it is the Tree of Life that God forbids to the human (utter confusion! Good and evil!):

> We may eat from the fruit of the trees in the garden,
> but of the fruit of the tree, which stands in the middle of the garden,
> God has said:
> do not eat from it and do not touch it, otherwise you will die.
> Gn 3:2–3

The human conceals the decisive argument *in favour of* God, of this God: that he is good and gives the human *everything* (all the trees!) that he needs to live. The conversation now revolves exclusively around the Tree of Knowledge of 'good and evil', the pros and cons of the myth's wisdom. Is it not really the case that reality's secret is unspeakable? And that God 'means' this unspeakability? Is the knowledge of this fact not precisely a sign of reverence, to deem God's will unfathomable? Is this not real, true religiosity? Does the biblical testament to God and to the human not in some way have to comprehend itself through this religiosity? Are myth and revelation not 'somehow' compatible? Is Israel's avowal: 'Hear, Israel, YHWH, your God, YHWH is one, you shall have no others next to him', not a bit too simple, after all? Do we not have to speak of a double knowledge of God: God who speaks the word of deliverance in the Bible, *and* God who we know as the unspeakable secret of the 'universe'? Thus, the battle between God and the 'gods' is 'sublimated' in a conversation about religion, that logically degenerates into ambiguity: Did God really say ...? Yes, who will utter the word of deliverance?

This conversation about religion is prototypical for the confusion that biblical anthropology constantly faces: biblically speaking, the compromise with the so-called natural theology is impossible. It is the compromise between *hearing* God's word and what humans by nature can *see* as divine. This can be all sorts: the superiority of nature, the course of history, the bond of blood and soil, people and fatherland. Thus the God of Israel ultimately finds himself on the coupling-strap ('belt'!) of the soldiers: God-with-us.

Up until this point this is the narrative of the human who is liberated and falls: the tragic course of all liberation movements. But this narrative does not let the human fall: his fall cannot have the final say. Biblical anthropology does not close its eyes against the seriousness of this fall, but maintains the possibility that there will be humans, who will hear the word of the liberator-God again as a message of their deliverance from slavery, and that this word will be fulfilled.

Then it will transpire that the fall, thank God, was no more than an incident, an accident.

Crying for Deliverance

Despite the fact that the human has drawn a line under the history that God started with him, God stays in conversation with the human:

> YHWH, God, called to the human and said to him:
> Where are you?
>
> Gn 3:9

And he asks him:

> What have you done?
>
> Gn 3:13

In this conversation the human in all his misery is given the floor one more time. He can think of nothing better but to accuse the other of what he himself should answer for: the human accuses his wife, woman accuses the snake. This is the myth's wisdom put into practice: a chain of accusations with the effect that ultimately nobody is responsible for the fact that things went wrong. It will always go wrong – if the snake is the beginning of all wisdom.

It is the woman who leads the fall in this narrative. Thus she comes close to the malicious notion of woman as man's temptress. When man follows woman, this is fatal for him. He has to control himself, he has to control her. Male sexism is based on this fear of woman, this fear legitimates it. This is why it is important to remember that the narrative of Gn 3 is a perversion of the *condition humaine*.

But God's word puts the 'fall' in the perspective of its being overcome: *la lotta continua*, the fight goes on! The snake is cursed, and from here on a compromise between the woman and the snake's wisdom – here, too, the woman leads the way, in battle! – is unthinkable, enmity is the only option:

> I [YHWH] place enmity
> between you [snake] and woman,
> between your descendants and her descendants
>
> Gn 3:15

In the meantime, the human, who squandered his liberation, lives in a world lacking deliverance. In this world, human becoming-human means pain for the woman when she gives birth to her children, and dependence on the protection of the man, who cannot help but rule over her:

> I will multiply your pain, your pregnancy,
> you will give birth to children in pain,
> you will desire your husband,
> and he will rule over you.
>> Gn 3:16

The male human's (*adam*) becoming-human consists of toil and labour in the field (*adama*), which in this undelivered world is condemned to only barely nourish the human:

> cursed be the field on your account,
> all the days of your life you will eat from it in pain,
> thorns and thistles will spring forth from it
> you will eat the weeds of the field,
> you will eat bread in the sweat of your brow.
>> Gn 3:17–19

It has to be understood that this refers to a *lacking* world! Biblical anthropology leaves no doubt that the prevailing relations in this world are thoroughly broken. This world cries for deliverance. It is a world in which humans cry out: women to be liberated from what a male-dominated world subjects them to; men to be liberated from the exploitation of their labour power.

The fantastic narrative of the human, raised from the dust, placed in the garden where life is good, has turned utopian: the garden turns into a place where the human is *not*. The human is chased from the garden:

> So YHWH sent him from the Garden of Eden,
> to *serve* the field from which he was made.
>> Gn 3:23

But the garden is also 'preserved':

> he [YHWH] made the cherubim live at the gate to the Garden of Eden,
> and also the flame of the flashing sword,
> so as to *preserve* the path to the Tree of Life.
>> Gn 3:24

Admittedly, the human is sent to the field, cursed to toil from dawn to dusk. But his mission remains to 'serve' it. This labour is not hopeless: 'serving' the field is still tied to 'preserving' the path that leads to the Tree of Life. The garden has turned utopian, but that means: it 'survives' as utopia for the human.

The Tree of Life reappears in the Book of Revelation, in the middle of the New Jerusalem (Rv 22:2). Here, the process of humans becoming-human has finally reached its good end and the Tree of Life is available to all.

This is not the case for the anti-utopia that has now become thinkable: that the human, 'like the gods', has eternal life.[11] In any case, the God who has the floor in this narrative does not have to think of that:

> The human has become like one of us
> in his knowledge of good and evil.
> Now he could even reach out his hand
> and take of the Tree of Life and eat
> and live forever!
>   Gn 3:22

In the meantime – between fall and the fulfilment of utopia – the human returns to the field he came from:

> For you are dust and to dust you will return.
>   Gn 3:19

This is a 'blessing in disguise' (Deurloo):[12] the word 'return' is reminiscent of exile, life in foreign lands. There, Israel lives off the hope that God will 'return' to his people in order to raise them from the dust and return them to the path towards the Promised Land (to let them return!). God knows:

---

11 The horror scenario that the human of the ambivalence of 'good and evil' should live forever could become a reality if science really does manage (in this still undelivered, still inhuman world) to overcome physical death. We should not wish for it.

12 For Deurloo, the 'blessing in disguise' is constituted by the fact that woman 'will bear children': life will go on, there is a future! (1988, pp. 88 f.). I also hear the blessing (in disguise) in the 'return'.

for he knows what 'forms' we are,
remembering that we are dust.

Ps 103:14

He knows because he himself 'formed' this human, 'from the dust of the field' (Gn 2:7). And he returns to his people – *remembering* that they are dust – not to let them fall after all, but:

like a father has mercy on his children,
YHWH has mercy on those who fear him.

Ps 103:13

The people can know that they live in an in-between-time: the time between the fall *and* the rising.[13] This is why the human 'calls' his wife's name full of hope: Eva (Hebrew: *Chawwa*, life!). And this is why the human does not have to go through life only 'girdled for battle'. Because:

YHWH, God, made garments of fur for the human and his wife,
and clothed them.

Gn 3:21

Elsewhere in the Bible, the word 'garment' is used for the king's gown (Gn 37:3f.; 2 Sm 13:18), but it is named as the priest's robes (Ex 28). So in adversity, the human may clothe himself with armour, but God clothes him with the office of priest. He, the Israelite human, can be a 'kingdom of priests' (Ex 19:6), destined to exemplify a society that lives priestly: in reconciled life.

So in this biblical anthropology, priesthood is not an exclusively male matter: this honour is bestowed on the human as a whole, including women.

The Human and His Brother

Before the story of Israel's becoming in the midst of the peoples begins, we will look at the other storyline: the story of Cain and his descendants.

---

13   In this light, Luther's *'simul iustus et peccator'*, humans are simultaneously just and sinners, is very sensible. But this does not mean that he remains fixed on this 'simultaneously' forever (good *and* evil). The time will come when the just rule the earth and it can be said: everything is good, very good.

Cain is the human who does not follow God. God keeps an eye on Cain's *brother*, Abel. His name (Abel means 'vapour') says it all: he is nobody, his life evaporates into nothingness. God prefers this Abel, he acknowledges his gift:

> YHWH acknowledged Abel and his gift,
> He did not acknowledge Cain and his gift.
>> Gn 4:4–5

This has nothing to do with arbitrariness. But it has everything to do with God's partisanship: to be the God of 'nobodies'. He wants to include Cain in this partisanship: by keeping an eye on the weak, who is his *brother*.

The word 'brother' appears eight times in this relatively brief narrative!

The narrative is concerned with fraternity. Cain, however, does not want to acknowledge his brother, 'his face *falls*' (Gn 4:5). And then he *stands up* ... to *kill* his brother (Gn 4:8). This is the reversal of the rising of the human from the dust of his misery. The right of the stronger to be the 'preserver' of his brother is perverted into survival of the fittest. YHWH says to Cain:

> he [Abel] desires you,
> do not rule over him.
>> Gn 4:7

What else could be meant by this but that Cain should rule in such a way that his brother, who depends on him, does well? Survival of the fittest, however, means murder and mayhem.

So Cain is the exact opposite of the Israelite human embodied in Abel's nothingness? But then Cain also means '*servant* of the field' (Gn 4:2), and so he corresponds with the human who is called upon 'to serve and preserve' the field. Except that, for Cain, the link between 'serve' and 'preserve' has been broken:

> YHWH said to Cain:
> Where is Abel, your brother?
> He said:
> I do not know. Am I my brother's '*preserver*'?
>> Gn 4:9

It is precisely the breaking of this bond with which the Israelite human is familiar. Cain's actions also correspond with the fall of the liberated human to his opposite. Biblical anthropology is not Manichean: humankind is not condemned to a fight between absolute good and absolute evil. The human, destined to be the image of the liberator-God, must know that he himself is looking for light in darkness and can lose his way before he knows it. For him, too, it is good news that God does not cease communication with the fratricide:

> but he said:
> what have you done! [see Gn 3:13]
> the voice of your brother's blood is crying out to me from the field.
>> Gn 4:10

Cain understands these words to mean that his brother's murder calls for vengeance. In his view, this murder is the beginning of a vicious circle – always having to be on the run, for he says:

> Anyone who finds me will kill me!
>> Gn 4:14

This is the law of blood and thunder: Whoever murders will be murdered, an endless blood feud. But God disrupts this logic:

> Anyone who kills Cain
> will be avenged seven-fold.
>> Gn 4:15

Kill Cain once – the fratricide, rightly on the run, rightly guilty of death – and God will avenge him seven-fold. That is how absolutely God condemns the fatal law of the blood feud!

In the first instance, the Israelite human is being addressed here in the first instance. He is called upon to demonstrate a law that is not the blood feud:

> do not be vengeful and vindictive towards your people's children,
> but hold dear your neighbour, like yourself.
> I am YHWH.
>> Lv 19:18

If he fails to follow this, his calling, then God calls him strictly to order:

> If then you still disobey me,
> I will continue to chastise you,
> *seven-fold*
>> Lv 26:18 and 24

This is not a lesson in Manichaeism, but in the difference between good and evil: between a social order based on solidarity and a social order based on the survival of the fittest and the consequent aggression. Cain the human is spared; he too, falls within the circle of merciful light. But the order he 'establishes' is not spared. For Cain 'establishes' himself, but he does this in the Land of Nod, and that roughly means: homelessness (Gn 4:16). This appears contradictory: an established order and a homeless existence at once. But it is the contradiction of this order itself, in which humans can never be sure of their existence, always have to be on their toes: rulers today, fugitives tomorrow.

Realism and Hope

What is narrated next is the history of civilisation, the beginning of *our* civilisation. Cain builds a city (Gn 4:17), his descendants create the conditions for the shift from nature to culture: Jabal, the father of animal husbandry (tent and herd), Jubal, the father of music (and the instruments it requires: the harp and the flute), Tubal Cain, the inventor of smithery (Gn 4:22–24). But the narrative implies that these achievements are not 'neutral': the father of these fathers of civilisation is Lamech. And Lamech is the embodiment of violence. He interprets the prohibition of the blood feud as the motivation for excessive, endless violence:

> Yes,
> I kill a man for a wound
> And a boy for a welt!
> [compare the expression 'wound for wound, welt for welt' in Ex 21:25,
>> which limits violence]
> Yes,
> Cain is avenged seven-fold,
> but Lamech is avenged seventy-seven-fold!
>> Gn 4:23–24

What is generally ignored or dismissed as 'collateral damage' is the core of the matter here: our civilisation is a Lamech-civilisation. It is the Israelite perspective on world history and the so-called advanced civilisations, the perspective of the victims, the critical knowledge that '[t]there is no document of culture which is not at the same time a document of barbarism' (Benjamin).[14]

But this general history is not 'the' history. And it is not the conclusion drawn by biblical theology from the outset, so as to frustrate all hope for the possibility of a different world. At the end, the narrative returns to the human who was chased from the garden but remains destined to be God's likeness (Gn 5:1). Life does not simply go on – in the spirit of Cain, ignoring Abel – but Eve, whose name means life, bears her son in Abel's lineage: Seth (Hebrew: placed). God 'places' him as the 'other descendant, in Abel's stead' (Gn 4:25). The word 'descendant' refers back to the enmity God 'placed' between snake's 'descendants' and the woman's 'descendants' (Gn 3:15): the fight continues! And it also points forward: to the 'descendant' (*tsara*), who constitutes the line that, via Noah, runs to Abraham and further: to Israel, the people, who are salutarily different from all other peoples.

In the Book of Genesis, the Hebrew word *tsara*, which actually means 'seed' but is usually translated as 'descendant' or 'offspring', is reserved almost exclusively for the line of Israel. Having descendants is part of the blessing with which God binds the future of Israel to the future of his liberation project. For it is never self-evident that there will be descendants in Israel: the 'mothers of Israel' (Sarah, Rachael, Hannah) are often too 'barren' for this; the birth of a son turns into a miracle. It is the blessing with which Abraham is blessed, once he has shown that he was prepared to 'offer' his son Isaac to the liberator-God:

> by myself I swear
> – YHWH's word –
> yes, because you have done this, have not spared your son, your only one,
> I bless, yes, I bless you,
> I will multiply, yes, multiply your *descendants* (*tsara*)
> like the stars in the heavens and the sand on the seashore
> > Gn 22:16–17

But the line of Israel is not entirely exclusive. Israel is given a people at its side, which God also counts among Abraham's descendants. These are the descendants of Ishmael, the son of Hagar, Abraham's slave:

---

14   Benjamin 2003, p. 392.

The slave's son, too, I will make into a people,
for he is your *descendant* (*tsara*).
<blockquote>Gn 21:13</blockquote>

Israel has to share its blessed existence with this people – and why through this people not all peoples?

Seth's son Enoch leads his line. His name basically means the human in all his precarious existence, the opposite of the *Übermensch* who makes himself at home in the ruling civilisation: the 'homunculus'. He cannot be absent from the narrative of 'the' human: as the 'homunculus' who is 'remembered' by God, who God 'checks in on':

What is the homunculus,
that you remember it,
the child of man,
that you check in on it!
<blockquote>Ps 8:4</blockquote>

Here, biblical anthropology turns into the history of the becoming of Israel in the midst of the peoples. Next comes the 'book of the history [begettings / *toledot*] of Adam, the human' (Gn 5:1).

This history is enduringly characterised by what the human is 'in principle': image and likeness of the liberator-God. Which is also where it starts:

On the day when God created the human,
he made him in God's likeness,
he created them male and female
and blessed them
and called their name: Human (*adam*)!
on the day of their creation.
<blockquote>Gn 5:1–2</blockquote>

This is not the story of the human who has fallen for all eternity, but the story of the fall *and* ... the rise.

But the story cannot start before what constitutes the essence of being-human has been articulated, the *a priori* of all history:

In that day one began to call out the name of YHWH.
<blockquote>Gn 4:26</blockquote>

This is what makes the human human: calling out the NAME. Bowed low in the dust he protests: Your kingdom come, hallowed be your NAME, your will be done, in heaven as it is on earth. Prayer as resistance (Miskotte), and resistance as the act of his becoming-human *par excellence*.[15]

---

15   In his 'The roads of prayer', Miskotte summarises the content as follows: 'In all its praying, therefore, there is a *belligerent element*. The community takes its stand, watchful and warlike at the front, on the battleground of powerful demons. Neither defeat nor victory is certain, but only this: that they must and can hold their ground for the benefit of mankind, for the welfare of fellowmen in the sufferings of the times. Then prayer is often like the resistance of the underground, like prudent unlawfulness' (1968, pp. 159f.).

Entry

The exodus from the 'house of bondage' happens with a view to entry into the Promised Land. Delivery from slavery is not complete until the slave people actually live in a society in which the order of liberation has been established. Liberation and a stable order do not contradict each other. On the contrary, ceding liberty to the open play of social forces opens the doors to survival of the fittest. In the 'ten words' (Ex 20:1–17) – the covenant's *Magna Carta* – the God of Israel identifies himself as the liberator, but not without his 'instruction' for the path to the land where the salvation of the 'neighbour' has the final say.

The first word is:

> 'I am YHWH,
> your God,
> who brought you out of Egypt,
> out of the house of bondage.'
>> Ex 20:2

and the final word:

> do not desire
> your neighbour's house,
> do not desire your neighbour's wife,
> his male slave, his female slave, his oxen, his donkey,
> or anything else that belongs to your neighbour.
>> Ex 20:17

The land (*adama*, the 'field', the 'farmland') is the pivotal point of the 'ten words'. It appears in the fifth word:

> Honour
> your father and your mother
> so that your days may be numerous
> on the *farmland* that YHWH your God gives to you.
>> Ex 20:12

This fifth word is the last word relating to the relation between humans and God. Father and mother relay the Good News of the Liberator-God to the sons and daughters of Israel. That is why they are to be honoured.[1] Israel will not be able to save itself in the Promised Land without this divine knowledge, it will not know how to 'serve and preserve' the 'farmland' (Gn 2:15). This word is the transition to the following five words, which are concerned with the relations between humans. So they are concerned with what Israel is bidden to do in the land, with the society that is to take shape in this land. But the land and the society are presupposed as early as in the first five words: the 'farmland' in the fifth word and the Sabbath in the fourth word, the great feast day that God grants his people, '[being] like him':

Remember
the Sabbath Day
– keep it holy.
Serve (*abad*) and do all your work for six days,
but the seventh day
is a Sabbath for YHWH, your God:
no work is to be done
by you, your son, your daughter,
your male slave, your female slave, your animal,
and the stranger who stays in your house.
For in six days
YHWH made
heaven and earth, the ocean and all that is within it,
and on the seventh day he rested,
which is why YHWH blessed the Sabbath Day and made it holy.
          Ex 20:8–11

This God is no stranger to earthliness or to society; it is part of his 'nature' to furnish humans with a view to a land and to include them in his Sabbath from the start. Here, from the first to the final word, service to God is service to the human. And this is not the case because we came up with this idea in order to harness God for our own desires. It is God's own idea, to be God in this and no other way: the God of liberation, the God who wants a land where his people will prosper – because it is well organised.

---

1   A different explanation would be that this commandment concerns the care of the elderly: Those who care for their father and their mother when these have grown old, thus prolong the dignity of their lives while prolonging his own life through living an example.

Land as Livelihood

All five books of the Torah revolve around the land. The first book, Genesis, closes with the 'court Jew' Joseph's words to his brothers:

> I die,
> but God will look out for you, yes ensure
> that you will ascend from this *land*
> into the land she promised to
> Abraham, Isaac and Jacob.
> And Joseph swore an oath to the sons of Israel and said:
> God will look out for you, yes, God will ensure,
> so let my bones ascend from here.
>   Gn 50:24–25

The second book, the Book of Exodus, repeats the Sabbath commandment in words that already presuppose the land as a given:

> serve for six days,
> but on the seventh, celebrate (*sabat*),
> even during seedtime and harvest.
>   Ex 34:21

The grand finale of the third book, *Leviticus* (from Chapter 25) announces the two big structural measures that affect the land's economy (sabbatical and jubilee). The fourth book, *Numbers*, closes with regulations that only come into effect once Israel has taken possession of the land (34–36 = the final chapters).

The fifth book, *Deuteronomy* (in Hebrew: *debarim* = words, specifically the words Moses speaks to the people), is concerned with the entry into the land and what Israel is commanded to do there right from the start:

> Look,
> I have taught you the regulations and statutes,
> as YHWH my God commanded me
> to practice them in the *land*, to which you come, in order to inherit it[2]
>   Dt 4:5

---

2 Translating the Hebrew word *jrs* with 'to inherit' (and in the hifil form: dis-) is perhaps too innocuous for what is factually taking place. Isn't the land simply conquered, aren't the peoples who live there simply expelled? But, no matter how violent, this is not an imperialist

In these books, this land is still totally and entirely the *Promised* Land. Joseph is still buried in Egypt, the people of Israel are still in the desert, of Moses it is said that while God lets him see the land, he will never enter into it (Dt 34:1–4). Viewed from the Torah, it remains a vision, utopia.[3]

It is difficult to provide a precise meaning of the word 'utopia'. It is taken to mean so many different things. My use of the word derives from the Greek *ou-topos*: 'no place'. I take this to mean: that which has no place or has not yet found a place. The content and shape of the utopia are not prescribed in this case. It can be the poetic description of a blessed end state or an idyllic beginning. But it can also be a movement such as socialism that has no place or has yet to take place. In this chapter it is a programme whose execution is still outstanding. Its shape is hence 'programmatic': laws, rules, instructions.

But the imagination is not simply given free rein to paint a picture at will of how wonderful things could be in the Promised Land. Admittedly, the talk is of a land where life is good. It is repeatedly referred to as a land 'where milk and honey flow'. Israel does not have to settle for anything less. The promise is: Abundance! But the promise is not of a land of plenty where the roasted pigeons fly into your mouth of their own accord. First, the land is viewed from an organisational perspective: 'regulations and statutes of law' are given alongside the land. The Torah tells stories – of liberation, of the desert where the liberation movement threatens to lose its way, of the moving on 'despite everything' – but above all it represents legislation. It regulates everything from societal structure to the details of everyday life. The 'joy of the law' (*Simchat Torah*), which the synagogue celebrates and which the church unfortunately does not know, is founded on the promise that it is possible to organise the good life:

> I am YHWH, your God.
> Keep my regulations and my statutes of law,
> For: the human, who keeps them, will live through them.
> Lv 18:5

---

conquest, but a disowning for the benefit of a society in which the land is not privately owned, but belongs to everyone together. And hence after all: inherit.

3   'The people's entry into the land is not part of the text of the Torah. That is part of another book and that tells of other worries' (Naastepad 2001, p. 361). This is the qualitative difference between the Torah as the 'constitution' of the project 'Israel' and the 'first prophets' (Joshua– 2 Kings) as the history of the real Israel (ibid.).

We tend to avoid the word 'law' nowadays, and prefer to say 'guidance', in line with Buber and Rosenzweig's Germanisation of Scripture. 'Law' sounds too lawful to our ears, not at all like the Gospel, which is full of grace rather than 'work' in the sense in which we tend to use it. But is it not Gospel that amid the many oppressive legislations, one law is given that liberates – and that, as we may believe, can be done?

The society in which the God of Israel intervenes in order to liberate is an agrarian society. The means of existence for these people is the land, or more precisely: the field, which the human must 'serve' in order to survive. But this is too abstract a formulation. 'The' human is specifically the human who works the field, *adam* on the *adama*,[4] the farmer with his 'business', his wife, his sons and daughters, farm hands and maidservants, his livestock, his machines. But this human is not the human who actually profits from what the land produces. The *adam* on the *adama* usually works for others who are placed above him: the lord close by, to whom he owes money, the king far away, to whom he must pay tribute. He is at most only partially in possession of the land, or the means of production required for cultivating this land. He is threatened by the danger of no longer being able to pay the debt or the tribute and becoming a slave, a threat the majority of people faced under the social conditions of the time. This is the society from which the people of Israel are liberated: a house of bondage.

In the Torah this house of bondage is called (in Hebrew) *Mitsrayim*, 'Land of Oppression'. This 'Land of Oppression' is ruled by Pharaoh, the embodiment of the centralised state.

We are faced with an act of backdating here. The redaction of the Torah that we have inherited dates from no earlier than the time when Egypt has become a Hellenic state (the Ptolemaic Empire, 304–30 BCE) (see Chapter 4). This backdating 'alienates' the biblical Egypt from its historical origin. For the Bible is concerned with the slave-holding society in its generality as it oppresses humans on the underbelly of society, the essence of the political system that enslaves humans *en masse*.

The Organisation of the 'House of Bondage'

The story of Joseph who, as Pharaoh's 'vizier', makes all Egypt's inhabitants into slaves (Gn 47:13–26) illustrates this state for us. We are told how the mechanism

---

4 *Adam* and *adama*, 'human' and 'field' (Gn 2): the 'materialist' play on words, which expresses how the human cannot be 'groundless'.

of the great dispossession works: famine rules and the only authority that can make seed available in large quantities is the state. The people are forced to sign over to the state first their money, then their herd (their means of production), then their field (natural resources) and ultimately themselves. The story offers a clear analysis of the development of the state. It presupposes a society in which lack is structural. Nobody can withdraw from the law of the 'up and down' of good and bad harvests. What they can no longer produce, the people have to *buy*. Those who cannot do that – and most cannot – perish. An authority is required to solve this 'social question'. It has to be an authority that stands above society, in order to organise the problem of lack 'from above' in such a way that the masses can still eat. In this story the work is done by the state, which takes in hand the process of production by means of the total nationalisation of the means of production in order to provide everyone with an equal share of the distribution and production of foods: everyone is given the same amount of seed, everyone gives the same amount of the yield to Pharaoh (one fifth) and can keep the rest for themselves in order to live.

This is the 'Land of Oppression': free people become slaves. But the story does not conceal the fact that this 'oppression' is generally appreciated by the 'oppressed':

> They said [to Joseph]:
> You kept us alive,
> May we find mercy in the eyes of my Lord and become Pharaoh's slaves.
>> Gn 47:25

They submit to the subjugation of their own free will. Otherwise they would be hopelessly at the mercy of the discipline of the market. They would rather be Pharaoh's slaves than the playthings of the free play of social forces. For in that game, the weaker is the loser from the start. The Torah 'teaches' this at the end of the Book of Genesis by showing us a 'welfare state' such as we did not encounter until the twentieth century – and which already threatens to disappear again.

But is it not surprising that the Torah, which shows the path out of the house of bondage and into the Promised Land, paints such a positive picture of this house of bondage? Except that considered more closely, the picture is not all that positive. For as we were told, this is the story of a great dispossession: forced by their poverty, the people lose the power of control over the means of production, without any hope of ever regaining these in the Pharaoh's order. One will not encounter the converse side of the welfare state organised by

Joseph in the self-image of Pharaoh's order. Let us listen to the song of one of Pharaoh's 'viziers' (so the function Joseph had) from the so-called New Empire:

> I have elevated the Ma'at [Egypt's holy order] into the heavens,
> And have spread its beauty to the ends of the earth.
>
> ...
>
> I have dispensed justice between the poor and the rich,
> I have protected the weak from the strong,
> I have warded off the rage of the angry,
> I have pushed back the greedy in his hour
>
> ...
>
> I have dried tears ...,
> I have protected the widow who has no husband
>
> ...
>
> I have given bread to the hungry
> and water to the thirsty,
> Meat, salve and clothes to those who have nothing.[5]

The power that speaks here praises itself to the skies but says not a word about the very earthly foundation of this heavenly realm: humans who are left with no choice but to look for their salvation above (*sursum corda*), because all they find below is a valley of tears – even though they are the ones who produce the food that sustains all humans, including Pharaoh and his 'viziers'.

The critique of this order articulated in the story of Joseph and his 'viziers' hits the mark precisely, though, because it also shows this order's strong side. For the 'vizier's' song is not pure ideology. His state really does provide bread for the hungry and water for the thirsty; it really does take care that the widow, who has no husband to protect her, should not be entirely without rights. Concealing this and suggesting that the state causes only misery to the oppressed does not correspond with reality, nor does it correspond with the experience of these oppressed people themselves. Such a 'theory of immiseration' does not account for the fact that not all subjugated people automatically rebel against the order that subjugates them. Those who want to emerge from the house of bondage must realise that not only the lords will resist, but that the labourers, too, will not simply co-operate. The Kingdom of Freedom is calling? Let us hope so. But that Kingdom is also intimidating. When the people of Israel,

---

5   Quoted from Assmann 2000, p. 211.

having been delivered from the house of bondage, pass through the desert on their way to this Kingdom – as the narrative says, it is a miracle – they long for 'Egypt's pots of meat' (Ex 16:3) before long. This yearning is not merely a nostalgic mirage. The pots of meat were reality. It is the story of Joseph's 'viziership' that guards the listeners of the Torah against imagining the path of the liberation movement as all too easy.

But the Torah also knows how precarious total dependence on the state is for the labourers. The other experience is also recorded:

> A new king arose in Egypt, who had not known Joseph.
> Ex 1:8

The boom of the welfare state is over, the situation has (once again) deteriorated, which means the time is ripe for increased exploitation. Soon enough the slaves cry out: Who will deliver us from our misery! This is the beginning of the Book of Exodus, the document of the emergence.

The story of Joseph's 'viziership' points to yet another aspect of the Pharaonic system. Not all people turn into slaves; there is a privileged 'class': priests.[6] Even the great dispossession has its limits:

> It was only the priests' field that he [Joseph] did not acquire,
> because the priests received a fixed income from Pharaoh, and they ate
>   from their fixed income, which Pharaoh had given to them,
> which is why they did not sell their field.
> Gn 47:22

The priests are functionaries who are responsible for ideology. They manage the power of the imagination – in accordance with the fantasy of power. They lead the rituals that hammer the dominant order into the people – as divine, eternal, omnipotent. They 'guard' the secret of this order: created by God himself and hence elevated above all doubt. They possess fields, but do not depend on their harvest. They are too important for the reproduction of the state to be exposed to the play of social forces. They have to be protected from

---

6 Gramsci, too, perceived the priests of his own time in a similar fashion: 'The category of ecclesiastics can be considered the category of intellectuals organically bound to the landed aristocracy. It had equal status juridically with the aristocracy, with which it shared the exercise of feudal ownership of land, and the use of state privileges connected with property' (Gramsci 1971, p. 210). Evidently, he never knew priests who served the people (Camillo Torres!)

experiencing the discipline of the market, of sharing the fate of the oppressed. Otherwise, they might be tempted to assist an entirely different idea to seize power; come up with rituals that awaken the longing for liberation: a Pesach liturgy, for example. The threat posed by such a great coalition between people and clerics has to be avoided. This is why the priests are subsidised by the state: you do not bite the hand that feeds you. Thus they are 'alienated' from the people, who hunger and thirst for justice.

Impoverishment through Debt

The society in which the Torah intervenes and liberates is based on an agriculture that produces not much more than what the quality of the soil and the climate permit. The possibility of increasing productivity with the help of technical means is very limited. The limits of growth are obvious. The best possible case is an 'Economy of Enough':[7] it suffices for the producers as well as for those who cannot (not yet or not anymore) produce: children, the elderly, the 'disabled'. So if one wanted to produce more than what was 'normal', wanted to produce more and more, then this was only possible by property expansion or by forcing others to contribute a share of their own harvest (tribute). Large-scale land holding, though, is only possible on the basis of slave labour. And this is where the 'logic' of the social system of the time 'takes effect'. Most people own only a small piece of land and it is all too frequently the case that this yields so little that its owner is forced to borrow food or seed, later cannot repay the debt, hence loses his property and becomes the creditor's slave. So this process releases both land and labour and makes it possible for only a few lucky people to accumulate property, yield and wealth. According to this logic, it is logical that there is no longer space, no field, for the great mass of people – they have no choice but to work for others.

> Woe be unto them,
> who build one house next to the other,
> and lay field against field,
> until there is no more space
> > Is 5:8

---

7   The term is taken from the Dutch economist Bob Goudzwaard. He pointed towards an economy where the needs of humans and of nature took precedence, rather than capital growth. Because: *There is enough for everyone* (as sung by the Dutch band Bots)!

We encounter this critique with the prophet Isaiah, and he is envisioning what is happening in the real Israel. This is food for thought: the project 'Israel', as it turns out, has itself succumbed to the logic it wanted to escape. Here, though, I am quoting this critique as a clear-sighted observation of this logic.

So while society does rely on agriculture, on the 'serving and preserving' of the field, its mode of production is based on large-scale property ownership and slavery. In this society, the field (*adama*), which the Torah's anthropology binds to (bands with) the *adam*, the human without any earthly lord and master, is stolen from the human. This system's motivating principle is private property. The Latin word *'privare'* means 'to rob', and this is what is happening systematically here. In this society, property truly is robbery.

This is also what this social system shares with all social systems to date: the logic of private property, which means: the increase of property through the dispossession of others. A logic of enrichment by impoverishment.

There is also a big difference to the society in which we live. In our social system, too, the great majority of people do not own the means of production and are forced to make their labour available to others. But the owners of the means of production use this labour in order to increase enormously the yield of what the earth – and who knows, in future perhaps the universe – has to offer. Here, what people previously could only dream of is made a real possibility: there is more than enough for everyone; work is so easy it seems to complete itself. The reality, however, paradoxically contradicts this real possibility: people die of hunger, automatisation 'liberates' people from their workplace. But paradox is the core of the system itself. The power of capital stands between the needs of the people and food production: the inability to deal with this food in any other way than selling it for profit. For without profit, the system cannot function.

The system cannot persist without an authority responsible for 'law and order'. This authority comes from above. Where should the people, who have lost the power of control over the means of production, find the means to ensure 'law and order' themselves? So, there is a king who imposes 'law and order', and a priest who renders this 'law and order' sacrosanct by declaring it holy. King and priest, state and state ideology – they constitute the superstructure of this society that has robbed the people of their property. They manage this society, but they also mirror it. For – the story of Joseph's 'viziership' tells us this – the king robs the people of their 'land' and the priests rob the people of their ability to find the right words for their discontent ('this cannot be true') – a different narrative, a different ritual.

What remains unconsidered in this system's logic is the wholly different possibility of an 'Economy of Enough', rather than an 'Economy of Always More' in the hands of ever fewer people; a different society, where what one person has left over is left over to the other person who is suffering scarcity; a society where one person helps the other, because they share the same right to live:

> Be in solidarity with your neighbour,
> he is like you yourself.
>> Lv 19:18

In order for this wholly different possibility to come into view, the logic of a society based on large-scale property ownership and slavery has to be broken. In this asocial society we *cannot* 'be in solidarity with our neighbour' – unless we organise ourselves in opposition to society. If we want to make room for 'love of the neighbour', then we must want a different society, where 'law and order' are organised very differently, and where the commandment to 'love thy neighbour' is no longer a purely ethical question, but is a matter of the law. This can only happen on the condition of emerging from the house of bondage and its ideology. This emergence is the start of the project 'Israel', the attempt to organise this entirely different society.

In the beginning of the book of the emergence, Exodus, is written this laconic notification:

> A new king arose in Egypt, who had not known Joseph.
> He spoke to his people:
> The people of the children of Israel are more numerous and stronger
>> than us.
> Onwards, let us trick them,
> before they become even more numerous,
> lest in the case of war breaking out,
> they ally themselves with our enemies
> and wage war against us and issue forth from the land.
> And they put slave masters in place, in order to oppress them with slave
>> labour.
>> Ex 1:8–11

This is the converse side of the welfare state. The people, who, driven by need, came there to stay alive, are overwhelming for the state. A new king arises who has no interest in Joseph's social policies – they have probably become 'unaffordable' in the meantime. For him, the people represent a threat above all else: they are too numerous and hence too strong. He fears power in numbers and suspects that they might serve his enemy with this power. This suspicion, incidentally, rings of projection: he intends to exploit them even more and so has to expect that their loyalty to his regime will diminish. There is a danger of their rising up against him and his losing their labour force. And he can already sense what will then happen: their emergence from the house of bondage. So he turns to *his* people: they – those over there – are overtaking *us* in numbers and strength. It is the classic solution of any dominant order that gets into difficulties because the social question can no longer be solved: divide and conquer. They are all slaves, but with the principle of 'our own people first' the system successfully appeals to another distinction: that between Egyptians and 'Hebrews', 'us' and the 'foreigners'. This also serves an economic purpose: the foreigners can now do the dirty work, the forced labour that nobody likes doing.

Otherness as Formative Experience

This historical experience is formative for Israel. The Book of Genesis narrates the 'becoming' (*genesis*) of the people of Israel in the midst of the peoples. Abraham is told already:

> You should know –
> that your descendants will be strangers (*ger*) in a country that does not
>   belong to them,
> they will be enslaved and oppressed.
>> Gn 15:13

He knows it:

> I am the stranger and the settler (*toshab*)
>> Gn 23:4

In the social hierarchy of the time, there are two more categories of humans aside from slaves who depend on the (dis)favour of the ruling class. They are the *ger* and the *toshab*. The *ger* (stranger) enjoys the right to hospitality, so he is an authorised 'guest'. The *toshab* (from *yashab* = to settle) is the settler whose rights are not even included in the right to hospitality. The Torah, too, distinguishes between them: the *ger* has equal rights, 'one Torah' exists for the Israelite and for the *ger* (Ex 12:49). This is why the *ger* is allowed to partake of the Pesach feast, the *toshab* is not (Ex 12:45–48).

But when the Torah wants to drive home the point that there are no property owners apart from YHWH (the abolition of all private property!), then Israel, too, is told: you are 'strangers and settlers' (Lv 25:23) – *nota bene*: in a country where they can live as free people! But that is precisely the point. Israel is absolutely not allowed to think itself the lord of its manor. So that they remain free people! And liberate others!

And just like Abraham, Isaac knows it too (Gn 26:3; 32:5); and so finally does Israel. His sons tell Pharaoh:

> We have come in order to live as strangers in this land.
> Gn 47:4

The paragraph about the king who did not know Joseph reminds us of the precarious state of the stranger, by definition: once hospitably welcomed he turns into an unwelcome guest before he knows it, someone whose foreignness threatens the integrity of the country. He is in danger of disappearing: into foreign lands or into the anonymity of slavery. He experiences first-hand: he is not permitted to have a name (a swear word at most). It is telling that the book of the exodus starts by explicitly naming the 'sons of Israel':

> These are the names of the sons of Israel, who came to Egypt
> Ex 1:1

The Hebrew Bible's rule of entitling the books of the Torah in accordance with the first line makes a lot of sense here: *shemot*, names. They are the names of all those who remain nameless within the dominant order, who are saved by the exodus, who are given space for a project that may carry their name: the project *Israel*.

In this book, their names are tied to the exodus. But their names also remain tied to their existence as strangers in the house of bondage, where they were in danger of losing their names. The story of the project 'Israel' is not the usual story of an established order. This, too, bears affinity to a pre-history: nomads who settle; a people that starts off small and then grows large; a period of 'sectionalism' that builds the foundation for the current empire. This rule governs all national histories: small turns large, barbaric turns civilised, weak turns strong. Small, barbaric, weak – they are all defects that have been mastered, that can be confidently left behind. And should the nation ever 'collapse', then it can be 'normalised' by becoming a major power once again.

Israel's history is the exception:

Do not torture the stranger:
you know the soul of the stranger,[8]
for you were strangers in the Land of Egypt.

    Ex 23:9

Israel must always remember that they were strangers – not in order to set off their current state of being, but in order to help the strangers in their own country receive justice. Those who know what it means to be a stranger – 'know their soul' – will think carefully before they submit the stranger in their midst to the same things to which they were submitted elsewhere. At least, this is what the Torah hopes to achieve by reminding them of this existence as strangers in such a way that it becomes constitutive of the organisation of the land that God gave to Israel. Delivery from slavery does not give Israel the freedom to simply leave behind the problem of slavery and to proceed with 'business as usual'. They are given the freedom to do what God the liberator commands:

Keep the day of the Sabbath, keep it holy, as YHWH your God com-
    manded you to.
Serve and do all your work for six days,
but the seventh day is a Sabbath for YHWH your God:
do not do any work,
you, your son, your daughter, your male slave, your female slave, your ox,
    your donkey, all your cattle,
and the stranger within your gates –
so that your male slave and your female slave may rest,
(*he is*) *like you.*
Remember that you were a slave in Egypt
And YHWH your God brought you out with a strong hand, with
    outstretched arm
which is why YHWH your God commanded you to honour the day of the
    Sabbath.

    Dt 5:12–15

---

8   Leo Baeck points out that the only place where the phrase 'know the soul' appears is in Prv 12:10 ('He who is just knows the souls of his animals'), and then writes: 'Stranger and animal – they are as the mute; their voices are not heard and their words are not understood. Therefore, their souls must be understood; the living breath of their questions must be felt' (Baeck 1964, p. 47).

Being told that their God is God the liberator and that he leads them out of the house of bondage is Israel's privilege. But Israel is given this privilege so that it can ensure this right for everyone in the Promised Land – those who are 'within their gates', to be sure, but according to God what happens within these gates is exemplary: a feast day for everyone, including the stranger. The perspective of the project 'Israel' is universal. As YHWH already assures Abraham, the project's patriarch:

> May all peoples of the earth bless each other by invoking your descend-
> ants
> because you have heeded my voice.
>> Gn 22:18

It is determining of the project 'Israel' that the 'children of Israel' must never again fall victim to slavery while they are there. For as YHWH says:

> they are my slaves,
> who I brought out of the Land of Egypt,
> they shall not be sold
> as slaves are sold
>> Lv 25:42

Here the word 'slave' (*ebed*) is revolutionised: the slave is liberated from the house of bondage, not because it is his turn to be the master, but, quite the contrary, in order to be YHWH's slave (*ebed*), liberated in order to organise a society without slaves. And in the books of the 'second prophets', *ebed* YHWH also turns into a figure of redemption that keeps the hope for justice alive through its solidarity with the condemned of the earth to the depths of the depths:

> The righteous, my slave, will make the many righteous,[9]
> by shouldering their debts.
> That is why I give him the many
>> Is 53:11–12

Granted, YHWH permits Israel to buy slaves from the Goy and to 'draw on' their descendants 'for ever' immediately afterwards (Lv 25:44–46). The project 'Israel' does not take place in a social vacuum. Nor is it yet the 'ideal world'

---

9   In the Bible 'many' often means 'everyone'.

where the Kingdom of Freedom reigns without limits. Although the Goy, if they are enslaved in Israel, can count themselves lucky. Here, the slaves share the Sabbath rest that Israel is commanded to grant to *everyone*. Is it possible that Israel is allowed to draw on them in order to demonstrate to the Goy that a world different from theirs is possible?

Here, too, we can suspect a play on words with *abad*. Israel is allowed to 'draw on' (*abad*) the Goy for slaves (*ebed*). Must we not also hear the ring of the 'serving' of the 'garden' from Gn 2 here? And is not that 'serving' the 'serving' of the garden in order that it is 'preserved': to 'serve' *and* 'preserve' the garden? Is it too far-fetched to presume that Israel is also commanded to 'draw on' its slaves from among the Goy in order to 'preserve' them for the Kingdom of Freedom?

The Right to Live for Everyone instead of Free Enrichment for the Few

This very decisive provision – that the Israelite is a free human – is not an abstract principle left untranslated into specific legislation. Social life has to be arranged in such a way that it demonstrably breaks with that other principle of freedom: the freedom to rob other humans of their freedom, to render them dependent on an owner who has free command of their labour, in short: the slaveholder's freedom.

Our 'enlightened' world, that made freedom its 'guiding principle' like never before, is tainted by a radical contradiction with respect to the realisation of this principle. It is the contradiction between the principle of a freedom based on equality with a view to togetherness, and the principle of free enterprise that draws on the labour of others. They are the principles of the 'Declaration of the Rights of Man and the Citizen': 'These rights are liberty, property, security, and resistance to oppression' (art. 2). Here, liberty and property are found together. In capitalist practice, however, liberty amounts to the commandment to secure business profit (euphemistically called 'returns') at all costs.[10] Everything else – liberty, equality, social security – is secondary.

The injunction on selling a fellow Israelite into slavery is a matter of legislation which Israel is bound to follow day to day. It is not a principle, but a regulatory statute, directed at a specific situation:

---

10   'accumulate, accumulate! That is Moses and the prophets' (Marx 1996, p. 591). The endless
        accumulation of capital: this social order knows no other Torah, nor another prophecy.

> *When* your brother falls into ruin next to you,
> and sells himself to you [*then!*]
>> Lv 25:39

But this legislation is not purely a matter of casuistry: investigating case by case what should be done. The Torah is written with a view to the organisation of a society that is *structurally* distinct from the rest of the world. The attention to detail coincides with structural measures that break down the logic of a social order that encumbers humans with debts and enslaves them.

Thus, it is the law that all debts be forgiven every seven years:

> Every seven years you shall forgive all debts.
> This debt relief will proceed as follows:
> All creditors will cancel the loans they have given their neighbours:
> He can no longer force his neighbour, his brother, to pay up,
> because a debt relief in the name of YHWH has been proclaimed.
>> Dt 15:1–2

Debt relief also occurred in Israel's surroundings. But there it happened only occasionally and was more a matter of the economic cycle. In Israel it is part of the lawfulness of the society itself.

And the law says that a fellow Israelite who is forced to sell himself into slavery shall be liberated in the seventh year:

> If your brother, a Hebrew man or a Hebrew woman, has to sell them-
>   selves to you,
> He shall serve you for six years,
> In the seventh year you must send him forth as a free man.
>> Dt 15:12

And this liberated fellow Israelite is not sent into the desert where he has to fend for himself:

> When you send him forth as a free man,
> do not send him without wages!
>> Dt 15:13

It is absolutely forbidden to invoke the 'law of the jungle' by forcing the weak to pay more than they owe; in other words, to demand interest:

If you lend money to my people, the oppressed by your side,
then do not practice usury,
give it interest free.

Ex 22:24; the same prohibition in other words: Lv 25:36 and Dt 23:20

But the word 'interest' is really far too innocuous to accurately express what is at stake here. For in the social order of that time, it was impossible to use money borrowed with interest to make a profit. Then it is hardly unjust that he who lends money should also demand interest. After all, he is providing the borrower with capital to 'work' with. The capital is invested and normally (according to the 'normality' of capital) this transaction yields more than was invested. Interest can then be paid. Those who had to pay interest at that time usually only indebted themselves even further – until they could no longer pay it at all and were forced to sell themselves into slavery. The Hebrew word *neshek*, which is translated as 'interest', literally means 'that which is bitten off'. And that is what happens when interest is collected: it is mercilessly 'bitten off' of the debtor.

In today's society, too, people have to borrow money in order to buy things they cannot readily pay for themselves (consumer credit). The interest calculated in this case comes close to what the Torah calls *neshek*: the debtor frequently ends up in a hopeless spiral of debt. The same thing happens on the level of macroeconomics. Countries are forced to borrow capital in order to develop, but given the dominant conditions, they cannot borrow in such a way as to return a profit. But the interest has to be paid off, so the debt increases; IMF and World Bank demand that 'non-productive' costs (in other words, social welfare expenses) be drastically reduced: so *neshek*.

Ultimately, though, what needs to happen is that *everyone* has access to the means of production without which life as a free man is impossible: land. The law of the 'jubilee', the decree that says that a general 'land reform' should be 'proclaimed' every fifty years, serves this 'final goal':

Consecrate the year, the fiftieth year,
proclaim liberation for all inhabitants throughout the land:
may it be a 'jubilee' for you,
you will return,
each to your property,
each to your clan
...
in this 'jubilee'

> you will return,
> each to your farm.
>> Lv 25:10–13

This permanent 'land reform' would render the accumulation of property through the robbery of other people's means of production fundamentally pointless. The vision that this measure offers is the communisation of the means of production. The fact that everybody has the right to own property is the opposite of the prerogative of the few to own everything: this is not master and slave, here everybody owns everything communally.

The 'jubilee' is the climax of the revolution prescribed by the Torah: the communisation of the means of production is the material foundation for the Kingdom of Freedom, which is what the project 'Israel' is ultimately aiming for. Without this foundation, the Kingdom of Freedom is a total washout, a pipe dream, a fool's paradise, utopia, condemned to failure before it even starts. Hence, the 'jubilee' has something of the fullness of the time, the fulfilment of everything the legislation aims at. The debt relief and the liberation of the slaves happens every seven years; it is the regularity of the Sabbath that 'disrupts' the ordinary run of things (in modern Hebrew, Sabbath can also mean 'strike'). It is like a preventive measure that pre-empts the danger of the project 'Israel' turning back into an 'Egypt', a *Mitsrayim*, a 'Land of Oppression'. The 'jubilee' is the sum of seven such Sabbath years, the sum of everything the Sabbath year promises to the land and the people:

> The seventh year
> will be a Sabbath, a Sabbath for the land,
> a Sabbath for YHWH,
> you shall not sow your field
> nor harvest your vineyard
> ...
> The Sabbath of the land will yield your food,
> you, your male slave and your female slave,
> your farmhand and your settler, who enjoys the right to hospitality in
>   your house,
> your livestock and the wild animals on your land,
> shall eat all its yield.
>> Lv 25:4–6

This is quite amazing: the land is given a vacation and there is food for everyone. But then the verses continue:

Count seven Sabbath years,
seven years times seven:
thus the days of the seven Sabbath years
amount to forty-nine years.
Then let a shofar
make the rounds with a blare

...

let the shofar make the rounds
throughout all your land,
and consecrate the year, the fiftieth,
proclaim the liberation of all its inhabitants throughout the land:
let it be a 'jubilee' for you

    Lv 25:8–10

Seven times seven Sabbath years; the time is fulfilled, something will happen. And then it does happen, in the fiftieth year: the blaring of the shofar announces the great all-encompassing liberation, the return to one's own land, and no lord can interfere any longer. This is the project's *ultima ratio*, this is its ultimate commandment: to establish an order where slavery is over once and for all, where liberty really reigns.

The institution of the 'jubilee' demonstrates that this is not a 'reformist' project. It does not make occasional adjustments to the logic of an economy where the one person's advantage is the other person's disadvantage (so long as the economic cycle permits!) but the reverse. An entirely different logic is to be made into law: the general dispossession of the dispossessors, who 'lay field against field'.

Whether the 'jubilee' was ever really proclaimed in the real Israel is highly questionable. Apparently, the project Israel never advanced past, at best, the practice of Sabbath years, when debts were forgiven and slaves were liberated – over and over again, because people always indebted themselves to such a degree that they were forced to sell themselves into slavery. So was it a reformist project after all, one that limits the laws of the marketplace but does not abolish them? Or is the effort to render the endless accumulation of property to the advantage of the few impossible, 'over and over again', in fact a *permanent revolution*? Making use of the 'jubilee' as a 'regulating idea': doing Torah with a view to its fulfilment, not settling for anything less?

Promise and Realism

This is the real purpose of the Torah: to serve as the Law for the project 'Israel', the fundamental instruction for the organisation of a society without rulers in the land.

But the Torah does not offer a programme of one piece, no blueprint for a new smooth-edged society. The design it offers is realistic and accounts for the gradualness that is crucial to any revolution. The Torah knows that the people, who want to radically renew the world, having grown up in the old, incorrect world, is a problem. It does not simply provide *one* language that allows the precise articulation of how life in the Promised Land will be organised. The Torah approaches the problem of shaping a complete novelty in different ways. Thus, there is neither a king nor a locally centralised cult in the Book of Leviticus, while the Book of Deuteronomy explicitly counts on the institution of a monarchy and virtually makes centralised bureaucracy into a commandment. Both books talk about how the Promised Land can be arranged in order that it can become a Kingdom of Freedom. Is a king part of that? That is the question. Or centralised politics? This, too, is unclear – even if underneath the pressure of circumstance it cannot always be left unclear.

Things were no different in the socialist movement. The *Communist Manifesto* (1848) makes the sketch of a socialist society concrete by opening with the necessity of 'despotic inroads on the rights of property'.[11] It does not examine the problem of a *despotic* liberation movement – how to prevent liberation from degenerating into pure despotism. This problem is then the topic of Lenin's *The State and Revolution* (1917). Lenin predicts that the state, which is necessary in order to consolidate the socialist order, will gain independence from the revolution, and devises measures meant to prevent this from happening. The fact that what he sought to prevent did happen in the end is another story. That is the story of real socialism, which is so terribly similar to the story of the real Israel.

The revolution is programmed in three ways:
Leviticus focuses on the question of land. Its revolutionary principle is:

> The land can never be sold forever,
> for the land is mine [YHWH's];
> you are strangers and settlers.
>> Lv 25:23

---

11   Marx and Engels 1976b, p. 504.

The expression 'the land is mine' is in complete opposition to the logic that submits land ownership to the law of purchase and sale. God opposes it. He appropriates the land in order to grant it to the 'strangers and settlers', who had been duped by it. Those who avow this God as the creator of heaven and earth (the Hebrew word *erez* not only means 'land', but also 'earth'), involve themselves in the movement of the land-less, who distribute the land in God's name in such a way that everyone can find a place within it.

Deuteronomy speaks of the project 'Israel' as a vision for the poor:

> Ultimately, there will be no more poor people with you.[12]
> Dt 15:4

This is why the debts have to be forgiven every seven years (Dt 15:1–3). If this is practised regularly, then ultimately there really will not be any more poor people, then wealth will become general. But the 'regularly' is crucial:

> for the poor will not stop in the middle of the land.
> Dt 15:11a

The problem of poverty cannot be resolved with one fell swoop; the path towards a world without poverty is long. The fact that poor people continue to exist is no reason to resign oneself to that fact. On the contrary, the statement 'the poor will not stop' constitutes the prelude to a commandment:

> Therefore [!] I command you:
> open, yes you will open your hand to your brother,
> the oppressed, the poor, in your land!
> Dt 15:11b

The option for the poor never ends. For as long as there are poor people, the world is not in order.

Exodus is interested above all in the revolutionary subject that is itself responsible for the execution of the project:

---

12   The translation as 'ultimately' is taken from Rinse Reeling Brouwer: 'The word that I translate as 'ultimately' is elsewhere used to signify 'the end of the world', so it invokes the furthest view possible. This statement hence concerns the Promise' (1992, p. 29).

And you, when you heed my voice and preserve my covenant,
then among all peoples
you will be my own
> Ex 19:5

Just as the land, because it is owned by the Liberator-God, is an entirely different land from those that surround it, so Israel will be an entirely different people from the other peoples, because it is God's property:

for mine is all the land [the whole earth]
but you
will be a
Kingdom of Priests for me,
a holy people.
> Ex 19:5–6

The order of the peoples is grounded in kingship and priesthood, throne and altar, state and ideology. These are authorities beyond all critique, authorities that the people have to look up to. A 'holy alliance' of violence and conviction: those who approach the king too closely have to deal with the priest. The priest then convinces him that things are as they should be and not otherwise. For the highest Being, God, wishes it.

The project 'Israel' knows no holy authorities. The people themselves are called upon to be 'a holy people'. In other words, the people themselves are responsible for this project. After all, it is their own project: delivered from slavery in order to institute a Kingdom of Freedom. Kingship and priesthood are democratised: the people rule the state, the priesthood is priesthood of the community.[13] This is tantamount to a revolt against the gods, who want the people to kneel down before their enslaving law. But the instigator of this revolt is that God who turns a slave people into a 'Kingdom of Priests'. If that is not a revolution!

The phrase 'Kingdom of Priests' is unique in Scripture. And what it expresses is also unique: a people who can, in principle, get by without king or priest, because they are themselves kings and priests. To be sure, the phrase is cited once in the apostolic writings (1Pt 2:9). There it is describing the messianic community, that jumble of Jews and Goy who previously were a 'non-people', but now can be God's people (1Pt 2:10). This community's vision is to be 'kings for ever and ever' (Rv 22:5).

---

13   'Judaism is humanity on the brink of morality without institutions' (Levinas 1996, p. 122).

Ideology and Liturgy

The people are called upon to *become* holy; they are not declared holy. The programme also reckons with the fact that the people will lose their way, that they will approach their God too closely and annex him for purposes that are alien to this project. This is why distance must be created between God and the people so that the relation remains 'pure' and the covenant does not degenerate into an ideology of 'God-with-us', and the project 'Israel' into a complacent *entre-nous*. With a view to this wholesome distance, Israel, the Kingdom where everyone is a priest, also has priests. But from the beginning these are functionaries in the service of the people. They cannot make themselves into an independent special caste with specific privileges as they did in Egypt. For there the priests were given a dedicated, protected allowance by Pharaoh; and as we know, you do not bite the hand that feeds you. On account of this allowance they were also the only ones who did not have to sell their field; they were property owners, unfamiliar with the miserable living conditions of the slaves. In Israel, on the other hand, it is precisely the priests who are not allowed to own land and who are supported by the people. They are set free to devote themselves to the liturgy without reaping any benefits:

> At that time
> YHWH selected the tribe of Levi
> to carry the Ark of the Covenant of YHWH,
> to stand before YHWH,
> to exercise the office of priesthood for him
> and to give blessings in the name of YHWH,
> to this day.
> Hence the tribe Levi has no part or property amongst its brothers:
> YHWH is its property
>> Dt 10:8–9

One tribe, the Levites, is 'selected' for the practice of the service. They are exempt from the commandment to 'serve and preserve' the field, which means they do not have to work hard for their livelihood. They are granted permission to concentrate wholly on the service which ensures that Israel remains true to its God – because only then will Israel be a blessed people. But they will render this service without any self-interest. They are even denied the right to own the means of production, which is granted to all Israelites. What they do is entirely *pro Deo*. That is why they have to experience first-hand what it means to depend on others. For their service to God should remind the people that God's heart belongs to the damned of the earth. Their status is lowly, they share a level with the stranger, the widow and the orphan – like them they rely on the mercifulness commanded to the people of Israel:

> Every three years
> you are to bring out one tenth of that year's yield
> and deposit it within your gates,
> then the Levite will come –
> for he has no share nor any property like you –
> and the stranger, the orphan and the widow, who live within your gates,
> and they will eat and be satisfied
>> Dt 14:28–29

These 'degraded' priests constitute the authority that marks the distance between God and people. On Sinai, where God cancels his covenant with the people, they, standing by the people, do this by themselves keeping the distance that God's proximity demands. Only Moses and Aaron, the high priest (Ex 24:1), with his sons Nadab and Abihu and 70 'elders' (Ex 24:1), are permitted to proceed further and to ascend towards God. But this, too, serves to reinforce the distance, for ultimately God allows only Moses to climb the mountain in order to hear his word directly (Ex 24:2). But this distance does not introduce a social hierarchy, a caste society where everyone knows their place, the people, obviously, being at the bottom. This 'hierarchy' purely serves God's message to the people:

> Moses came
> and told the *people* all YHWH's words and all legal statutes.
> Then the whole *people* responded, with one voice they said:
> all the words that YHWH has spoken,
> we will do them.
>> Ex 24:3

It is not the priests' purpose to prevent the community from approaching God. Their task is to accompany this 'approaching' in order to prevent the encounter between people and God from degenerating and to prevent the people from approaching their God too closely. Leviticus, the book in which the role of the priests plays a central part, starts by declaring the 'approaching' of God to be a right enjoyed by everyone:

> Speak to the sons of Israel and say:
> Adam, a human,
> When he approaches YHWH with his offering
> >   Lv 1:2

Adam! The human free from domination, with whom the biblical anthropology starts and ends, is addressed first. That which elsewhere is the privilege of a single caste is here democratised from the beginning, a matter for all the people (Berthil Oosting).[14] The appearance of the priests is secondary; they are part of a liturgy that does not revolve around them but around the act of the bond between the people and their God.

This role of service is life threatening. For priesthood incurs the temptation to manipulate the liturgy to one's own advantage. It is not enough for the priest to play the modest part that God assigned to him. He commands his task autonomously:

> Aaron's sons Nadab and Abihu each took their pan,
> lit a fire inside
> and laid incense atop it.
> They offered up 'strange' fire
> to YHWH
> which he had not commanded them to do.
> >   Lv 10:1

This passage speaks of taking initiative in a way that is 'strange' to what the priest is commanded to do. It does not clarify what precisely is meant by 'strange fire'. The context, however, gives a good indication about what it could be. After all, the commandment says to demonstrate in the liturgy how much the project 'Israel' challenges the usual aim of service: submission. In this 'usual' service, the priest's 'approaching' of God is an action that leaves the people standing behind. This seems to be what Aaron's sons are doing here – they especially, the sons of the high priest, who were allowed to ascend Mount Sinai, their prominence ultimately rests on their being the first, who become 'the last of all' (Mk 9:35). The 'strange fire' that they prepare must come from *Mitsrayim*; they are behaving like Egyptian priests.

---

14   'The tent of the encounter is the place Adam can seek out *on his own initiative*, to be closer to Adonai' (Oosting 2004, p. 66).

The Hebrew word that is translated as 'strange' is *zar*. It sounds like the middle part of the word *Mitsrayim*: *t-s-r*. Does this perhaps hint at the place where we can expect to find this 'strangeness'?

While priesthood is untouchable in Egypt, it remains a precarious affair in Israel, one that must be followed with critical care. The critique of Nadab and Abihu's approach is fatal:

> And then fire issued forth
> from the face of YHWH
> and consumed them,
> and they perished in the face of YHWH.
>> Lv 10:2

Thus the priest in the context of the project 'Israel' is violently put in his place: he is a priest in the service of the covenant between God and his people.

Celebrations of Memories that Liberate

The liturgy which the priest has to practice in Israel is an 'anti-liturgy',[15] the opposite of everything that is customary elsewhere. The celebrations commemorate the liberation which sustains Israel. This is not only the case for Pesach, which celebrates the exodus from slavery. The celebrations that are tied to the land and to agriculture are also related to the liberation movement – that does not end in the land, but proceeds towards its realisation.

Shavuot, the Feast of Weeks (Shavuot means 'sevenfold'), is the celebration of the beginning of the harvest, but it is also directed towards:

> Remember that you were a slave in Egypt,
> So keep and practice these commandments!
>> Dt 16:12

According to Jewish tradition, Shavuot celebrates the gift of the Torah. For the Torah is the instruction for the practice of commemoration in the land: the organisation of a society without domination.

---

15   The term is taken from C.W. Mönnich: 'Anti-liturgy is a term that he himself [the author] "charged" as a parallel to Ionesco's antithéatre. That, too, is theatre, and how! In the same manner, anti-liturgy is not the refusal of a stylish liturgical celebration *per se* ... but

Sukkot, the Feast of Booths (sukkot are the tents where labourers live during harvest season), is celebrated when the harvest is brought in. The celebrants live in 'booths' for seven days. Thus they are put into the situation between the exodus from slavery and the entry into the Promised Land:

> All those, who call Israel their home,
> shall live in booths
> so that the future generations shall know
> that I let the sons of Israel live in booths
> when I led them out of Egypt, –
> I, YHWH, am your God!
>> Lv 23:42–43

Living in booths was the way of life of the people during their journey through the desert. Under no circumstances can the people forget this once they have arrived in the land.

This is why the Torah includes a book that is devoted entirely to this journey through the desert: Numbers, named after the first words of the Hebrew Bible: *ba-midbar*, in the desert. Initially, the people delivered from slavery do not enter into a land 'where milk and honey flow'. They end up in the desert where the liberation movement runs the danger of losing its way, of losing its vision and beginning to yearn for the 'meat pots of Egypt'. These are miserable conditions and agitators understandably emerge who try to convince the people to turn back. Numbers is the story of the counter-revolution ('Korach's gang'), which is suppressed with a strong hand (it is the hand of God himself), but which permanently traumatises the relationship between God and his people: the generation that was delivered from slavery perishes in the desert. The book does not conceal the fact that the revolution that God intends to start with this people is humanly impossible. But it also announces that God makes the impossible possible: a new beginning, a new generation that enters into the land in spite of the adverse conditions. The people have to bear in mind that when they hear the Torah they always also hear Numbers: they are returned to the desert in order to learn afresh what it means to be engaged in this God's liberation movement (Hos 2:16–18).[16] The path to the

---

expresses the desire precisely not to perform a play, not to allow spectators, to involve all those present in the work' (1966, p. 5).

16   This desert reminds the prophet Ezekiel of diaspora: 'I will let you come into the *desert of peoples*, there I will judge you, face to face: as I judged your fathers in the Egyptian desert' (Ez 20:35 f.).

Promised Land runs through the desert, again and again, towards the despair that no
liberation movement is spared. But not without the God whose name is: I will be there.

Entry is not just another aspect of the story of the transition from a nomadic
way of life to an established society – after which the establishment quickly
forgets that they themselves were once nomads who had no fixed place to lay
down their head. Israel is established in the land and it remains in process: its
liberation movement can only come to rest when all peoples in Jerusalem have
found their salvation (Is 27:13; Jer 3:17; Mi 4:2; Zec 8:22). In view of this, though,
the feast days are already days of rest. Leviticus, in particular, the book of the
Torah where everything revolves around the commandment to the people to
be 'holy' – to distance themselves, like their God, from the law of ruling over
and hence oppressing others – makes explicit that no work may be done in the
context of any feasts (Lv 23). The building of the new society cannot equate to
labour without any rest. For then the people lose sight of the real purpose of this
building: precisely to liberate humans from eternal drudgery. The liberation
movement's liturgical ground rule is the regularity of the Sabbath, the day of
rest.

In the festival calendar in Leviticus 23 the Sabbath leads the way:

> These are my festivals: for six days
> you will work,
> but the seventh day
> is Sabbath, it is the Sabbath day
> > Lv 23:3

Afterwards it resounds again:

> These are YHWH's festivals
> > Lv 23:4

And then come the other celebrations that are all connected to the Sabbath in one
way or another. The Sabbath is the common thread that runs through all the feasts
celebrated by Israel: liberation from labour.

Yom Kippur is a particularly special celebration; it is the day when God recon-
ciles with his people – by giving them the opportunity to 'cover' (*kapar* = cover)
their misdeeds.

So Yom Kippur literally means: Day of Covering. The common translation is: Day of Atonement (or Reconciliation). Hence this feast is also known as the great day of atonement in the Jewish and therefore also the Christian tradition. This is what is so great about this celebration: the people's offences are 'covered' in order to wipe the slate clean; God and his people are reconciled, i.e. come together again, so as to proceed along the path to liberation together.

Yom Kippur presupposes that the people will 'sin' once they have arrived in the land: rather than staying beside their liberator, they go their own way, 'like the other peoples'. The programme for the project points this out from the start. Not to have an eye for this would constitute poor Idealism. The real Israel, 'a tiny people' (Breukelman)[17] surrounded by a hostile world of peoples, can hardly help itself but 'sin'. The great danger is that they deny this and idealise the reality, suppress the problems, resist (self-)criticism, ultimately go to waste. If there is no space for the public expression and discussion of the flaws of one's own regime, then the project is doomed. By suppressing criticism, the liberation movement inevitably loses its way; it does not know here from there.

Yom Kippur is the celebration at which this is openly articulated: We lost our way, we lost our way terribly. It is the celebration of the admission of guilt:

> Aaron shall place his hand on the head of the live ram,
> and admit
> all the misdeeds of the sons of Israel and all their disloyalties,
> all their sins
>> Lv 16:21

Forgiveness and a Fresh Start

Now, a confession of guilt can be very oppressive – if this guilt persists. In that case, self-criticism is purely destructive: the realisation that the project has failed, that the people who are meant to carry out this project are not fit for the task. For better or worse, humans are sinful beings; it is sheer pride to think that they, who are 'naturally inclined to hate God and their neighbour',[18]

---

17   'A tiny people' involved in a history that 'in terms of world history is a history of nothing'. But they are not without hope, because it is *pars pro toto* the history of God-with-us-all' (Breukelman 1999, p. 192).

18   Thus the Heidelberg Catechism – one of the reformist confessional documents – replies the following to the question as to whether the human can uphold what God demands of him in His commandment: 'No, for I am naturally inclined to hate God and my neighbour'.

could ever escape their nature. Then it truly would be a mockery to celebrate the confession of guilt – as though God demanded that humans cultivate their incompetence and immaturity as the other gods do! This God's great liberating deed is the human's emergence from self-incurred immaturity, after all.[19] Yom Kippur is a feast day, a great feast day, because self-criticism opens the way for a fresh start.

Just how radically this fresh start is conceived of in Judaism becomes apparent in the custom of wearing a burial shroud for Yom Kippur. The Jew meets his God, 'a dead man in the midst of life … already beyond the grave in the midst of life'.[20] The hour of the Judgement Day, the hour of absolute penitence, strikes in the midst of life. Here the transition from this world into another world, God's world, takes place. But as Rabbi Moses Teitelbaum warns, we are not entering into the afterlife: 'But repentance does not help after death. It does help now; therefore let us be remorseful with all our hearts for our sins, and truly resolve not to sin again'.[21] This is why the following is emphasised: 'Yom Kippur effects atonement for human transgressions against God, but atonement for transgressions against fellow humans can only be made if the two have first made their peace with each other' (Joma 85b). The offer of a fresh start, reconciliation with God, is simultaneously the commandment to make a fresh start, to reconcile with the people.

The Torah is not the law that kills, but the Testament of the God of Israel who approaches his people, who gives them the opportunity to account for their sins in order once again to walk the path of liberation. This is no 'cheap grace' (Bonhoeffer).[22] Self-criticism is the condition for God's 'acquittal from outside' (Miskotte).[23] This is about a *fresh start*, a reversal. So it is not a matter of proceeding along the wrong path but with a clean conscience, as though nothing had happened.

But thank God this is not the last word that is spoken about the human. The Heidelberg Catechism continues: he is a sinner, indeed, 'except we are regenerated by the Spirit of God'. In opposition to 'natural anthropology', biblical anthropology proclaims: God made the human good!

19   If the liberated person lets himself be talked back into this immaturity, however, then it really is 'self-incurred'. In this case Kant is absolutely right.

20   Rosenzweig 2005, pp. 346f.

21   Hertzberg 1961, p. 144.

22   'Cheap grace is grace without discipleship, grace without the cross, grace without the living, incarnate Jesus Christ' (Bonhoeffer 2001, p. 44).

23   *De vreemde vrijspraak* ('Acquittal from outside') is the title of a volume of sermons by Miskotte.

Does this not contradict the reformist *sola gratia*, through 'grace alone'? Does this not derogate the Gospel, the good news that God wants to be our God unconditionally? But is the commandment to self-criticism not already part of God's grace towards us when he cleanses us from sin and so comes clean with us? Is it not a 'costly grace' (Bonhoeffer) to be given the freedom to make a fresh start?[24]

The confession of guilt is embarrassing. Self-criticism cuts deep into the flesh. The liturgy of Yom Kippur visualises this through the ritual of the two 'scapegoats'. One of the goats is slaughtered for YHWH, as a 'sign of atonement' to show that the people are cleansed of their sins (Lv 16:15). The other goat is sent into the desert so as to 'carry away' from the people 'all transgressions' (Lv 16:21–27). What takes place here is reprehensible, but then what is represented is also reprehensible: the perversion of the project 'Israel'. The people are given an object lesson of the hardest kind. In the 'scapegoats' they find embodied the criminality that they would have had to endure first-hand.[25] It bears witness to its own disorientation in the desert. But it is a lesson in the spirit of the Torah; it is in celebration of Yom Kippur, the Day of Atonement:

> For on this day you will be
> reconciled ('covered'),
> you will be cleansed:
> you will be cleansed of all your sins
> in the face of YHWH.
>> Lv 16:30

The 'scapegoats' take the place of the people who watch as their sins go up in flames, their transgressions carried away. The ritual creates space for the people to come clean with their God. This is embarrassing for the people, very embarrassing, but not fatal.

---

24 'It is costly, because it calls to discipleship; it is grace, because it calls us to follow Jesus Christ ... Costly grace is the incarnation of God' (Bonhoeffer 2001, p. 45).

25 The great Jewish commentator Ramban (1194–1270) has the following to say with respect to the blood sacrifice: 'He [the one making the sacrifice] must sprinkle the blood that corresponds with his blood on the altar. He does this in order to be conscious of the fact that he has committed a transgression towards his God, with his soul and his body, and that really it should be his own blood that is spilled ... And without God's loving loyalty that would surely be the case, too. But God accepts a substitute sacrifice that offers the opportunity to the human to better his life through insight'.

A liturgy of this kind, in which animals are sacrificed and sent to their death, seems alien to us today. We look on it as animal abuse. Religions that still involve animal sacrifices (Islam, for example) are suspect – apparently, they have not (yet) reached the humane level of our enlightened culture. The (our!) Enlightenment still lies ahead of the faithful of these religions; they have yet to 'undergo the (our!) Enlightenment'. Then they will arrive in a culture where animals are no longer sacrificed but are industrially processed, in the world of bio-*industry*. Of course, this does not mean that we should reintroduce animal sacrifices into our liturgy. But perhaps we should search for liturgical practices that represent the admission of guilt and the forgiving of guilt so that they show us just how embarrassing this is. Harsh words of criticism should be spoken in this ritual – not about others, but about ourselves. For, in the words of Huub Oosterhuis, 'to be human on earth means to be blessed in *embarrassment*' – not as a general anthropological truth, but as a sign of those people who know grace, as *notum ecclesiae* ('sign of the community').[26]

But this begs the question of whether sacrifice is not a hugely problematic issue at an even more fundamental level. Should it be the case that others are sacrificed so that we can escape? This is how capitalism works: the economy demands sacrifices in the service of business that could not survive otherwise. Does God perhaps work in the same inhumane manner? Does he require an 'atoning sacrifice' because otherwise he is not prepared to deliver us from our misery? Is the God of Israel – no other gods are spoken of here – the god of capitalist metaphysics, after all: Chronos, who eats his children and chronically demands sacrifices, without the intervention of a kairos that says *basta*, enough? Now, when it comes to human sacrifice, the Torah is quite clear: YHWH does not want it, ever (Gn 22:12). The God of Israel is not concerned with himself, as though he needed sacrifices in order to feel affirmed in being God:[27]

> For benevolence pleases me
> not sacrifices,
> knowledge of God more so than burnt offerings
> > Hos 6:6

Our knowledge of God is thoroughly misdirected so long as we think that YHWH is a 'God-in-himself', who demands that he be served 'in himself'. This God exerts himself entirely in his liberation movement: he *is* not *per se*; he *is there* for his people. All that he wants is that they follow his Torah, implement it, put it into practice. The entire

---

26   Song 489 in the Dutch *Liedboek voor de kerken* ('Book of Church Songs').

27   There is a passage in the Talmud where it is permissible to extinguish God's name in order to keep the peace between man and woman (jSota 1:4). That is how radical this God is when the issue is human wellbeing, prepared to renounce himself!

service, including the sacrificial rites, is directed towards that: that the people find their way back – not to God-in-himself, but to the Torah.

When the people, or a representative of the people, overstep the accepted liturgical boundaries and sacrifice themselves in order to radically do Torah, then that is a different matter. So that the will of God the liberator be done, not only in heavenly utopia, but also finally on earth. And human sacrifice finally has an end.

In this celebration, the priests lead the way. This means they lead the way with self-criticism. The priest has to come clean with God first of all. He in particular, given his role of preventing the people from approaching God too closely, runs the danger of himself becoming overfamiliar with 'divinity'. He goes in and out of the holy place, as if it were his home. This is why the message to him is:

> that he [Aaron] better *not* enter into the holy place *at all times*,
> beyond the curtain
> to the covering over the ark
> so that he will not die
>> Lv 16:2

The priest does not elevate himself above the people; he is on their side. When he asks for the 'covering' of sins in his priestly function, then this is inclusive:

> He will ask for cover, for himself, for his house
> and for the whole community of Israel.
>> Lv 16:17

The priest is not pure; the people are purified. This is the liberation that is celebrated at Yom Kippur:

> For on this day
> there is reconciliation ('covering up') for you,
> so that you can cleanse yourselves:
> of all your sins
> you are cleansed before YHWH
>> Lv 16:30

Having come clean with God, the people are at liberty to renew their devotion to the project, to take upon themselves once more the 'yoke' of the Torah. From now on, they will once more 'bow' to the law that dictates the organisation of society in such a way that bowed and oppressed people receive justice:

Let this be your permanent instruction:
In the seventh month on the tenth day
You shall *bow* your souls, –
[and this means]
do no work whatsoever,
neither the native nor the stranger in your midst.

    Lv 16:29

The idea that taking up the 'yoke' of the Torah is an act that is not only done in complete liberty, but is in itself also liberating, is often hard to imagine for us as Christians, especially of the reformed variety. We think that liberty and obedience, grace and work, fundamentally contradict each other. Liberty then means not being bound, and mercy: knowing that our (by definition sinful) actions have no bearing on that. Hence, we are not particularly well suited to be the loyal allies of those people who tenaciously want to change the world. It would do us good to celebrate the feast of '*Simchat* Torah', the '*joy* of the law' with the Jews.[28]

Yom Kippur is the celebration of the fresh start that Israel can make again and again. The order of the covenant, which God made with his people with a view to the coming of the Kingdom of Freedom, is reinstated. The people convert – to revolution. The people's transgression was their wish to return to their old circumstances, to the house of bondage. Yom Kippur opens the way for a radical renewal of society. The most incisive structural measure known to the Torah, the jubilee, is 'proclaimed' on precisely this day:

Let a blaring shofar
make the rounds,
in the seventh month, on the tenth day,
on the Day of Atonement ('the Day of Covering Up' – *Yom-hakippu-rim*),
let the shofar make the rounds
through your entire land.

...

and call forth liberation throughout the land,
for all its inhabitants

    Lv 25:9–10

---

28   See Friedrich-Wilhelm Marquardt in an essay from 1995: 'The Torah: God's gift of freedom: for Israel, and for us. This law of the spirit of life – thanks be to Jesus – liberated me from all other laws of sin and death' (Marquardt 1997, p. 30).

A key word that ties the liturgy of Yom Kippur to the institution of the jubilee is *kol* (translated as 'all' or 'entire'). At Yom Kippur '*all* transgressions ... and *all* their disloyalties' are made known (Lv 16:21), the 'scapegoat' carries off '*all* their sins' (Lv 16:22), Israel is cleansed 'of *all* [its] sins' (Lv 16:30), the priest asks for 'cover' 'for *all* the assembled people' (Lv 16:33). At the beginning of the jubilee, the shofar goes around 'through the *entire* land', 'liberation ... for *all* its inhabitants' is proclaimed, 'delivery' has to be dispensed 'in *all* the land' (Lv 25:24). That is how radically the following is true, here: The old is past, see, everything is become new!

Disassociation from the Logic of Domination

Yom Kippur is 'anti-liturgy' in *optima forma*. It is the revolutionary opposite of the great feast celebrated in the Babylonian empire, the New Year's Feast. Certainly, there are similarities. This feast, too, includes the ritual of the 'scapegoat': a sheep whose cadaver is thrown into the river and whose head is taken into the desert. The king appears as the representative of the sinful people. The priest relieves him of the signs of his dignity, hits him across the face, and lets him speak a prayer of penitence in which the king professes his innocence and is absolved. But the similarity is also the difference. The king (who never even makes an appearance in the Yom Kippur liturgy) leads the dominant order's god, Marduk, in a procession through the city and into a subterranean holy place, where he, together with the king, then spends three days. In the meantime, the victory of order over the force of darkness is acted out for the people. A complete reversal of social roles takes place during these three 'chaotic' days: slaves become masters, masters turn into slaves, a mock king reigns. But at the end of the feast Marduk is again placed on his throne, which is on the highest step of the temple tower. Order has been reinstated: masters rule again, slaves serve. The liturgy of this New Year's Feast implies that a world in which the slave turns master is tantamount to the eruption of 'chaos'. The people are meant to share with relief the celebration of the returning of power to the firm grasp of the great coalition of king and priests. And that this will be the case forever and ever. The Yom Kippur Feast teaches the people something better: a different world is possible; confessing to it makes a difference, always:

> Let this be an eternal regulation for you:
> to ask for 'cover'
> for the children of Israel for all their sins
> once a year!
> > Lv 16:34

According to the festival calendar in Lv 23, Yom Kippur is celebrated ten days after the New Year's feast (Rosh-ha-Shana). The synagogue calls these ten days the 'ten days of penitence'. The New Year's feast is the start of the retreat preceding the reversal that 'happens' at Yom Kippur: 'eternal' renewal as opposed to the Babylonian 'perpetuation' of the status quo.

In Israel, the priest serves the people. This service, however, is not populist: it does not mean always telling the people what they want to hear.

That is what Aaron does in the story of the 'golden calf' (Ex 32:1–6). The people think that the liberation movement cannot manage without the performance of swagger and demands a 'God' who embodies this swagger. Aaron acts according to the populist principle: *vox populi, vox Dei* (the voice of the people is the voice of God) and creates a 'bull calf', a caricature of the God of Israel who shows his power in his bond with the weak.

The service that the priest must render is to hold the people to the promise they willingly made: to do Torah, the law of liberation. His task is to teach the people to live differently from those peoples who are subjected to the fatal cycle of mastery and slavery. For the people must demonstrate through the way of life that delivery from slavery is possible – not just a utopia, but real. The priest leads the people in this task:

> YHWH spoke to Aaron and said:
> you shall not drink
> wine and beer,
> neither you nor your sons with you,
> when you enter into the tent of the encounter,
> so that you do not die:
> this is an eternal prescription
> for all generations! –
> to *separate* the holy from the unholy,
> the flawed from the clean
> and to teach the children of Israel
> all the regulations
> that YHWH said to them
> through Moses.
>
> Lv 10:8–11

This 'separating' invokes the story of the creation. There, God accomplishes the exodus from *Tohuwabohu* by 'separating' (light from darkness, the 'waters' above and beneath from heaven, day from night): it is possible for the oppressed to orientate themselves, to find ways of escaping their fate. The people, this God's image and his likeness, now have to learn to translate this orientation into practice. They have to show in their everyday practices that anything does *not* go, that there is a difference between holy and unholy, flawed and clean.

The areas of life where it is crucial to separate concern food (the dietary laws) and sexuality (discharge, ejaculation, menstruation). Why certain foods are 'flawed' and others 'clean' is unclear. The taboo of certain aspects of sexuality could be caused by the fascination that sexuality exudes, weighed down as it is by fear. This is a danger zone that has to be carefully regulated. Liberation does not mean anarchy where 'anything goes'.

Trying to regulate a way of life is a very risky matter. Condescension or worse are never far off. What ends up in the sphere of the taboo depends on the dominant gender relations: the woman suffers more from this than the man. The instructions that the people receive, however, are instructions – following them means to redefine them continuously – because circumstances change, we now know better. This, at least, is the Talmud's method: to ask continuously for the proper lifestyle, if need be through a very liberal handling of the instructions provided in the Torah.[29] It is the practice of liberty in the knowledge that the way in which one lives cannot be ceded to the free play of social forces: bio-industry, for instance, or the sex industry.

The instruction for how to proceed with the 'Egyptian illness', contagion with the enslaving ideology, from which Israel is liberated by its God, is a special case.

The Hebrew word for this illness, *tsara'at*, is usually translated with a word that refers to a kind of skin condition (King James Bible: 'plague'). But the Hebrew word includes the root *tsara*, which can also be found in the word *Mitsrayim*. Hence the association of this illness with Egypt forces itself on me, at least.[30]

---

29   Hermann Cohen offers a nice example of this liberty: in the Yom Kippur liturgy, the
       Talmud reads 'he purifies' (cleanses) rather than as is written in the Torah, 'he will not
       leave [the guilty] unpunished'. And he remarks: 'This change may, without exaggeration,
       be called an act of the deepest piety and of the most ardent love of man, which did not
       shrink from infringing upon the letter of the most holy words of revelation' (Cohen 1995,
       p. 222).

30   Monshouwer: 'In any case, it [the translation 'Egyptian illness'] expresses the fact that this
       is a frightening disease ... [I]n order to conceive it we have to ... consider the meaning of
       the [Hebrew] name for Egypt ... [I]t is by definition the land, from which one has to be
       liberated' (Monshouwer 1983, p. 47).

Israel has to protect itself against this contagion through excommunication:

> He who is afflicted with this frightening disease
> ...
> remains 'flawed'
> all the days that he is afflicted with this disease,
> he is 'flawed';
> he shall live alone,
> his place is outside the settlement.
>> Lv 13:46

While this is terrible for those afflicted with this disease, this is a bitter necessity for Israel. The infiltration of the ideology of the slave-holding society corrupts the project of liberation. If it does not want to fall entirely to ruin, it must stand up against this with all its might. But the excommunication is not absolute. Those who have been infected are not carelessly disposed of as sick elements on the ash heap of history. They reside outside the settlement, but with a view to their 'cleansing' and their return into the community of Israel. The Torah that refers to this disease ends with the 'Day of the Cleansed' (Lv 14:57). The liberation movement has to come clean with its dissidents.

This practice of excommunication, in particular, has led to terrible derailments in the history of the liberation movement. 'Cleansings' turned into slaughter, 'heretics' and 'enemies of the party' were stigmatised as 'sick' and 'dealt with' accordingly. What was meant to avoid ruin was itself ruinous. Apparently, excommunication in line with the Torah is inoperable. If it still needs to be done, then it should only be during a state of emergency, as a final emergency measure. A temporary measure, then, that aims to reintegrate the excommunicated. It is a measure, furthermore, that is bound by the strictest rules, which must be publicly announced. This is also the case in the Torah concerning this disease: the priests who decide whether somebody 'has been infected' or is 'pure' are subject to strict regulations that are made public. Normally a liberation movement has to be strong enough to fight the ideological battle within its own ranks without having to resort to excommunication. But what does 'normally' signify here? Is Walter Benjamin not right when he writes: 'The tradition of the oppressed teaches us that the "state of emergency" in which we live is not the exception but the rule'?[31]

---

31   Benjamin 2003, p. 392.

The priest is characterised by its *Aufhebung* [sublation]. He teaches the people to do Torah (Lv 10:11), but in such a way that the people can do Torah themselves. The priest is an intermediary and a transitional figure in the Torah. Ultimately, the Torah addresses the people. The land is given to the people, the people are held responsible for the fulfilment of the liberating law. The people are told:

> Do not follow the regulations of the 'Goy' people
> ...
> I [YHWH] said to you
> you will inherit their [the Goy's] field [*adama*];
> I give it to you, to inherit:
> a land, where milk and honey flow
> ...
> thus separate
> the clean from the flawed cattle
> ...
> You will be holy to me,
> for I, YHWH, am holy,
> I separated you from the peoples
> so that you would be there for me.
>> Lv 20:23–26

The priest serves the people. Whenever the liturgy that he 'serves' might imply that he is in charge, he is called to order. He can give the people his blessing, but his priestly ego is explicitly ignored in the process. What he does is nothing more than pass on YHWH's blessing:

> YHWH speaks to Moses and says:
> speak to Aaron and his sons and say:
> *this* is how you shall bless the children of Israel,
> by saying to them:
> may YHWH bless you and keep you! –
> May YHWH let his face shine for you and be affectionate to you! –
> May YHWH raise his face to you and give you peace!
> They will give the children of Israel my name,
> *but I will bless them*!
>> Nm 6:22–27

A Different Kind of Holy Place

In the cult of the dominant order, the holy place takes centre stage. It is a building in which everything revolves around what is holiest of all in this order: survival of the fittest, embodied in the image of a god that is intended to represent what is holiest of all. Therefore, the fact that it is a building – a man-made creation, a construction – should remain hidden. The holy place has to leave the impression of having always already been there: the order that venerates it is eternal; not man-made, but built 'by nature'[32] or by the god himself.[33] In reality, the holy place relies on labour, forced labour. But that remains a mystery, opaque even for the people who perform this labour: the slaves. The product of their manual labour is the means of oppressing them. First they toil to erect the building, then they bow down before the image of god that they themselves have made. It is a mystery, yes, it is the great secret of world history to date: the oppressed help construct their oppression. A particularly enlightened mind is required to see through this secret, a mind enlightened by the Holy Spirit that emanates from the God who wants to deliver the slaves from slavery. Such an enlightened person can sort the matter out:

> They [who make god images in order to bow down before them]
> neither know nor comprehend,
> for their eyes are glued shut so that they cannot see,
> their hearts so that they have no insight
> ...
> They have neither knowledge nor comprehension
> when they speak:
> I have burnt half [the wood block] in the fire [to keep myself warm]
> and I also baked bread on the [wood] coals,
> fried and ate meat, –
> the rest I made into an abomination,
> I bow down before a block of wood![34]
>
>   Is 44:18–19

---

32   'before building is begun it must be quite definitely ascertained whether the place selected is suitable for the "position". This really means that we cannot make shrines and cannot select their "positions", but can never do more than merely "find" them' (Van der Leeuw 1986, p. 398).

33   As the Babylonian myth of the creation of the world, 'Enuma Elish' says of the 'Tower of Babel'.

34   Tom Naastepad notes that immediately afterwards the wood joins in the joy at Israel's

And he can ask, with liberating sobriety:

> who builds a god or casts an idol without purpose?
>> Is 44:10

A secularised 'translation' of this prophetic enlightenment is Bertolt Brecht's poem 'Questions of a worker who reads':

> Who built Thebes of the seven gates?
> In the books you will find the names of kings.
> Did the kings haul up the lumps of rocks?
> And Babylon, many times demolished
> Who raised it up so many times? In what houses
> Of gold-glittering Linma did the builders live?
> Where, the evening that the Wall of China was finished
> Did the masons go? Great Rome
> Is full of triumphal arches. Who erected them? Over whom
> Did the Caesars triumph? Had Byzantium, much praised in song
> Only palaces for its inhabitants? Even in fabled Atlantis
> The night the ocean engulfed it
> The drowning still bawled for their slaves.
>
> The young Alexander conquered India.
> Was he alone?
> Caesar beat the Gauls.
> Did he not have even a cook with him?
> Philip of Spain wept when his armada
> Went down. Was he the only one to weep?
> Frederick the Second won the Seven Years' War. Who
> Else won it?
>
> Every page a victory.
> Who cooked the feast for the victors?

---

liberation: 'Rejoice you depths of the earth, break forth in cheers you mountains, you forest and all the *wood* within. For YHWH has liberated Jacob and shows his divine might in Israel' (Is 44:23). 'As though they were humans! The cosmos is anthropomorphised', while idolatry de-humanises humans by making them freeze in awe in front of a block of wood (Naastepad 1979).

Every ten years a great man.
Who paid the bill?

So many reports.
So many questions.[35]

The Torah also makes room for a holy place. But it gives voice to a God who makes no secret of the fact that this is a building made by humans, a construction. What is more, he commands them to construct it:

they shall *make* a holy place for me
    Ex 25:8

What the gods take great care to keep secret is openly declared by this God: the holy place does not make the people (into obedient subjects) – but the people make the holy place (into a place where the miraculousness of this philanthropic God is made visible). This by itself is already a miracle; what the holy model represents is a miracle above miracles. For the people shall make the holy place:

exactly like I am letting you [Moses] see it:
the construction plan for the tabernacle and
the construction plan for all its features,
that is how you shall make it.
    Ex 25:9

And what this God makes visible nobody has ever laid eyes on before: the utopia of a world in which life is good – in the first place for the people who are miserable in this world. It is the utopia of the Promised Land, the vision that is offered to Abraham when God calls upon him to go – down the path to the land 'that I will let you [Abraham] *see*' (Gn 12:1). In other words, it is the vision of the 'good creation', which starts the narrative of the delivery from slavery (Gn 1:1–2:4a). The holy place that is made is intended to be a likeness of this creation: 'YHWH gives his instructions to Moses in seven speeches, which – in correspondence with the story of the creation – reach their climax in the commandment to remember the Sabbath (Ex 31:12–17)'.[36]

---

35   Brecht 1976, pp. 252 f.
36   Deurloo 2004, p. 44.

And once the holy place has been 'completed' (Ex 39:32) – just as God 'completes' his creation (Gn 2:2) – Moses will see in it what God saw in his creation:

> God saw everything he had made:
> yes, it was very good.
> Gn 1:31

Thus Moses now also sees:

> Then Moses saw the whole work:
> yes, they had made it
> as YHWH had commanded,
> thus they had made it.
> Ex 39:43

The purpose of the holy place is the visual representation of utopia. It is meant to make visible what is so terribly invisible in the desert where the liberation movement is located: the beautiful life that lies ahead of the people. God commands to make the holy place in such a way that the people can affirm, through the mouth of Moses: It is very good – even if Moses only implies this, but it is clear enough for the reasonably keen-eared.

But the *making* of the holy place itself also includes a likeness: between creator and created in their labour. The God of the Bible is not a natural phenomenon; he has not always existed as the gods have always existed, symbols of all the things that cannot be changed. This God is a practitioner from the outset; the word 'in the beginning' reads: he *created*. This is a deed of radical difference: creation out of nothing, out of *Tohuwabohu*. He *makes* reality. He makes it in such a way that he can say: it is good, very good, and he is not forced to do so. It is liberated labour.

Thus the human, too, made in his image and his likeness ('let us make humans', Gn 1:26), is allowed to make the holy place as the product of liberated labour.[37] The emphasis is entirely on the people (all the people: men and women!) labouring of their own free will, and sincerely:

> Everyone, man and woman,
> whatever their heart *allowed* them to bring

---

37   Reeling Brouwer 1992, p. 27.

for all the labour YHWH commanded, through Moses, to be done,
they brought it, the children of Israel,
of their own *free will* for YHWH!

  Ex 35:29

The builders of the buildings that perpetuated their oppression remained
unnamed: 'In the books you will find the names of kings. Did the kings haul
up the lumps of rocks?' Here, the labourers with their specialist knowledge are
also named:

Moses speaks to the children of Israel:
see, YHWH called *by name*:
Bezalel ...
he filled him with God's spirit
in wisdom, in skill and in knowledge,
of all possible labours,
to imagine designs,
to make them ...
... to make all possible labour according to a design,
he also gave him the heart for teaching –
him and Aholiab

  Ex 35:30–34

The splendour of the holy place reflects the creativity of its makers. And it is
God who commands them: to be free to make such a holy place! This holy place
may only be called a 'work of service' (*abodah*, from: *abad*) because the 'service'
of the liberation is celebrated there:

exactly like YHWH commanded Moses,
thus the children of Israel did it,
all the work of *service*.

  Ex 39:42

From the beginning, this work was intended to serve as the habitation for the
NAME that breathes liberation:

They shall make a holy place for me,
I shall *live* in their midst.

  Ex 25:8

No image of God can be found in this 'habitation', for this God is not concerned with himself, but with the project he has set in motion with Israel. This project is written in the Torah, and only the Torah can be found in the holy place.

That this is the case is gradually made evident in the instructions for making the holy place. First, there is the instruction to make the 'ark' (Ex 25:10), then the instruction to make room in this ark for the 'covenant' (Ex 25:16). Later it turns out that this 'covenant' is written on two stone 'tablets' (Ex 31:18), and finally that the 'words of the covenant, the Ten Words' (so the summary of the Torah) are recorded on these 'tablets' (Ex 34:28). And the 'ark with the covenant' is located in the 'habitation' on the 'inside of the curtain' that 'separates' the 'holy' from the 'most holy' (Ex 26:33), so in the centre of the 'habitation'.

The NAME only wants to live in a holy place in which the Torah takes centre stage.[38] And God the liberator will not rest until his NAME has been firmly established 'across the whole earth'. Once the 'habitation' is 'completed', it turns out that 'fulfilment' is a cloud that guides the people 'on all their travels':

> For YHWH's cloud
> was above the habitation during the day
> and a fire during the night
> before the eyes of all the house of Israel
> on all their travels!
>> Ex 40:38; end of the Book of Exodus

In light of the coming Kingdom of Freedom, any established order, even the best of them, is temporary. The gods live in a building that emanates solidity, this God's holy place is a tent, made with a view to a liberation *movement*.

Nevertheless, a 'habitation for YHWH' solid as a house will be built in the real Israel. And the NAME confirms that he wants to live there, too. Could this possibly mean that despite all the temporariness there can be something akin to the realisation of utopia after all? Or are we sure that the liberation of labour will never be celebrated in St. Peter's in Rome?

---

38   'The tent of the holy place contains the tablets with the Ten Words, the tent is hence the symbol of God's presence in the midst of his people. Not an image, much less an image of the law of the jungle, but a tent with the Ten Words, the charter *against* the law of the jungle' (Naastepad 2001, p. 122).

The instructions for the making of the holy place are interrupted by the story of the golden calf (Ex 32:1–6). The people's assembly, tired of waiting (Moses, their charismatic leader, 'hesitates to descend from the mountain', Ex 32:1), has the fatal idea to demand the following of Aaron, the priest:

> make gods for us
> that will lead us
>> Ex 32:1

And Aaron does as the people say and makes a bull calf, a golden beauty that bursts with strength, the visual representation of the 'will to power'. The people avow:

> These are your gods, Israel,
> who brought you up out of the Land of Egypt.
>> Ex 32:4

This profession of faith(lessness) shows just how far the people are alienated from their God. He makes humans ('let us make humans') – image and likeness of his humanity. The people make gods – image and likeness of superhuman power. This is not only the return to the religion of the house of bondage, this is worse: the perversion of the liberation movement. The revolution embodied in the image of a muscle-man, one great leader: Command, we will obey you.

One of the programmes that is written in Torah with a view to the organisation of the Promised Land, the Book of Deuteronomy, also accounts for the possibility of this perversion. From the beginning it reins in the free play of religious forces that enact the 'will to power':

> You shall destroy, destroy all places,
> where the peoples, who you will succeed, have served their gods
> ...
> thus you shall not act before YHWH, your God,
> but in the place
> that YHWH, your God,
> will elect from all the tribes,
> there you shall search for a habitation
> to establish his name,
> that is where you will go.
>> Dt 12:2–5

The centralisation of the cult in one place; there are nicer things. But it can be necessary in order to maintain the uniqueness of the holy place that is meant to represent the utopia of liberated labour.

This is contrary to our pluralist disposition. Should not everyone be able to do what their heart desires – especially concerning something as intimate as religion? The Torah, however, is of a different opinion: in it, religion manifests especially as 'unbelief' (Barth)[39] – the lack of faith in the coming of the Kingdom. That is why the rich world of religion making way for the utopian fantasy of the good creation in one place at least can be more important than religious freedom.

However, the issue is less that all roads lead to Rome than that there is so little to see in Rome that is utopian. But Rome is not yet Jerusalem, is it ...?

A King Characterised by His *'Aufhebung'* [*Sublation*]

The dominant order is unimaginable without a 'king' who reigns over his kingdom 'from above'. The king: this is not the symbolic figure of today, but the embodiment of state power. The state, superior to the people, decides what is good for the people. State *authority* ensures that the people follow the law – the law that stipulates the honouring of the state itself. For chaos rules without the state; without the state the people are not able to defend themselves against their enemies. The state also commands the instruments that make it a state: the judiciary, the police, the military. That is why the state forces the people to pay the price: tribute, financial or of natural produce. And the state impresses: the people look up to the palace, watch as the king ascends the throne, admire (and perhaps fear) the parades that demonstrate the power of the state.

According to the Torah, it is very well possible that the people could do without a state to order their affairs.[40] The people are quite capable of helping themselves – if they recognise that this self-help consists of solidarity. YHWH liberates them from slavery with a view to just this: to organise a society based

---

39   'Religion as unbelief' is the title of the second section of § 17 of Barth's 'Church Dogmatics' ('The Revelation of God as the Abolition of Religion'). What Barth means is: 'It is a concern, indeed, we must say that it is *the* one great concern of *godless* [!] man'. Nota bene: 'Above all it affects ourselves also as adherents of the Christian religion' (Barth 1956a, 299 f.).

40   Friedrich Engels could also imagine this well: 'the first act by virtue of which the state really constitutes itself the representative of the whole of society – the taking possession of the means of production in the name of society – this is, at the same time, its last independent act as a state. State interference in social relations becomes, in one domain after another,

on solidarity. The measure of the great land reform that renders large-scale property ownership impossible – the jubilee (Lv 25:8–34) – knows no king. The book of the emergence, Exodus, knows only the king befitting of this name, YHWH:

> YHWH shall be your king
> for ever and ever!
>> Ex 15:18

YHWH is the 'anti-king', the opposite of the king of Egypt. He liberates the slave people who Pharaoh does not want to let go. YHWH declares the people themselves a 'Kingdom of Priests' (Ex 19:6). He is the king who descends in order to lead his people forth into the Promised Land: the king characterised by his *Aufhebung* [sublation].

The pronouncement of YHWH as king comes at the end of the song that Moses sings after the passage through the Sea of Reeds (Ex 15:1–19). And Moses is the 'intermediary' between God and his people who (because of that) is himself characterised by his *Aufhebung* [sublation]: not a king, not a priest, but a prophet, who himself longs for all people to be prophets and for the Spirit to wash over them.
    If this were allowed to happen:

> All the people YHWH's prophets,
> because YHWH gives them his Spirit!
>> Nm 11:29

Moses is serenading the kingdom of the God who wants to be all in all.

The Book of Deuteronomy, though, predicts that the people will still try to 'save' the project 'Israel' by instantiating a king. It anticipates this situation:

> When you arrive in the land that YHWH gives to you,
> and inherit it and settle within it,
> and you say: I want to place a king above myself,
> like all peoples who surround me
>> Dt 17:14

---

superfluous, and then dies out of itself; the government of persons is replaced by the administration of things, and by the conduct of processes of production' (Engels 1987, p. 268).

This is the situation that Israel will permanently find itself in: it is *surrounded by* the peoples who fight the project with fire and arms and work their best to make Israel disappear from the face of the earth. These peoples permanently problematise the project simply by being there. The pull of their 'Goy' ideology has always been present: the law of ruling or being ruled that is inescapable because the 'gods' have decreed it, 'the gods of the peoples who *surround you*' (Dt 13:8). How will a 'grass-roots democracy' be able to stand up for itself under these circumstances? Is it even possible to avoid a state authority that ensures Israel's 'autonomy and equality' (Veerkamp)?[41] Or will the project 'Israel' inevitably boil down to a strong state, characterised by a 'controlled economy' that forces happiness on its people?

Deuteronomy does not eschew these questions out of idealism, but looks for the answer in the concept of the 'anti-state' – a state that is never given the opportunity to treat the people as the object of its power:

> [if you must institute a king]
> then institute a king above yourself
> whom YHWH, your God, chooses
> you shall institute a king above yourself
> from the midst of your brothers:
> you shall not give power over yourself to any foreigner,
> who is not your brother.
>
> Dt 17:15

The king in Israel will be 'YHWH's chosen one'. And that, by definition, is not the kind of king familiar to the peoples. On the contrary, YHWH chooses the oppressed and stands with those who take the side of the oppressed. This king is called upon to be the saviour of the poor:

> He saves the poor man who cries out for liberation,
> the oppressed who has no one to help him.
>
> Ps 72:12

---

41   According to Veerkamp, authority and equality are not only ideals but also constitute the basis of a real 'Torah Republic' under Nehemiah: 'He [Nehemiah], in the context of a limited but real autonomy, based the polity on that Torah, which demands the maximum of equality possible under the circumstances of limited autonomy' (Veerkamp 1992, p. 81). The 'given', not especially favourable, circumstances also give Deuteronomy's 'design' pause for thought.

This king will come 'from the midst of the brothers'. For he knows very well what it means to be oppressed, knows their sorrows are his own sorrows. The situation of the oppressed is alien to a king, who is unfamiliar with this brotherliness, from the start; he simply cannot empathise with their fate.

This king should not act grandly in the way that defines kingship among the peoples. He should refrain from military demonstrations of his power, not 'acquire many horses' (Dt 17:16): 'horses and chariots' are biblical symbols of imperialist militarism. He should not keep a harem: not 'have many women' (Dt 17:17). A harem full of princesses from other royal houses is a component of political diplomacy: marriages that are intended to bind other states. Respecting the ideology of these other states is also part of this diplomacy: the harem is a place of religious pluralism and the king would obviously participate ('his heart goes astray', Dt 17:17). And he should not enrich himself (at the cost of the people, obviously): not 'excessively accumulate silver and gold' (Dt 17:17). For then his monarchy would merely be a prelude for the kind of monarchy from which the people have just been liberated ('so that he may not turn the people back round towards Egypt', Dt 17:16).

The king's task, once he has ascended to the throne, is to study the Torah:

> This is how it will be:
> when he has taken his seat
> on the throne of his kingdom,
> then he will have a copy written in a book
> of this Torah
>
> ...
>
> this [book] will stay with him,
> and he will read from it all the days of his life,
> so that he may learn to fear YHWH, his God,
> to keep all the words of the Torah
> and these regulations.
> in order to do them!
> > Dt 17:19

This is a constitutional monarchy of a very special kind. For the constitution by which the king must abide is the Torah, which binds the kingship to the project of a society without domination. The throne on which this king sits is like a school bench, and his existence as king is a process of life-long learning – he has to learn that his glory consists only in 'soli Deo gloria', 'God, this God alone, the advocate of the poor, be honoured'. His elevation to king hence merely serves the Torah:

> So that his heart may not be elevated above his brothers
>> Dt 17:20

He can be king so long as he 'learns' that he has to be an absolute 'anti-king':

> so that he may be king for a long time,
> he and his sons,
> in the midst of Israel
>> Dt 17:20

His kingship will only last if the king is ultimately wrapped up 'in the middle of Israel' again, finds himself 'in the midst of his brothers' again, together with them in the kingdom of liberty, equality and solidarity. Chosen from the midst of his brothers to be a king who does not rise above his brothers, he ends up in their midst: a king characterised by his *Aufhebung* [sublation].

> 'In the middle of Israel', in the Promised Land. The land where the poor stand 'in the middle': 'For the poor man will not end *in the middle* of the land; therefore [!] I command to you: you will open, yes open your hand to your brother, the oppressed, the poor man, in your land!'
>> Dt 15:11

This is similar to the great socio-economic measure of the jubilee in Lv 25. Just as the introduction of a permanent land reform renders the systematic permanent accumulation of property impossible, so the introduction of such a non-kingly kingship ultimately renders the king impossible. Who would want to be king under these circumstances?

Deuteronomy also indirectly signifies that there is ultimately no place for a king in Israel. The 28th chapter details the salvation awaiting Israel if it heeds YHWH's voice, and the misery awaiting it if it does not. No mention is made of a king in the blessings for obedience (Dt 28:1–14), in the curses for disobedience (Dt 28:15–68), significantly, it says: 'YHWH will let you *and the king*, who you instituted above yourself, go to a people that you have never known ... there you will serve other gods, made of wood and stone' (Dt 28:36).

Deuteronomy's programme, which can see the project 'Israel' taking the shape of a state, also tends towards the *Aufhebung* [sublation] of kingship, the withering away of the state.[42]

The sublation of kingship into the universality of God's Kingdom constitutes the climax of the apocalyptic John's fantasy: 'There will be no night anymore and they will need neither the light of a lamp nor the light of the sun: YHWH God will shine above them. And they will rule as kings, for ever and ever' (Rv 22:5).

Total War?

Deuteronomy's programme also anticipates that the real Israel will not be spared from having to wage war. As a rule, it will be war against a militarily superior enemy:

> When you set out to war against your enemies
> and you see horses and chariots,
> people more numerous than you
>> Dt 20:1a

Above all, Israel's strength resides in its belief that the exodus from the house of bondage was not futile:

> Do not fear them,
> for YHWH, your God, is by your side,
> who brought you out of the Land of Egypt.
>> Dt 20:1b

It is the priest's task to remind the people of this:

---

42 Rudolf Bultmann can see only utopia here: 'Where their [the prophets'] ideals lead to some legislation or other, this outlines the picture of a utopia – for the continuation outlined in Deuteronomy ... is utopian; that is, they fail to recognize the real necessities of the organization of the state and are only capable of implementation at the price of the people constituted in accordance with these ideals not leading to any independent existence *as a state*' (Bultmann 1963, p. 69). Deuteronomy does not fail to recognise anything here. But it refuses to turn a society's 'not yet' into a 'never'.

> when you set out to war,
> then let the priest stand before the people
> and say to them:
> *hear, Israel*
> today you set out to war against your enemies
> ...
> it is YHWH who accompanies you,
> in order to wage war for you against your enemies,
> in order to liberate you.
>> Dt 20:2–4

This is addressed to a people who are militarily inferior and who, under normal circumstances, would lose the war. The God referred to here is God the liberator, who is the strength of the weak – an emphatic warning must be spoken against imperialist abuse.[43] The anti-imperialist character of the war waged by Israel is made immediately evident in the regulations that are to be distributed by the 'officers' (Dt 20:5–8). Under no circumstances is the war to escalate into 'total war'. That man who builds a house and has not yet been able to live in it: 'he must go, he must return to his house, *otherwise he might die in war*'. And the same applies to those who have planted a vineyard, but have not yet been able to enjoy its fruit, as well as to men who are about to get married, but who would leave behind only a widow if they fell at war. War must serve life; otherwise it is not only dubious but forbidden. Biblically speaking, the idea that it is 'sweet and honourable to die for one's country' is a perverse notion.[44] Only those who profit from these deaths profit from this saying. This slogan is used by the great men of the earth to motivate the people to sacrifice themselves for their imperial projects.

The man who 'is fearful and soft-hearted', too, 'shall return to his house' (Dt 20:8). It is a pragmatic measure, 'so that he may not melt his brother's hearts and make them like his heart'. It emphasises once more the non-heroic character of the Torah: People do not need to act the hero that they are not.

---

43   In the Jewish tradition, the blessing given to Benjamin (Gn 49:27: 'Benjamin tears apart the wolf') as the suggestion that it is precisely the weakest of the sons of Israel who will vanquish Israel's arch enemy, Amalek (wolf = Amalek).

44   Bertolt Brecht, when he was still very young, had to write an essay on this saying and wrote (as a friend later recollected it): 'The saying that it is sweet and honourable to die for one's country can only be classed as propaganda. It is always hard to take one's life, whether in bed or on the battlefield' (Völker 1979, p. 9).

But war does not only affect one's own people. War always also affects another. This is another reason to see war as an emergency measure. If the possibility of war occurs, then the possibility of keeping the peace takes precedence:

> if you approach a city
> in order to wage war against it,
> then first make it an offer of peace!
>   Dt 20:10

This peace is not necessarily especially idyllic. It is not the great peace, *shalom*, where everyone has everything together. The real Israel needs a *cordon sanitaire*, and peace, in this case, means that the city that wants peace is made to discharge a 'tribute'; that is, it will serve Israel's interests (Dt 20:11).

What specific shape does this 'service' take – in a society in which the liberation from servitude is Torah (Constitution)? Hopefully, Israel will 'remember' that it was itself a slave in Egypt when it takes up the role of 'occupying power'.

Should keeping the peace fail, then there is war and *à la guerre comme à la guerre* (war is war): the men are killed, women, children and livestock become loot; 'you shall enjoy the loot from your enemies' (Dt 20:14). The word of liberation is incarnated here in a way that is hardly pleasant.

But it gets even worse. For up until now, 'cities that are far away from you' (Dt 20:15) were at issue. Concerning the cities of the peoples who are expected to make room for Israel – so that 'utopia' finds a 'topos', a place – it is a whole different matter:

> However, of the cities of the peoples, who YHWH, your God,
> gives to you as property,
> you shall let no breath live,
> no, you shall 'ban' them, 'ban':
> the Hittite, the Amorite, the Canaanite, the Perizzite, the Hivite, and the
>   Jebbusite,
> as YHWH, your God, has commanded you.
>   Dt 20:16–17

It is these peoples who render life impossible for Israel. They hate the project of a society without domination. They will do anything to blight it. No compromise is thinkable with these peoples; their gods represent everything that the God of Israel detests: they debase humans, honour power, ensure that everything stays as it is. These peoples are destined to disappear completely, a *'decretum horribile'* (as Calvin called God's 'decree' to damn part of humanity). But how else can Israel and its project live?

This 'final solution' is too terrible to be true. It also contradicts what God solemnly 'decreed' after the 'great flood' that virtually annihilated the promise of a good creation:

> Never again shall all flesh be exterminated by the floodwaters, –
> never again shall there be a flood to destroy the earth!
> Gn 9:1

Hence, we cannot follow Deuteronomy's programme in this instance. A different solution has to be found. Certainly, Israel will make room for itself 'by means of the threat and exercise of force' to organise a new society.[45]And it will be uncompromising in its ideological battle with the 'peoples' – otherwise it would perish in the world of the peoples.[46] But the disappearance of these peoples is not without the expectation of their *Aufhebung* [sublation]!

Perhaps the 'borderline case' of Amalek, the prototypical anti-Israeli project intent on exterminating the people of Israel, points precisely in that direction.[47] It is clearly stated that Israel, when YHWH 'will have given you peace from all your surrounding enemies', shall 'erase [Amalek] from its memory' (Dt 25:19). Could this 'erasing' not represent the promise to Israel that all that is radically evil, embodied by Amalek, will one day truly be past, will no longer be allowed to have a name – because everything has turned good?

---

45 Fifth thesis of the 'Barmen Declaration' ('Theological Declaration on the Current Situation of the German Protestant Church' of May 1934): 'Scripture tells us that, in the as yet unredeemed world in which the Church also exists, the State has by divine appointment the task of providing for justice and peace. [It fulfils this task] by means of the threat and exercise of force, according to the measure of human judgment and human ability'.

46 Tom Naastepad reads Dt 20:16–17 itself as referring only to this ideological battle: 'Of course, this does not mean it is necessary to cause a bloodbath ... This commandment ['let no breath survive'] is a commandment *ad absurdum*. How else can the fact be articulated that absolutely no compromise is possible between God's people and the gods? So it is said like this' (Naastepad 2001, p. 222).

47 According to Dt 25:18, Amalek attacked Israel from the back, where its weakest members were located and the people were generally 'tired and faint'.

The story of the real Israel mentions YHWH's terrible charge to Saul to 'vanquish' Amalek 'from man to woman, from child to new-born, from oxen to sheep, from camel to donkey' (1Sm 15:3). But in a certain sense, it is also an 'anti-war story': 'anti' regular war, where elites spare each other and the common people are sacrificed. This is what Saul does (he spares the king, but the despised and the humble are destroyed) and why he is damned (1Sm 15:9–11).

The Talmud, incidentally, implies that Saul protested against this ghastly charge: 'Even if a human might have failed, how has the animal failed?' And when YHWH still is not prepared to retract the charge, again: 'Even if the great ones might have failed, how have the little ones failed?' (Joam 22b). We can only lament the fact that Saul let YHWH order him to silence too quickly.

Finally, the Torah on war concentrates on relatively minor things, like the trees that have to be disposed of on account of the occupation. If they are fruit trees, then the commandment is: Leave them standing. For:

> you shall eat from them
>> Dt 20:19

Once again the line is drawn at 'total war': no scorched earth tactic. We have to eat, after all!

In one of the final scenes of Brecht's *The Days of the Commune*, the communard Jean Cabet proposes to fell an apple tree in order to use it for building a barricade. In the end, he leaves the tree standing. The following act shows the commune's bloody defeat. Brecht provides the following stage directions: 'Place Pigalle, May, during Bloody Week. At the barricade, ready to fire, stand Geneviève Guéricault, Jean Cabet, François Faure and two civilians. The German cuirassier is dragging a crate of ammunition after Papa into the corner of the wall. A badly wounded woman, a stranger, is lying in a sheltered place. Heavy artillery fire. Rolling of drums, which signifies attacks in neighbouring streets. *The apple tree is in full bloom*'.[48] Not everything should be sacrificed to the (unfortunately) necessary force of arms. Something, however small, has to testify to the purpose: the good life.

The disillusionment is great. The project 'Israel', too, will not be able to make do without a king (state) and without war (military). And once the state and the military have established themselves, the question remains whether they

---

48   Brecht 2003, p. 123.

will ever allow themselves to accept their *Aufhebung* [sublation]. The state apparatus will likely always find a reason to postpone its withering away. And the saying 'if you want peace, prepare for war' will not be unfamiliar to the generals of the people's army, either. How can we ensure that the project's radical vision is preserved in the real Israel, that the institutions are not given the opportunity to declare themselves the be all and end all of revolutionary wisdom? What is required is a critical agent who can publicly call the established order to the order of permanent revolution. This critical agent is the prophet. He is the element that cannot be institutionalised in the society constituted and organised by the Torah; he is the critical public, without whom this society solidifies into a 'status quo'. It is the prophet who confronts the real Israel with its Law, the Torah. He prevents the deterioration of this Law into a principle that has no practical significance for reality.[49] And just as Deuteronomy anticipates that the real Israel will have a state and will have to wage war, so it draws the conclusion that there must be prophets who actualise the Torah by introducing it into real society as critical theory:

> YHWH will let rise
> a prophet from your midst, from among your brothers,
> like to me [Moses],
> you shall heed him
> > Dt 18:15

The people institute a king; it is YHWH who lets the prophet 'rise'. Critique can only be truly critical if it is independent. It needs the freedom to speak the truth to the people and the institutions instituted by the people (kingship and priesthood). In the real Israel (he rises 'from your midst, from among your brothers'), the prophet represents YHWH himself. And YHWH is the ultimate critical voice, the reason for the critique of every dominant order:

> I am YHWH,
> your God,
> who brought you out of Egypt,
> out of the house of bondage

---

49   Let us imagine for one moment that the Law's tenet, 'human dignity shall be inviolable' (the German Constitution's first article), were more than a cliché for Sundays and Holidays!

you shall have
no other gods
next to me
in my face
Ex 20:2–3

For him, no institution is holy. The liberation he initiated tolerates no sanctioning from whichever political or ideological entity it might be. The NAME, after all, means 'I will be there, as he who I will be there'; and he will be there in the figure of the prophet, the relentless critique of all circumstances that stand in the way of the final liberation.

The prophet is neither a fortune-teller, nor an oracle, nor a clairvoyant. These are figures typical of the world of the Goy, where fate reigns. There, nobody knows what awaits them (what will the stocks do?). The future is unpredictable and that is why experts are needed, who claim that they can make predictions. The things they predict remain tied to fate, though, moving along the up and down of good luck and bad luck, good and evil. The project 'Israel' is told to bid farewell to precisely these 'future prophets' (Dt 18:9–14).[50] For the future is the Kingdom of Freedom. This kingdom is coming and the prophet rises in order to announce it. Not as a pleasant afterwards that has no bearing on the present, but as its permanent critique:

Turn around,
For the Kingdom of heaven is nigh
Mt 3:2; 4:17

Entry can start, the Torah becomes flesh: the real Israel.

---

50   'It is well known that the Jews were forbidden to look into the future. The Torah and the prayers instructed them, by contrast, in remembrance. This disenchanted those who fell prey to the future, who sought advice from the soothsayers. For that reason the future did not, however, turn into a homogenous and empty time for the Jews. For in it every second was the narrow gate, through which the Messiah could enter' (Benjamin 2003, p. 397).

CHAPTER 8

The Real Israel

The real Israel has not managed to realise the project 'Israel' – yet. It is important to emphasise this 'yet': the Hebrew canon calls the books that tell the story of the real Israel (Joshua, Judges, Samuel 1 and 2, Kings 1 and 2) the 'first prophets'. It is a matter of *prophetic* historical narrative: history *to date* does not have the final say regarding the possibility of the future existence of the project 'Israel' one day existing.[1] The 'first prophets' ultimately leave history open-ended. The Second Book of Kings does relate how the tiny bit left of Israel – the Southern Kingdom of Judah – disappears into Babylonian exile, and how the symbol of its state autonomy, the king, is incarcerated in a 'dungeon house' in Babel. But the narrative then continues and ends with:

> When he turned King of Babel, Evilmerodach
> lifted the head of Jehoiachin of Judah from the dungeon house
> and spoke kindly to him
> and set his throne above that of the kings who were with him in Babel,
> he let him change his prison garments
> and from now on always ate his meal in his presence, all the days of his life,
> but he received his maintenance payment as a regular payment from the king,
> as much as each day needed,
> all the days of his life.
>
> 2 Kgs 25:27–30

Open-ended (Hi)Story

This ending is reminiscent of the ending of the Book of Genesis: the story of Joseph, who is brought into Egypt as a slave, is imprisoned, but is then miraculously liberated from his imprisonment by Pharaoh to become his highest

---

1 The sentence from the *Communist Manifesto*, 'The history of all hitherto existing society is the history of class struggles' (Marx and Engels 1976b, p. 484), also concerns prophetic historical narrative. It suggests that the fight may have been endless to this point, but it will one day end: in the classless society.

functionary (Gn 37–50). Following this story of 'exile', the end of which is not entirely without hope, comes the Book of Exodus which relates the even greater miracle of the delivery from slavery: the delivery of the people of Israel in the service of the project of a 'Torah Republic'. Thus the 'first prophets', too, open the possibility, albeit with caution, of a new exodus and the reinstating of the 'Torah Republic'. This is not the narrative of the 'end of history': another world is possible!

The third section of the canon, the *Ketuvim* ('Writings'), also tells the story of the real Israel in the spirit of prophecy. According to 'historical' sequence, the books of Ezra and Nehemiah should follow Chronicles, because they deal with the period after exile. But in the canon these Chronicles specifically come at the end. The reason for this is that the renewed attempt at establishing a 'Torah Republic' quickly runs into trouble. It desperately fights off the pull of assimilation through strict isolation (Build a wall! No marriages with non-Jews!). Chronicles, on the other hand, finishes with the *kairos* that enables a fresh start for the project 'Israel':

> But in the first year of Cyrus, king of Persia,
>
> ...
>
> he raised Cyrus, the king of Persia's spirit
> and he [Cyrus] issued a call through his entire kingdom,
> in writing, too,
> [that said:]
> Thus has Cyrus, king of Persia spoken:
> YHWH, the God of heaven, has given me all the kingdoms of the earth,
> and it is he who told me to build him a house in Jerusalem, in Judah.
> Those of you who are of his people:
> YHWH your God be with you, you may set forth!
>
> > 2 Chr 36:22–23

This promising ending also constitutes the beginning of the Book of Ezra. The fact that it is reserved for the very end means that the vision of this *kairos* looks beyond the problematic fulfilment in the shape of the 'Torah Republic' in Ezra and Nehemiah's time. Prophetically speaking, history is never without the possibility of *kairos*!

In its writing of the history of the real Israel, prophetic historical narrative keeps the option of fulfilment open, but it never sugar-coats it. Bar any ideal-isation, the 'criminal history' of this Israel is related: how a completely ruined people cry for a king, 'as the other peoples have one', how the kings that the people then receive permanently disgrace their messianic calling (to be kings in the spirit of the Torah) and reveal themselves as common oriental despots. The only liberation story that the Bible knows is the real one, and the only theory of history that it employs is to pursue this history without any illusions.[2]

The Bible gives people who have lost their courage the courage to make their own history. But they make this history under conditions that they did not make and that are usually miserable. Those who refuse to believe this disregard reality and with it the chance to change this reality. Belief in the possibility for change is one thing, actually changing reality quite another, and the latter is impossible without knowledge of the real conditions.

New Beginnings and Regression

In the first of the books of the 'first prophets', *Joshua*, we can still see the enthusiasm of new beginnings. Joshua, the protagonist of the people's entry into the Promised Land, is still characterised by his similarity to Moses, the protagonist of the exodus: just as YHWH ('I will be there, as he who I will be there') 'was there' for Moses, so he 'will be there' for Joshua (Jo 1:5).

Joshua belongs to the 'old guard' of the exodus generation; he has experienced the exodus first-hand. He was there when Moses climbed Mount Sinai, where the Torah was handed over (Ex 24:13). Even then he was a functionary: Moses's *mashoret* – from *sharat*, 'to exercise an office' (very often this refers to priesthood) (Ex 24:13; 33:11; Nm 11:28; Jo 1:1). But he is also, like Moses, a spiritual man (Nm 27:18; Dt 34:9), not some *apparatchik*. He knows what it means to arrive from the desert in the land. To his eyes the significance of the NAME is immediately visible: YHWH liberates (Yoshu(y)a is a combination of *yasha'* = liberate, and *Yah* = an abbreviated version of YHWH)!

The Pesach Feast, celebrated during the exodus as the celebration of 'transition' from slavery into liberty, can now be celebrated as a harvest feast in the land, as a joyous confirmation of the 'transition' into the land where the Torah can receive 'arms and legs' (Jo 5:10–12). The land is appropriated with relative ease. The first city that is conquered, Jericho, does not fall because of the force of

---

2   That is, albeit perhaps too optimistically put, the Marxist understanding of communism: 'Communism is for us not a *state of affairs* which is to be established, an *ideal* to which reality [will] have to adjust itself. We call communism the *real* movement which abolishes the present state of things' (Marx and Engels 1975d, p. 49).

arms, but because of insistent demonstrations: once the people have circled the city seven times and the priests have let the shofar ring, the city wall collapses (Jo 6:20).

It is the same shofar that is blown to announce the jubilee, the general land reform (Lv 25:9–10). Could what happens to Jericho perhaps be translated in the following way: the permanent demonstration under the slogan 'all the land for the people', because all the land belongs to YHWH, who makes it available to the people not to the masters, simply floors the inhabitants of Jericho? Except that our joy is immediately tempered when we hear how Joshua commands that the city and all its inhabitants be 'banned', which means exposed to destruction (Jo 6:17). So while there is an intimation of the possibility of a non-violent strategy and the power of demonstration, when these do not appear to impress the inhabitants of Jericho, they are ruthlessly 'stabbed, smitten, slain'.[3] Thank God we have a prophetic book that relates Jonah's demonstrative appearance threatening Nineveh with destruction should its inhabitants not convert. This demonstration actually does lead to the conversion of Nineveh's inhabitants, which is why YHWH spares Nineveh. And this really irritates Jonah. For us, however, it should be a reminder to try the power of demonstration, and when that does not work and we find ourselves forced to resort to violence, at least never to stab and beat ruthlessly.

And then the time has come: the fulfilment of the promise that liberation movement and liberated land come together:

> YHWH gave Israel all the land that he had promised to their fathers,
> they inherited and settled in it,
> YHWH created peace for them on all sides, just as he had promised their
>   fathers,
> None of their enemies could withstand them,
> YHWH gave all their enemies into their hand
>
> Jo 21:43–44

Is it surprising that the people should enthusiastically agree with Joshua when he asks whether they really want to 'serve' the liberator-God and practice all that is written in the Torah (Jo 23:6; 24:15)? Three times they promise:

---

3   As Luther recommended the princes do against the rebelling peasants: 'Stab, smite, slay, whoever can. If you die in doing it, well for you! A more blessed death can never be yours, for you die obeying the divine Word and commandment in Romans XIII' ('Against the murderous, thieving hordes of peasants').

> We want to serve YHWH,
> We want to heed her voice
>> Jo 24:18–24a; Jo 24:24b

After all, they have seen with their own eyes that the impossible is possible: the slave turns master, the common people rule the state. All that is left now is to establish this state so that it can wither away as quickly as possible after it has paid its dues: to make room for the Kingdom of Freedom.

It is Joshua who, with a prophet's realism, curbs the enthusiasm. When the people say 'YHWH is our God, we want to serve him' for the first time, Joshua reacts with the harsh remark: 'you cannot serve YHWH' (Jo 24:19). To be sure, those who witnessed the miracle of the revolution for themselves, who experienced first-hand how the old world had to make way for a new world, may well manage to sustain their commitment to the project 'Israel'. But how will those fare, who only know of these golden days of revolution through hearsay, whose lives are determined by the 'travails of the plains', who find themselves on the 'long march through the institutions'?[4] At the close of the Book of Joshua, the following is said:

> Israel served YHWH all of Joshua's days
> and all the days of the elders, who survived Joshua,
> they, who *knew all YHWH's deeds* that he had done for Israel.
>> Jo 24:31

The next book, Judges, will cite this sentence one more time ('they served YHWH, [they] who had *seen* all YHWH's deeds that he had done for Israel'), and then adds:

> But when Joshua, Nun's son, YHWH's servant, had died
> ...
> and all the others of that generation had also joined their fathers,
> a new generation rose up, following them,
> who *did not know YHWH*,
> nor the deed he had done for Israel.
>> Jgs 2:8–10

---

4   One of the leftist leaders of the student movement in '68, Rudi Dutschke, coined the phrase 'der lange Marsch durch die Institutionen' with reference to Mao Zedong.

And the first story that is told of this post-revolutionary generation is that they did something 'radically evil' in the eyes of the Liberator-God:

> they served the baals,
> they abandoned YHWH, the God of the fathers, who had brought them out of Egypt,
> they followed other gods, from amongst the gods of the peoples who surrounded them,
> they bowed down before them and angered YHWH
>
> Jgs 2:11–12

This is the beginning of the end: the liberation movement adopts its enemies' ideology, which excludes liberation *a priori*. After all, the 'gods' represent the ideology of the rulers that pronounces the rule of these rulers as the beginning and end of all wisdom. Those who believe this are lost to the practice of Torah: their practice conforms to the theory by which they have been fooled.

Marx was right: 'criticism of religion is the premise of all criticism'.[5] Only he was wrong when he said: 'For Germany is the *criticism of religion* in the main complete'.[6] For neither in Germany nor anywhere else is religion a thing of the past. It flowers in the power of the many ideologies that 'deify' the 'secular' – these days perhaps most impressively 'the' economy whose critique was and is Marx's great achievement: capitalism. The radical critique of religion: you shall have no gods beside me, is the abiding condition of this critique. For as radically as this God in heaven kills off all gods, so radically are we told to do the same on earth!

What is only mentioned in passing in the Book of Joshua turns out to be a major problem in the Book of Judges: the land is not completely 'liberated' (Jo 13:13; 15:63; 16:10; 17:12). The key word in the first chapter of the Book of Judges is 'they did not disinherit' (11 times!). Thus the following is impressed upon us: Israel has *not* completely banished the peoples of the land. Apparently, this 'disinheriting' is not a done deal; rather it is a process that Israel is called upon to complete. Whether this process actually proceeds depends on Israel's loyalty to the Torah (Jo 23:13). This is not, in the first instance, a military matter, but an ideological one: the process stops when the people break the covenant, when they do not heed YHWH's voice (Jgs 2:20–21). Israel must fight the ideological battle in order to be able to withstand its enemies.

---

5   Marx 1975b, p. 175.
6   Ibid.

The fulfilment articulated in Jo 21:43 (YHWH gave Israel all the land) does not contradict the fact that the peoples already in the land were not completely 'disinherited'.
This contradiction is connected to the fact that the Bible, when it concerns the fulfilment of the promise, wants to express two things: (1) The (hi)story of the liberation movement does not stay unfulfilled; (2) In turn, fulfilment is unthinkable unless
Israel fulfils the covenant by doing Torah ('should you turn your backs [on YHWH] ...
know for sure that YHWH will not continue to disinherit these peoples before you',
Jo 23:12–13). For YHWH does not want to be 'God' without his people. Only when
God the liberator and the liberated human have finally found each other does the
(hi)story of struggle come to an end and does the story of the Kingdom of Freedom
begin.

Failed Attempts at Self-Organisation Free from Domination

The first part of the Book of Judges (Chapters 1–16) narrates how the real Israel is
constantly embroiled in a desperate fight for self-assertion against its enemies,
the peoples that 'surround them'. There can be no talk here of an attempt
to do Torah – Judges is the only book in the 'first prophets' that does not
once mention the word 'Torah'. The fact that the people exist at all is owed to
'liberators', who 'arise' from time to time – a sign that God the liberator has not
entirely forsaken his people.

'Judges' repeats the beginning of Exodus, as it were: the people are enslaved, they
'cry' out and YHWH lets 'a liberator rise' for them (Jgs 3:9, 15). The difference is that
here the people were gone astray and it is YHWH himself who 'sells [them] to the
enemies who surround them' (Jgs 2:14). But YHWH cannot hear the cry of the slaves
without wanting to liberate them. He is moved by their misery, not by their high
morals. Even their moral misery does not keep him from declaring their cause –
and hence themselves – just. His justice is constituted by the justification of the
godless.

These liberators are given the name 'Judges'. Though they do 'judge', too, most of
what is said about them concerns their liberation of the people from slavery. In
light of the general immiseration, their appearance is a miracle. They all belong
to the 'underclass', to those people who are normally the last: the youngest son
(Otniel, Jgs 3:9), a physically disabled man (Ehud, Jgs 3:15), a woman (Deborah,
Jgs 4:4), a member of the poorest clan of his tribe (Gideon, Jgs 6:15), the son of a
prostitute (Jephthah, Jgs 11:1). These unlikely types have been chosen to be the
liberators of the people.

Perhaps the unlikeliest of them all is the last 'judge', Samson (Jgs 13–16): his mother 'infertile' (Jgs 13:2), his birth practically impossible – the story remains silent regarding the fact that his father sired him.

Even in their role as the representatives of the 'other Israel', while some of them appear to be the exceptions that prove the rule of the ruin of all previous liberation movements, they simultaneously sustain the hope for the future success of liberation. One such exception is Deborah, who calls upon Barak to lead the people in their fight for liberation, but simultaneously prevents him from being the great victor himself: the woman leads the way, the man follows and war in the fashion of men is limited. For Deborah says to him:

> I will go with you,
> but the fame will not be yours on the path that you follow,
> for YHWH will deliver Sisera [the enemy commander] into the hands of
>   a woman.
>
>> Jgs 4:9

It is Yael, a woman who brings down the leader of the enemies. Deborah commemorates her deed in a song – and Barak joins in – when she speaks of the 'Days of Yael' as the time when her own 'rising' also takes place (Jgs 5:6–7). What is usually written as 'men's history', in Israel, too ('It happened in the days ...' and this is followed by the name of a man), is here – unusually, but still – serenaded as 'women's history'.

And then there is Gideon, the judge who refuses to be crowned king. What makes the project 'Israel' distinctive, after all, is being a radically democratic project, not to need a king 'like the other peoples' to keep the order – an order that will inevitably be one of oppression. Only the NAME, who liberates slaves and commands them to serve no 'other master', will rule in the real Israel. This is what Gideon reminds the people of, when they ask him:

> Rule over us, you and your son, and your son's son,
> for you have liberated us from the hand of Midian
>
>> Jgs 8:22

His refusal is the avowal:

> I will not rule over you,
> my son shall not rule over you,
> YHWH shall rule over you!
>> Jgs 8:23

The judge and liberator is only a transitional figure. It is the NAME who liberates. And it is his people who are called upon to 'serve' this liberation by really existing as a liberated and liberating people themselves. Gideon safeguards Israel from forsaking its grassroots democratic constitution.

Gideon's – not coincidentally youngest – son Jotham gets to the heart of the anti-monarchic tendency of the first part of the Book of Judges. When his brother Abimelech (the name means 'my father is king')[7] sets himself up as king, he tells the fable of the trees that wanted to elect a king (Jgs 9:7–15). The crop plants, olive tree, fig tree, grapevine, reject their election, only the completely useless buckthorn accepts it – and then immediately threatens everyone who will not vote for him with destruction. The uselessness and destructiveness of kingship – of the state – can hardly be criticised any more crushingly than in this fable. Those who think this critique exaggerated must at least ask themselves: who does the state benefit – and at whose cost?

In the long run, however, the project 'Israel' cannot be maintained in its grassroots democratic shape. In the second part of the Book of Judges (Chapters 17–21), the following phrase is repeated: 'In those days there was no king in Israel' (Jgs 17:6; 18:1; 19:1; 21:25 – the closing sentence), when 'everyone did what they deemed just' (Jgs 17:6). The reason to change this is not the necessity for a strong man who can lead Israel in the fight against their enemies. The reason is the ruination on the inside, the total anarchy of the real Israel itself: the real Israel has turned into a complete caricature of the project 'Israel'. In Chapter 18, the tribe of Dan abuses the NAME in order to attack a people which lives as Israel wants to live, 'quietly and without worry' (Jgs 18:7). It is Dan's entry into the land, a bitter parody of the entry into the Promised Land which the Book of Yoshua narrates. In Chapter 19, hospitality is kicked with feet by the tribe of Benjamin in the middle of Israel. The victim is a woman. This triggers a fratricidal war against Benjamin in Chapter 20. The project 'Israel' has failed. The core of the project, the erection of a society of freedom, equality and solidarity (cf. Chapter 7), is destroyed.

---

7 Gideon has given him this name. His rejection of kingship was not all that obvious after all!

This fratricidal war is the disfigurement of the saying 'How good it is when brothers live together' (Ps 133:1). This 'good' is the opposite of the radically evil being alone and being apart. For: 'It is not good for the human to be alone' (Gn 2:18). That is the point of the good creation: humanity finally turned social.

The implied solution, though, is highly problematic. For where there is no king, the demand for the strong state appears before you know it. And the strong state would definitively end the project. But the sentence, 'In those days there was no king in Israel', is ambiguous. What is really missing? A king like the other peoples have? Could it not also be referring to the 'King' who abolishes all kingship: YHWH, the NAME, who delivers from slavery (May YHWH be your king for ever and ever! – Ex 15:18)? Or is the Book of Judges thinking of the impossible possibility (envisaged by the Torah (Dt 17)), of a kingship characterised by its *Aufhebung* [sublation]? A state determined to wither away happily? Judges remains open-ended.

It also remains open because Israel cares about the failure of its project. One key word in the Book of Judges is 'to cry'. It is the people's first as well as final reaction to what they themselves have brought about (Jgs 2:4; 21:2 – here it is intensified: 'a great crying'). They also cry once the fratricidal war has broken out (Jgs 20:23, 26). They are crying for the loss of what they were called upon to realise, all-encompassing brotherhood: 'Why, YHWH, God of Israel, did this have to happen in Israel that today a tribe is missed from Israel?' (Jgs 21:3). So long as the real Israel does not stop crying, there is still hope.

The Trap of a 'Solution' through Power Structures

The remaining books in the 'first prophets' (1 and 2 Samuel, 1 and 2 Kings) tell stories of kings. They do not, however, tell the common story that simply derives the necessity of the state, which ensures order from above because the people below are incapable, from the anarchy of everyone fighting everyone.

This is how Thomas Hobbes (1588–1679) imagined the state: because people are naturally inclined to compete with each other (everyone fighting everyone is the principle of all history), the solution is to transfer all power to one strong, authoritative state. For him, it was 'unnatural', and hence unimaginable, that people should rule themselves. His theory fit well into a time when capitalism still had to establish itself and so could only be implemented through force from above. But capitalism is itself based on the principle of general competition, which is why it will keep provoking the call for a strong state even when it has established itself. The Hobbesian state is not the solution to but rather the consequence of social anarchy.

The great alternative to this political theory, which declares the project of a society free of domination 'unthinkable' on principle, is Jean-Jacques Rousseau's (1712–78) concept of the state. He argues that humans are free and equal by nature and that the state of general competition only emerged as a consequence of the development of private property. His solution is the *'contrât social'*, the 'social contract', whereby humans freely organise themselves into a body politic led by the general interest. This state based on the 'social contract' could be read as the 'translation' of the project 'Israel' based on the Torah into the language of modernity. It is true, biblical theology is unfamiliar with the 'state of nature' where the human, purportedly, was free and equal. Its story of the 'beginning' is a story of liberation and presumes a state of domination and oppression (the *Tohuwabohu* of the dominant order). Can Rousseau's speculation on human nature as essentially free and equal not also be read as an avowal: against the empiricism of the prevailing fight of everyone against everyone that Hobbes's theory renders so plausible? The difference between the Bible and Rousseau is above all the fact that in the Bible the social contract (the 'covenant') presumes 'God's great revolution', while the revolution has yet to take place for Rousseau. However, without this revolution the state Rousseau hoped for is a fiction that needs the dominant order to distract from its asocial reality.

This authoritarian state is a state like the other peoples have. From the moment the people of Israel tire of their Torah-less anarchy, this state is defined without any illusions:

> This will be the right of the king, who will reign over you:
> he will *take* your sons,
> so as to divide them between the chariots and the horses,
> so that they run in front of his chariots,
> and so that they can be appointed as commanders of thousands and
>   commanders of fifty-thousands, –
> and in order to plough his fields,
> to harvest his crops,
> to make his weapons of war and his vehicles.
> And to *take* your daughters
> as makers of balms, as cooks, as bakers.
> He will *take* your fields, your vineyards, your olive groves, the best of
>   them,
> and give them to his servants,
> he will seize a tenth of your seed and of your vineyards

and give it to his courtiers and his servants,
and he will *take* your servants and your maidservants, your young men,
    the best of them, and your donkeys and use them for his business,
he will take a tenth of your small domestic animals,
and you yourselves will be his slaves.
    1Sm 8:11–17

The fact that this king will at least ensure order is not even mentioned once. Israel is only meant to know at what cost this order will come.

Antithesis: The Messianic King

But this 'law-and-order'-state is not the only state. In the prologue of First Samuel, Hannah sings her song of the 'messianic king'. It is the song that the oppressed cannot but sing because their longing forces them to hope for a king who will be 'different'. A king in the spirit of the 'different' God who 'sets upright from dust the small man, who raises the poor man from the dirt' (1Sm 2:8). Hannah sings for them all:

YHWH
judges the ends of the earth
that it grant victory to *his king*,
exalt the horn of *his anointed one*.
    1Sm 2:10

The king in the spirit of YHWH, who, like YHWH, uses his power to empower the people to become a society without domination. The Messiah!

'Anointed one' (Hebrew: *mashiach*) is the name given, in the context of kings, only to this king, chosen by YHWH to 'reign' over Israel in his spirit – with one exception: Cyrus, the Persian ruler, who enables the return from exile into the land, the opportunity for a fresh start (Is 45:1: Thus YHWH said to Cyrus, his *anointed one*). This is not simply a matter of finding a different word for 'king'; it refers to a distinctive king. A theology fixated on the opposition between the Israel 'of the Old Testament' and the 'Christian' (Greek for 'messianic') church has emphasised the discontinuity between Judaism's 'national-political' notion of the Messiah and its own 'non-political' Messiah. But the Messiah of the 'Old Testament' is no more simply political than the Messiah of the 'New Testament' is simply non-political. The continuity lies precisely in the fact that the Messiah 'of the Old Testament' embodies the hope – albeit repeatedly disappointed – for the Messiah, whose rule will sublate (*aufheben*) itself into a society free of domination. It is a matter of the extraordinarily political abolition of *all* domination.

The messianic king is not simply a utopian figure in the books of the 'first prophets'. He really exists! In the continuum of the chronology, in the *perpetuum mobile* of the eternal yesterday, there are also moments of 'now time', 'shot through with splinters of messianic time' (Benjamin).[8] This really exists: a king, who is not only of lowly heritage, but who also stands by the disgraced, who rules to serve them. The story of the choosing of David is told: in excess (the eighth son when seven are considered a complete set), the 'rest', the 'youngest', who is easily overlooked in the play of power (1Sm 16:11). He is the king who is heavily criticised by his wife, the princess Michal, when in the midst of his people he dances for joy at the return of the 'ark' with the Torah:

> How has the King of Israel honoured himself today,
> who exposed himself to the eyes of his female slaves and his male slaves,
> like the lowly exposes himself.
>> 2 Sm 6:20

To which he gives a response that will forever impress him on the collective memory of the Bible as a messianic king:

> Before YHWH,
> who has chosen me ...
> to appoint me as lord over YHWH's people, over Israel,
> I want to dance before YHWH,
> want to make myself even lowlier than this time,
> want to be lowly in my own eyes,
> and yet still be honoured
> by those female slaves you spoke of.
>> 2 Sm 6:21–22

To this un-kingly king, this Messiah of the lowly, whose only honour resides in 'being honoured by the female slaves', the promise is made that his kingdom will last 'forever':

---

8   Benjamin 2003, p. 397.

> Your house and your kingdom will endure forever
> And your throne is certain for ever.
>
> 2 Sm 7:16

This is a matter of the future. Not in the sense of a simple continuation of the *status quo* David consolidated. The promise is articulated after David has been explicitly forbidden to build YHWH a 'house' – as though the NAME were ready to conclusively 'consolidate'; as though the coming together of God the liberator and the liberated human had been fulfilled. Its fulfilment will be the 'son's' task:

> When your days have been fulfilled
> and you lay down with your fathers,
> then I will let your descendant rise after you
>
> ...
>
> and will consolidate his kingdom, –
> he will build a house for my NAME,
> but I will consolidate the throne of his kingdom forever,
> I will be his father and he will be my son
>
> 2 Sm 7:12–14

David is the Messiah, but he does not fulfil the expectations that relate to him. These are projected on to the son who really will lead the history of the project 'Israel' to its goal: the human in God's image, finally the successful process of the human being becoming-human. The 'son of David' who makes good the NAME's promise: to be the 'son of the father'.

David is not the first Messiah, though; Saul is. He is the Messiah who is *rejected* by YHWH (1 Sm 15:26). But what is it that is so reprehensible about him? Does he lack the ability to persevere, even in a despairing situation (1 Sm 13)? Is it that even after the victory over Amalek he 'spares' the king 'and all that is best' but 'bans', so kills, the 'despised and the damned' (1 Sm 15)? This really does disqualify him from being king in the spirit of YHWH. But does this also make him a bad king from the people's perspective? All in all, he is not a tyrant, after all, but a liberator – who will die in battle for and with his people. And no story is known of him that tells how he sends a loyal fellow soldier to his death in order to enrich his harem with his wife. That is the story of David (and Bathsheba: 2 Sm 11–12). Who is more despicable now?

The difference between David and Saul is not one of simple good and evil. They are both messianic figures. Saul is a messianic figure because his life demonstrates the impossibility of being in power and being a messianic king. David is one because this impossible possibility turns reality. David recognises this, too. To him, Saul remains 'YHWH's Messiah' to the end (2 Sm 1: 14–16).

David's successor is Solomon, the 'King of Peace' (his name promises *shalom*). He really does seem to be the son who fulfils the promise. No more war; *shalom*, peace, for which the people have hoped for so long, finally prevails:

> Peace was all around
> Judah and Israel lived in safety,
> every man beneath his grape vine,
> every woman beneath her fig tree
> > 1 Kgs 5:5

Israel is no longer the plaything of the peoples:

> Solomon reigned over all kingdoms
> from the stream Euphrates to the land of the Philistines and to the
> > borders of Egypt
> > 1 Kgs 5:1

Solomon is characterised by 'wisdom' – and what else could this be than the wisdom that is grounded in the 'fear of YHWH', in watching out for his Torah that is the beginning of all wisdom? This wisdom is said to be greater than 'the wisdom of all the people of the East and of all of Egypt's wisdom' (1 Kgs 5:10). It is recognised as greater by all the peoples, too:

> men came from all the peoples,
> to hear Solomon's wisdom,
> from all the kingdoms of the earth
> > 1 Kgs 5:14

What more could anyone wish for? Is this not when the utopia (the non-place) of the project 'Israel' finds its 'topos', its place? This is what Solomon thinks, at least. He plans to

> build a house in the NAME of my God,
> as YHWH said to my father David:
> your son, who I will place on the throne in your place,
> he will build the house in my name
> > 1 Kgs 5:19

This is fabulous. But is it not too good to be true? Can such an ideal world really exist amidst the wrong one?[9] Or is this nothing but a dream? Like Solomon's own dream, where YHWH asks him what he wants and Solomon replies in messianic spirit:

> give your servant a sensitive heart
> with which to teach your people
> to separate good from evil
>   1 Kgs 3:9

Real Rulers in Contradiction to the Messianic Expectation

This is really quite fantastic: a king who dreams not of power, but of justice. But this fantastic narrative ultimately serves mainly the clarification of one thing in prophetic historiography: this fabulous king, who, elevated above all toil and all pain, enjoys peace, is not the Messiah, is not 'son of the father' whom the people are expecting. On the contrary, he does precisely what should not be done according to the king's Torah (Dt 17:15–20): never to have enough horses (military power), women (the harem as a symbol of royal grandeur), silver and gold. Thus, his kingship is the first in a long line of kings who 'do what is evil in the eyes of YHWH' (1 Kgs 11:6) – until it cannot continue and the real Israel is scattered among the peoples. His realm breaks down. Henceforth, there are two realms: Judah and Israel, and the Israel of ten tribes will eventually be lost irretrievably.

But Israel is never given up for lost! Its absence is felt (cf. Jgs 21:3 and think also of Jer 31:15: Rachael, mother of Joseph = Israel and of Benjamin = part of Judah, cries for her children and will not be consoled) and hope is never given up. The 'people's' apostle Paul, in particular, holds out hope: *all* of Israel will be saved (Rom 11:26). Here speaks the obstinate hope of the Jew (let us never forget that Paul is a Jew) who persistently refuses to settle for the possibility that even one person might be lost.

Solomon will not go down in history as the 'son of David' (he is never called that in the Book of Kings, either). The promise to David, that the kingdom of the

---

9 'Wrong life cannot be lived rightly' (Adorno 1978, p. 39). This apodictic statement did not prevent him from persistently criticising the 'wrong life' – with the desperate hope for the right one.

'descendant after him' will be *forever*, is not the sanctioning of a dynasty. The promise founds the expectation: the Messiah is coming![10] At the same time, though, this promise remains linked to the name of David: the Messiah will benefit his people, the real Israel – not some abstraction.

In his novel *The King David Report*,[11] the GDR author Stefan Heym seems to have read this king's story, as the Bible tells it, as the legitimisation of a dynasty. A 'scribe' is given the task to revise what really happened in such a way that the dynasty of David is established for all times. It is a *roman à clef*: what is meant is the Stalinist writing of history that was aimed at 'perpetuating' real socialism and thus suppress all (self!-)critique that might have been able to save socialism.

Michel Clévenot's 'materialist Bible reading' reads the story of David's succession by Solomon as an 'ideological production, having for its purpose the religious legitimizing of the Solomon power', 'a beautiful story of a series of divine promises fulfilled by the coming to power of Solomon'.[12]

Prophetic historiography, however, legitimises nothing at all. It relates, relentlessly, what happens. Clévenot's 'beautiful story' is more likely to be the 'pre-history' that was critically revised by prophetic historiography (Kings). The promise is also only given a single time in the form of a pure indicative – without any ifs and buts – and that is to David (2Sm 7:16). All other kings are given an imperative: your kingdom will last forever, *if* you 'keep' the Torah (beginning with Solomon: 1Kgs 2:3–4).

The rest of the story of kings is primarily a story of disappointed hope: the kings come and go, but the majority do not follow YHWH's path. Nor does the real Israel, when it turns into a state, solve the problem of general anarchy, which has made the people long for a king. Those who have always thought that a 'Torah'-state was a contradiction in terms are vindicated. But then the story takes an unexpected turn: a king accedes, Josiah, who 'discovers' the Torah (2Kgs 22:8–11).

---

10   The 'Psalm of Kings' is devoted to Solomon (72:1), but the king who is asked for 'far exceeds Solomon ... There is no historical king who creates this level of justice ... no supreme ruler who is so uncorrupted that he could be compared to a field of grain, with green grass, with shiny fruit, with everything that is good and wholesome [72:16]' (Barnard 2004, p. 127). Not that the desire is put off until the day the cows come home: the Messiah does not silence the longing for deliverance, but arouses it.

11   Heym 1973 (*Der König David Bericht*; published in West Germany in 1972, later also in the GDR, 1981).

12   Clévenot 1985, pp. 19 f.

Or more precisely: the Torah *is* discovered, in 'YHWH's house', which meanwhile is in dire need of repair. A story of decay seems to take a turn for the better once more.

Josiah executes a radical 'reconstruction': all that is foreign ideology is discarded – nearly an entire chapter tells of the 'discarding', 'burning', 'dismissing', 'razing to the ground', 'disposing', 'slaughtering', 'eradicating' of the idols (2 Kgs 23:4–20). Then he commands the people to celebrate Pesach for the first time since Joshua (2 Kgs 23:21–22)! There, it signified the 'transition' into the Promised Land; here it could signify the 'transition' into breaking new ground, into the 'Torah Republic' that has never really existed in the real Israel. But it is too late:

> no king before him was like to him,
> who thus turned towards YHWH with all his heart, with his soul, with all
>   his might, [the sch'ma Israel!][13]
> entirely like the Torah of Moses,
> and after him nobody rose up, who was like him
> *Nevertheless*, YHWH did not turn back from the great flame of his wrath
>   2 Kgs 23:25–26

Likewise, Gorbachev the reformist also had to realise that his 'perestroika' [*reconstruction*] came too late. And he knew that those who are too late will be punished by life itself.

The Hope of Turning Back

After Josiah all that is left is the inevitable downfall. Israel has already been deported by the Assyrians, now the king of Babel does the same with Judah. End of story? No, end of one story.[14] For:

> King of Babel, Evilmerodach
> lifted the head of Jehoiachin of Judah from the dungeon house
>   2 Kgs 25:27

---

13   'So love then YHWH your God with all your heart, with all your soul, with all your might' (Dt 6:5).

14   Thus Ton Veerkamp qualifies the victory of the global marketplace: 'The end of history? No, the end of *one* history' (2005, p. 183).

Could not this 'lifting' – from the dungeon house! – be the intimation of an 'entirely different' lifting, that from the house of slavery? The premonition of a new exodus?

Of course, the question can be asked – prophetic historiography aside – whether a 'Torah Republic' is possible at all in *one* land in the midst of a 'wrong world'. Did not even the project of 'socialism in one land', which unlike the real Israel turned into a 'super power', fail? And not only because of its internal corruption, but also because international circumstances unfortunately mean 'it cannot be so'. Is revolution, in the age of 'globalisation', where capitalism has become omnipresent and impalpable, not imaginable, if at all, only as a world revolution?[15]

The 'second prophets', however, pin their hopes on a 'return' (Hebrew *teshuvah*, from *shuv*: to return, to turn around) to the Promised Land. It is a matter of a radical fresh start: the return should also be a turning around. The expectation is of new people whose circumcision (the sign that they are fundamentally different from the 'peoples') will be a 'circumcision of the *hearts*' (Jer 4:4). Finally the revolution's subject is a truly revolutionary subject. 'Heaven and earth' (Is 65:17) are renewed because what has never happened before will happen: YHWH, God the liberator's will as it is in heaven, so also on earth. This fresh start, however, will yet again attempt to demonstrate in one land that a different world is possible. For one day the peoples will catch sight of the real Israel as the 'light of the Goy' (Is 42:6; 49:6), and an Internationale will develop around it which, together with Israel, will fight for human rights.[16]

Pure illusion? The prophets announce that the precondition for this return is that YHWH turns around. He must create new conditions, conditions that have never existed in the same way before. Who can predict what kinds of conditions these will be? 'In itself' the hope for world revolution is just as fantastical as the 'second prophets' hope for a *kairos* that once more offers the opportunity to attempt the project of the delivery

---

15   Rudolf Bultman actually concludes the following from the failure of the project 'Israel': 'the idea of the rule of God is shown to be unrealizable within this world' (1963, p. 73). The 'idea of a covenant of God with a people' is thus also obsolete – except as 'an eschatological idea' (ibid.) He is certain: 'the new covenant is a radically eschatological dimension, that is [sic!] a dimension outside the world' (Bultmann 1963, p. 63). Israel's belief is more radical than this. It sticks to the notion: YHWH's will be done as it is in heaven so on earth!

16   Isaiah has YHWH call this out to the 'nations', too: 'Turn towards me and be liberated' (Is 45:22). This call 'is by no means only of religious significance ... but it is for the same nations, subjugated by Babylon and other ruthless powers, to turn to YHVH, Who wills to bring them into liberty in the great future historical hour' (Buber 1949, p. 215). The peoples: these are not only the enemy powers who mortally threaten the project 'Israel', but also those oppressed by these powers, who hunger and thirst for justice with Israel.

from slavery in *one* land. Those who hope have to be prepared for surprises: the spirit of the liberation blows wherever it pleases (Jn 3:8). World revolution, too, can become an obsession that blinds us towards the *kairos*. For instance, this *kairos* could happen somewhere in Latin America, and the question is then whether we'd even want to see it.

A 'Christian' theology that contends that its Christ has finally overcome such 'national political' boundaries, that the catholic, that is to say the general church, is the 'true Israel', overlooks the fact that the church developed in a specific, not necessarily repeatable, situation. The church, or more specifically, the messianic community, has its 'seat in life' in a very particular *kairos*. Jews and Goy avowed together: Jesus, not the emperor, is *kyrios* (the term for his royal highness the emperor, but also the intimation of the anti-emperor NAME). They organised themselves as a commune free from domination in the spirit of unbounded solidarity. Paul, the movement's strategist, thought that this organisation of communes was the only possible path in the Imperium Romanum: in view of the power of this Imperium, a 'national political' separate path was inconceivable. Perhaps that this is also our present situation. The 'Empire' (Negri/Hardt) really does give the impression of not permitting any place anywhere for trialling an alternative social formation. It has no notion of 'outside' and hence, at best, can only be subverted from within: the Pauline strategy. The concept of the 'community', however, cannot be played off against the possibility of a real, communally organised state. Neither should the one be *aufgehoben* [sublated] by the other. Church and state, more specifically, messianic community and 'Torah Republic', need to be separate, like 'two paths' that are not abolished *aufgehoben* [sublated] until the 'civitas Dei', God's Realm: God all in all.

The relation between these 'two paths' has to be clearly distinguished from the relation between the two 'empires' in Luther's so-called 'two kingdoms doctrine'. According to this teaching, Christians are allowed (if not indeed commanded) to see Christianity as something purely private and separate from their political existence. In politics, the Christian follows the laws of the ruling class, is a subject of the superiors placed above him or complies with the free play of social forces – and in one way or another he conforms to the respective 'mainstream' (Rom 12:2). As a private person, he is a sincere man who does no harm to anybody. The two paths – that of the Christian and that of the citizen – are wide apart here. This results in a tragic contradiction: the assumption that Christian and citizen will ever go together is hopeless. It is an entirely different matter for the community and the 'Torah Republic', the field of a politics of liberation. Both take place in the world that has not yet been redeemed. 'By divine appointment [the 'Torah Republic' has] the task of providing for justice and peace ... by means of the threat and exercise of force according to the measure of human judgment and human ability'.[17] It is doing battle in the old world for a new one. It is the community's task to represent the new world in the old, to demonstrate the right life in the wrong one. As such, it is also the critique of the use and threat of force without which a politics of liberation cannot make do. As the 'already' of a society free of domination, the community emphasises this society's 'not yet' even in the realm of its best politics. The 'right state', in particular, accepts this critique. The two have a strategic alliance. They are both intent on unhinging the old world and helping the new one break through.

---

17   According to the fifth statement of the Barmen Theological Declaration (1934) directed against the National Socialist state of injustice. To take this statement to be referring to our contemporary state of law is premature. Does it really provide justice and peace?

Paul and the Messianic Community

Paul was a Communist

That sounds more like a tasteless provocation than something that could help to explain what he was. Communism, after all, represents a rule of terror that disposed of millions of people on the ash-heap of history; it represents the complete perversion of the idea of general equality for which it stood.

But did the movement initiated by Paul fare any differently? Is Christianity not also a continuous 'criminal history', during which anybody who strayed from the 'right faith' (not least the Jews) was at risk of his or her life?[1] Tortured, murdered in the name of Christ, who for Paul was the realisation of the humanity of God the liberator? If we try to translate Paul's project into the language of today, though, communism lends itself to the task: as the belief in the possibility of a world that is completely different from the one that is real, as the practical recognition that this new world cannot be found in castles in the air, but can be found in the old world as the active hope for the *kairos*, where a 'novelty' occurs suddenly and surprisingly and has to be seized with courage. In modernity, only communism has dared this kind of radicalness, hence it alone corresponds to the 'early Christianity' conceived by Paul, which was still entirely messianic and not at all 'Christian'. Only if we understand the difficulties of communism can we understand the difficulties of the Pauline concept: its precariousness, its 'impossibility', the threat of its perversion into its totalitarian opposite. Those who read Paul purely as a 'dogmatist' are doubtlessly immune to the 'temptation' of engaging in the society propagated by Paul, a society where all have all together, a communist society. Those who read in that way do not know any better than to think that such engagement has nothing to do with their faith. But they are mistaken. If we take Paul as the founder of Christianity, then we cannot withdraw from his engagement. For better or worse, we will be communists, letting ourselves be led forth from Christianity into an extraordinarily questionable movement, one which barely even still exists at the moment, but which might recur at any time. For 'in it [the future] every second was the narrow gate,

---

1   Church critic Karlheinz Deschner's *Christianity's Criminal History* (8 volumes so far, 1986–2004), describes in great detail the transgressions of which the different Christian Churches, confessions, sects and their representatives, as well as the Christian rulers throughout the history of Christianity, are accused.

through which the Messiah could enter' (Benjamin).[2] Except, the question will be: will he find faith on earth (Lk 18:8)?

Currently, Paul is experiencing a renaissance as a 'Leninist'. In his book on Paul, Alain Badiou (1997) explains Paul's topicality with the observation that 'there is currently a widespread search for a new militant figure ... called upon to succeed the one installed by Lenin and the Bolsheviks at the beginning of the century, which can be said to have been that of the party militant'.[3] And in his book on Paul, Daniel Boyarin (1994), a Talmud scholar, writes that Paul's expression, 'There is no Jew nor Greek', reminds him of a phrase taken from Hillel Kempinsky, archivist of the 'Bund' in New York:[4] 'Paul was the first Bolshevik'.[5] But the association of Paul with Lenin can already be found in the first version of Karl Barth's *The Epistle to the Romans* (published in German in 1919). Barth refers to Lenin's *The State and Revolution* (1917) to show that *The Epistle to the Romans* is concerned with 'more than Leninism'.[6] But this 'more than' is an outbidding of the radicalness of Leninism and not its dismissal on account of being too radical. *The State and Revolution* is definitely radical: the state is not the end of all historical wisdom but its 'withering away' when 'the *necessity* of observing the simple, fundamental rules of the community will very soon become a *habit*'.[7] This is the 'great structural parallelism': the 'virtually religious veneration of the state which was to be superseded and replaced through revolution' that both Lenin and Paul 'fought against' (Marquardt).[8] In this context, the 'more than' does not mean that in Paul's framework the problem of 'the state and revolution' is only solved in the beyond: 'Your [the messianic community's] state is in heaven (Phil 3:20)'; but it does mean: 'He bursts forth from God and through God's strength with the aim not to improve the existing state, but to *replace* it; to *supersede* the power of injustice above and below with the power of justice'.[9] For Lenin, the prerequisite for the 'withering away' of the state is the socialist state, which can only come about through violent revolution. For Paul, the prerequisite for this 'withering away' is the messianic community, which is not

---

2   Benjamin 2003, p. 397.
3   Badiou 2003, p. 2. Similarly Žižek: 'there is no Christ outside Saint Paul in exactly the same way, there is no "authentic Marx" that can be approached directly, bypassing Lenin' (2000, p. 2).
4   The General Jewish Labour Bund, founded in 1897, was an autonomous Jewish workers' organisation in what was at the time Russian Poland, Lithuania and Belarus.
5   Boyarin 1997, p. 228.
6   Barth 1985, p. 506.
7   Lenin 1960, p. 474.
8   Marquardt 1972, p. 129.
9   Barth 1985, pp. 503 f.

founded on violent revolution, but in demonstrating an alternative practice, a practice of limitless solidarity. Whether the socialist state, sustained by a communist party, and the messianic community, in other words, Lenin and Paul are mutually exclusive, is a different chapter.[10]

So Paul was a communist. More precisely: he turned communist, because he experienced Jews and Goy coming together in a commune in which the differences were free of hierarchy:

> there is neither Jew nor Greek,
> there is neither slave nor freeman,
> there is neither 'male and female',
> for you are all one
> in Jesus the Messiah.
>> Gal 3:28

In Jesus the Messiah! For he embodies limitless solidarity; in biblical language: 'has become flesh'. In him, both Jews and Goy together recognised the becoming flesh of the word of deliverance, through which the NAME led his people out of slavery and onto the path towards the Promised Land, where all have all together. In him, the human in the image of God the liberator, who fulfilled the Torah, has finally come to light; who fulfilled the Torah by doing it. To them, he was the Messiah because he liberated them from the fatal thought that humans were not at all suitable for such a society based on solidarity; that humans were condemned to move within the fatal cycle of mastery and slavery for ever and ever.

Creatio ex nihilo

This creation was an absolute miracle, a *creatio ex nihilo*.[11] For that was Paul's nihilistic foundational experience: that everything he had hoped for as a Jew had petered out into 'nothingness'. Nothing had come of the promise that the Goy should recognise the experiment of the 'Torah Republic' as their light. Surely they should have recognised the deeds of God the liberator. For it had

---

10   See Chapter 8, at the end.

11   'Resurrection ... is pure event, opening of an epoch, transformation of the relations between the possible and the impossible' (Badiou 2003, p. 43).

become thoroughly visible how the NAME delivered a people from slavery, how these people actually started to build a society without domination, how they insisted that a world different from the prevailing one was possible, even if the attempt at actualising it had failed for the time being. The Torah was written not in a secret code, but in a language that could be translated: the Hebrew Bible into Greek (the Septuagint). Everywhere in the Roman Empire, where Paul lived, there were synagogues.[12] What happened there happened publicly. The notion 'we did not know' is inapplicable here; only God the liberator's anger at this guilty blindness holds true, for:

> God's rage unfolds from heaven
> against all godlessness and injustice of humans,[13]
> who suppress the truth with injustice.
> For what is knowable of God is overt to them.
> For God has revealed it to them.
> His invisible aspects have been seen
> in his deeds since the creation of the world:
> namely his enduring strength and divinity.
>   Rom 1:18–20

The word 'deeds' (Greek: *poièmata*, from *poiein* = to do/to make) is crucial for the correct interpretation of this text. This is not 'God in nature'. It hardly offers an obviously joy-inducing sight, either. Nature is sublime, it is terribly sublime, but it does not proclaim the Gospel of the delivery from slavery. This is not the occasion for a 'natural theology' that can found a 'gay science' (Nietzsche). At issue are the great deeds of God the liberator, from the creation (which is not visible, but which we are told of!) to the exodus. It is a matter of the movement of the liberated people in the Promised Land, which takes place entirely in public. At issue is also the failure of the project in the misery of the real Israel. But can the Goy be excused for expressing nothing but mockery for this failure – 'we are now a disgrace to our neighbours, mockery and scorn for those who live all around us' (Ps 79:4)? Could they not also have let themselves be moved, in turn, to save the project? But that is precisely what is typical of Goy

---

12   'During an advanced phase of the harvest [the entry of the Goy into the messianic community] Paul writes: "they are not to be excused" [Rom 2:1] for they have seen God's works and the synagogue is one of the works, everywhere on earth' (Naastepad 1986).

13   The fact that this refers to Goy in particular is demonstrated by what characterises their particular 'godlessness': turning the glory of the everlasting God into the image of a mortal human or animal (Rom 1:23). Not recognising the ban on images, that is the typical Goy sin!

then and now: gleefulness at the fact that the liberation project failed yet again. All that is left for Paul to say is: inexcusable (Rom 2:1).

But nothing, either, had come of the Jews who shouldered the yoke of the Torah in order to show the world that the 'Torah Republic' was possible. They cultivate the Torah and boast the true God whose will they know. When it comes to God's law, they are the experts, they are the chosen ones:

> to be the leaders of the blind,
> the light in the darkness,
> educators of the uncomprehending,
> teachers of the immature,
> owners of the knowledge and the truth that take the shape of the Torah
> > Rom 2:19–20

But 'not those who hear the Torah are righteous with God – those who do Torah are declared righteous' (Rom 2:13). And it is precisely the doing of Torah that falls short:

> You, who proclaim: do not steal!, you steal?
> You, who say: do not commit adultery!, you commit adultery?
> You, who loathe idols, rob temples?
> You, who boast of the Torah,
> You dishonour God by transgressing against the Torah!
> > Rom 2:21–23

How can the Goy then see and recognise that the Torah is the path to life?

> God's name,
> because of you it is blasphemed
> among the Goy[14]
> > Rom 2:24

What else is left for the Goy, then, but the deadly realisation that, ethically, the Torah expects too much, which at best occasions sanctimonious hypocrisy:

---

14 This is why, for the rabbis, the discrimination against non-Jews weighs heavier than that against Jews: 'Robbing a non-Jew is worse than robbing a Jew *because of the desecration of the divine name*' (Tosefat Bava Kama 10, 15).

Behold, why don't you, the superiority of our morality? And all they can see is the inferiority of its practitioners.

Paul fails to showcase the people of the Torah as a wholesome example of living the right life in the midst of the wrong life. But he is just as unable to propagate the path of the Goy as the actually reasonable, the more reasonable one: the *pax romana* as the more realistic solution to the problem of how people can live together in some kind of order as opposed to the unreal ideal of a 'Torah Republic'. He can only stay on target with respect to the delivery from slavery by bluntly drawing the conclusion:

> There is no righteous, no not one.
> There is no one who understands.
> There is nobody, who searches for God.
> Everybody has deviated, all together are corrupted.
> There is nobody who does good,
> No not one.
>> Rom 3:10–12, all quotations from Tanakh!

And this despair at the impossibility of any way out is concentrated in a 'negative anthropology' that literally cries to heaven:

> I, miserable human!
> Who will save me from the body of this death?
>> Rom 7:24

The 'I' crying out here is not Paul the individual, who yearns for his personal deliverance. It is the 'I' that we also hear crying out in Psalms: the 'I' of a collective, Israel, or its functionary, the king; or if it is an individual, the 'I' speaking for the collective, representative of it. It is 'the human', representative of the species humankind, but that 'is no abstract being encamped outside the world. Man is the *world of man*, the state, society'.[15] Anthropology remains an abstract entity so long as we do not consider the fact that humanity 'in its reality [is] the ensemble of the social relations'.[16] This 'ensemble', though, is not a peaceful coexistence; the social relations are grounded in the oppression of one human by another. 'The human' who is crying out here is the 'miserable human', who has not yet, not ever, come into his humanity. The deliverance that he is crying for is social: delivery from slavery, or in the words of Paul:

---

15   Marx 1975b, p. 175.
16   Marx 1976a, p. 7.

from the body of this death.[17] The 'body' is the Pauline metaphor for 'society' ('public *body*'). Here, it is society that is fatal for 'miserable humans'. It is opposed by the 'body of the Messiah', the messianic community, where 'miserable humans' come into their own.

Paul is crying out as a Jew who knows that the Torah is good, and who wants to do it (Rom 7:21). He is not lacking in 'morality'; his ethical conscience is deeply influenced by the '*Simchat* Torah', the joy at the Torah:

> The Torah gives me joy according to the inner human
> Rom 7:22

But he is forced to realise that the world he lives in, the world of the Roman Empire, is ruled by a different 'Torah', a different law:

> That campaigns against the Torah of my [Jewish] heritage and takes me
>   captive in the Torah of sin
> that resides in my limbs.
> Rom 7:23

'Sin', like 'I', should not be read as individualist here. For just as much as Israel's Torah is the constitution of a society, so the 'Torah of sin' is the constitution of a society that takes the Jewish 'I' captive, the 'body of this death'.

Where this Torah, this *pax romana*, reigns, a 'Torah Republic', be it in a land or as an opposing empire (the Eastern bloc against the 'free West'), is absolutely impossible. At most, 'doing Torah' can be a tolerated *Sonderweg* that does not much affect the ruling society, a niche 'just for Jews'.

This really was provided for in the domain of the *pax romana*: the Jewish Torah as *religio licita*, permitted religion. Permitted on the condition that it respect the Roman political order. This respect was demonstrated by the Sanhedrin (the state-approved representatives of Judaism) when they delivered Jesus, who was accused of being a revolutionary, to the Roman authorities: 'we find him guilty of agitating the people and forbidding them to pay taxes to the king, and claiming he is the Messiah, the King' (Lk 23:2).

---

17   'Nothing remained but the cry of those who had been violated, this cry, which arose among the sons of Israel in Egypt, who cried for their delivery from slavery' (Jankowski 1998, p. 170).

Out of this nothingness, where nothing is possible, novelty erupts, utterly sudden and totally surprising. As it did in Egypt, when the people cried out because they saw no way out of slavery, only endless oppression, and then the incredibly new happened: a God unlike the other gods, a God who heard their 'moans', remembered his bond with their fathers, saw their misery and recognised their suffering. Thus, this call here, who will deliver me from body of this death, also finds an answer:

> Thank God
> through Jesus, our Lord's (*kyrios*) Messiah!
> Rom 7:25

Jesus

Thank God (Greek: *charis*)! *Charis* is often translated as 'grace' and that is exactly what it is: the messianic event Jesus is by no means the result of any deserving effort on the part of the real Israel, the result of its liberation movement. The entirely messy story turns into its wholesome opposite: a renewed exodus, purely through grace, *sola gratia*. Those who are held captive by the Imperium Romanum are shifted out through the gift (another possible translation of *charis*) of liberty. Paul actually experiences this liberty. Not as an inner experience: 'according to the inner human' he can rejoice at the Torah as much as he likes, he will reap only frustration. Thoughts are free, but the exodus is not a mental leap; it is the leap into real liberty that transforms reality. Paul experiences how Jews and Goy have faith that Jesus's limitless solidarity is the human equivalent of the solidarity of the 'wholly different' God of Israel; who, in other words, 'believe' what he himself 'believes':

> The righteous
> will live off of 'faith'
> Rom 1:17, cited Hab 2:4

The fact that only those are 'righteous' who do Torah (Rom 2:13), and that only those who do Torah will live (Rom 10:5), in no way contradicts this 'faith'. 'Having faith in' Jesus means precisely 'being faithful' and avowing:

Aim (*telos*) of the Torah:[18]
the Messiah
justice for all who believe
    Rom 10:4

What else can the Torah's aim be, but that it (finally) be done? And how else can Jesus be called Messiah than as he who (finally) does Torah? The Torah's fulfilment, after all, is not its abolition, but on the contrary, its final instantiation. For the question as to whether Torah can even still be done at all is no longer open. It can: The righteous lives!

'Belief' does not contradict the Torah; it is the condition of its fulfilment. Recognising the Torah as the way of life is not self-evident in the world in which the righteous must live. The path into the Promised Land leads into the desert; Jesus's path does, too (Mt 4:1–11; Mk 1:12–13; Lk 4:1–12: the story of his temptation!). There, the temptation is great to return to the land of the Goy, where the 'other Torah' reigns. The fact that the Torah is the path to life can only be 'believed'. 'Faith' alone, *sola fide*, moves us to do Torah.

The church of the Reformation interpreted the *sola fide* as well as the *sola gratia* as anti-Jewish. 'Judaism's nature' was 'lawful': for it, the Torah is a 'law' that should be fulfilled through 'works'. Salvation, then, is the 'payoff' for that: the Jew wants to justify himself through the 'works of the law' instead of making himself dependent on grace. In opposition to this, 'Christianity's nature' consists of the 'faith' in grace, which can only be obtained through Jesus Christ. So Jewish belief was vilified as a 'payoff attitude'[19] and was associated with the purportedly Jewish commercialism that ruthlessly profited from others (i.e. from Christians).[20] By definition, the Gospel

---

18   The Greek word *telos* can also mean 'end'. Reading it here as the suggestion that Paul thinks the Torah has been abolished, however, is erroneous.

19   In the 'Excurse' on 'The Parable of the Workers in the Vineyard Mt 20:1–16 and the Old-synagogal Doctrine of Recompense' included in their 'Commentary on the New Testament from the Talmud and Midrash', the editors Hermann Strack and Paul Billerbeck speak of 'the old synagogue's official doctrine of recompense' and 'the greed for recompense' as 'the true driving force' behind the 'religious ethical practice' of Jews (Strack 1928, 495). Bultmann, too, understands 'The Jewish ethic of obedience ... as a legal contract relation ... the religious man expects to be able to call God's attention to his merits' (Bultmann 1958, pp. 65, 70f.). 'The real result is that motivation to ethical conduct is vitiated' (Bultmann 2007, p. 11).

20   Marx, too, appears to have been taken in by this Christian prejudice: 'What is the wordly religion of the Jew? *Huckstering*. What is his wordly God? *Money*' (Marx 1975a, p. 170).

represented the positive opposite to this 'law'. The Torah – and with the Torah all of the so-called *Old* Testament – now only served the negative purpose of illustrating human sinfulness. Spoken with the Reformation, 'joy at the Torah' was typical Jewish insolence.

All we know is that Paul himself definitely knew '*Simchat* Torah' and that for him Jesus signified the goal and not the abrogation of the Torah. What we do not know, though, is what the Jews of the time thought of his critique that the Torah was not a Jewish privilege, and in particular of his argument that not only the Goy but the Jews themselves had also lost the way in their (not) doing of Torah. This critique only pertains to those Jews who have organised themselves in the messianic community anyway: after all, the addressee of his Roman epistle is the community in Rome, not the synagogue. The customary Jewish critique of Paul does not criticise Paul the Jew, but rather the Christian Paul. This critique can only reject the argument that Jews know neither grace nor belief as malicious defamation.

Paul's polemic against Jewish chauvinism (Boyarin) that insisted on 'having' the Torah – as though the Goy could not also do Torah and the Jews should do Torah – was hence not at all 'Christian' but properly Jewish.[21] The truly difficult aspect, where the synagogue could not and would not follow Paul, was much more his polemic against circumcision as the unavoidable condition for Goy to become full members of the synagogue. For that would contradict 'the essence of Judaism' because it really would mean abolishing the Torah in a key point.[22]

Thank God, through *Jesus the Messiah*! The novelty that makes everything new is called Jesus. But why is that? And why does Paul dare to call this Jesus the Messiah? Apparently, the crucial fact about Jesus's life is that he was crucified. Paul writes the following to the community in Corinth:

> I decided to know nothing while with you
> except for Jesus the Messiah, and him crucified
>> 1 Cor 2:2

---

21   'in Romans 2 Paul is not condemning Jews who *keep* the Law – as Reformation readers
       would have done it – and certainly not attacking Judaism in general but rather criticizing
       Jews who believe that they are exempt from divine judgment ... simply by virtue of
       their being Jewish' (Boyarin 1997, p. 87). He ironically adds: 'Undoubtedly, certain Jews
       misunderstood the notion of Chosenness and indeed were led into the error of *sola gratia*'
       (Boyarin 1997, p. 93).

22   'keeping the Law while being circumcised is simply an oxymoron from the perspective of
       rabbinic Judaism, because being circumcised is part of the Law!' (Boyarin 1997, p. 96).

Only he who decides that with the 'word of the cross' (1 Cor 1:18) everything really has already been said about Jesus can speak with such exclusivity. This means: the novelty that comes to light in Jesus is related to what appears to be the end. The cross is the manner of execution the Romans reserved for all those who rebelled against their order, especially slaves: hanging on the cross, the crucified person demonstrated the futility of their actions. Jesus perishes in this way, with the terrible cry:

> My God, my God, why have you abandoned me?
> Mk 15:34

But this ending is the ultimate affirmation of the will of God the liberator, who demands only one thing of his humans: that they 'love' him with all their hearts, with all their reason and with all their ability by 'loving' their neighbours, who, like them, are not able to save themselves, who would hence be hopelessly lost without 'the love of fellow humans'.

It cannot be emphasised enough: the 'love' meant here is solidarity. Speaking with the apostolic writings: not *eros*, but *agape* (a rare Greek word, which is why it was useful for this special kind of 'love' that is not 'erotic' but all the more solidary).[23] This has nothing to do with an aversion to the erotic that is antagonistic towards passion. As if a solidary human were not allowed to be passionate.

Jesus, a good Jew, a student of the Torah, hears this demand. He hears it and he does it, to the bitter end:

> obedient to death –
> the slave's death on the cross.
> Phil 2:8

---

23   '*agapen* does not mean "to love" and *agapè* does not mean "love". The labour movement does not demand that you love all proletarians ... It is possible to feel sincere, emotional affection for certain people, but also to feel a profound personal dislike, in both cases it is possible to fight in solidarity with them'. Also, 'You cannot "love" "God" ... You can revere Him, because you bend to what you think to have identified as his will'. This means: 'It is necessary to be solidary with what HE demands of us, to keep the commandments ... you cannot love Him in the Christian cultural tradition of that word's meaning! In the covenant that the NAME formed with Israel, Israel represents a common cause: "to love God"' (Veerkamp 1996, p. 37).

That which from the perspective of the Roman Empire can only be seen as a demonstration of impotence affirming the dominant order is seen by Paul as proof of the weak man's strength: to avow rather than betray solidarity, even on the cross. Jesus did Torah, and thus he proved, once and for all, that the human is 'created' in the image of God the liberator.

This focus on the cross does not mean that Paul has no interest (any more) in pronouncing the resurrection: knowledge that is too 'gay', too optimistic. He does not advocate a cult of pain in order to denigrate the courageousness of rising up against the dominant order. Right at the start of his Roman epistle, he avows:

> God's son,
> born as David's blood descendant,
> appointed to Son of God in strength,
> by the Holy Spirit,
> because of his rising from the dead,
> Jesus the Messiah, our Lord (*kyrios*)
>> Rom 1:3–4

This 'strength because of his rising', however, consists precisely in the fact that not only Jews but Goy too are inspired by this solidarity revealed in Jesus: they rise from their despair to avow this crucified man as their 'Lord', and to follow him. They are the dead rising. Their rising, however, is not the triumphal procession of history's victors, but the rising of the crucified: to live his solidarity.

This rising is political. The avowal, Jesus is the Lord, i.e. *kyrios*, is an avowal against the *kyrios* who was the ultimate lord in the Roman Empire, the emperor, and an avowal of the *kyrios* who alone, according to the Torah, may be called 'Lord', the unspeakable NAME, who is hence gestured towards in Hebrew with *adonai* (Gr. *kyrios*). Those who avow this are articulating their inability to serve two lords (Mt 6:24; Lk 16:13). For them, the following holds true: *aut Christus, aut Caesar*, either the Messiah, or the emperor.[24]

The NAME and the Messiah go hand in hand to such an extent, here, that the 'Song of the Son of Man' cited by Paul (Phil 2:5–10) goes as far as saying that God the liberator 'gives' his NAME to Jesus as a 'gift':

---

24   This was the demand the Roman state made of the Christians: to avow Caesar unequivoc-
       ally.

> [because of the death on the cross] God answered his prayer
> and gave to him as a gift the NAME above all names
>> Phil 2:9

Here, an incredible transgression of boundaries takes place. But it is not the transgression of the boundary that is intended to prevent the human from acting up as *Übermensch*, who wants to be like a god (the emperor!). This boundary is drawn in the ban on images:

> Make no image of God, nor of any idol
> of anything in heaven above,
> on earth below
> or in the water beneath the earth
>> Ex 20:4

This boundary transgression is incredible because it inverts the logic of striving higher, of careerism, of wanting-to-be-the-lord-of-everything. It elevates the human who did not practice the wanting-to-be-like-God in terms of seizing power, but who is humiliated, who refuses to deliver himself from slavery by distancing himself from his equals and looking for something higher. He is given the NAME as a gift because through him the will of God the liberator is done, as it is in heaven, so finally also on earth. He hallows the NAME in such a way that it can ally itself with him completely from then on.[25] What happens here is not the usual 'human becoming God', but its revolutionary opposite: the humanisation of the NAME. The avowal, Jesus is *kyrios*, does not come at the cost of God the liberator, who gave himself this NAME. Jesus is given the NAME:

> so that, in the name of Jesus
> all knees of those in heaven and on earth and beneath earth be bent
> and all tongues avow:
> *adonai/kyrios* is
> Jesus [Joshua: the NAME liberates] the Messiah
> *In honour of God the Father*
>> Phil 2:10–11

---

25   Bert ter Schegget puts it beautifully: 'Henceforth the Scripture will have to be read from the perspective of this identification of the *adonai* with the cause of the solidary Son of Man' (1975, p. 141).

The fact that he trusts Jesus with this boundary-crossing, this 'transcending' of the human being[26] that exists only for itself, that is only ever in competition with others, bestows honour on this God: to share his NAME with a human. The human, this human, is the end of all God's, this God's, wisdom!

The synagogue was wary of this. Did the church not want to make a god of Jesus after all? The dogma of the trinity, which taught the 'consubstantiality' of (God the) Father and (God the) Son, was also prone to misunderstanding, to say the least. Did not the church father Athanasius explain the humanisation (incarnation) as follows: God became human so that the human could become God?[27] This wording, however, reverses 'God's revolution', which consists precisely in the fact that the NAME is tied to the finally successful *human*isation.[28] The tri-unity of Father, Son and Holy Spirit cannot mean the trinity of a God. What it can mean, though, is the unity that exists between God, the Father of his people of Israel, and Israel, this God's Son, and the Spirit of this Father and this Son that inspires humans to follow the path of the NAME. It is the unity of the covenant that God the liberator made with his people.

The Community's Strategy

The place of this avowal is the community. The novelty that is Jesus the Messiah is not an isolated historical occurrence. Jesus is the *path* – that truly leads to life (Jn 14:6). He makes history: the Messiah exists as community (Bonhoeffer).[29] The purpose of 'The Political Theology of Paul' (Taubes) is to straighten out this community's path.[30] Paul is not a systematic theologian and his letters are not

---

26   'The transcendence is not infinite, unattainable tasks, but the neighbour within reach in any given situation ... "the human being for others", Therefore the Crucified One, the human being living out of the transcendent' (Bonhoeffer 2010, p. 501).

27   Although Athanasius probably meant something different: It is the God become *human* who lets humans share his *human* nature. But to Jewish ears this causes frightful confusion.

28   'But by virtue of the same moment by which it lifted the spell of natural religion [grace and love as liberation from the iron law of guilt and retaliation], Christianity is producing ideology once again. To the degree as the absolute is brought closer to the finite, the finite is made absolute ... The progress beyond Judaism is paid for with the assertion that the mortal Jesus was God' (Adorno and Horkheimer 2002, p. 145).

29   'Through the Holy Spirit, the crucified and risen Christ exists as the church-community [*Gemeinde*], as the 'new human being'. For Christ truly is and eternally remains the incarnate one, and the new humanity truly is his body' (Bonhoeffer 2001, p. 220).

30   Taubes 2004.

dogmatic treatises – on sin, 'the' law, grace, salvation. He is the theoretician of concrete practice. The community should not simply set out, into the blue. They should know what they are doing, have a concept, think about the way they organise themselves. The fact that Jews and Goy 'find' themselves in Jesus the Messiah, that they avow him as the true *kyrios*, should be not only enthusiastically celebrated, but also consciously seized as an opportunity for a strategy that will fully shock the power of the Roman Empire.

Strategic thinking is not alien to 'questions of belief'. Biblically speaking, belief is always tied to 'paths'. The Torah gives 'guidance' and the people should contemplate it, day and night (Ps 1:2). Equally, Jesus the Messiah shows the way and Paul gives 'guidance' in his spirit concerning this path. Those who think that strategy detracts from belief forget that the believer may be seen as a 'stranger' by the world, but cannot be a stranger *in* the world.

To Paul, the other strategies that suggest themselves in order to make space for the Torah in the world of the 'Empire' are hopeless. The attempt to reinstate the 'Torah Republic' through the use of weapons, as the Maccabees did, is illusionary, even more so the plan to turn the world 'Jewish', as propagated by a certain Jewish party (the Zealots). Equally illusionary, though, is another party's strategy (the 'Pharisees'): wanting to survive as Judaism by erecting a 'fence' around the Torah and leaving the world of the Goy to itself in the hope that they would then also leave the Jews in peace.[31] The only hope is held out by 'breaking through' into the world of the Goy. This produces a society that publicly subverts the hierarchies on which the Roman Empire is built. The society (the 'body') of the Messiah where 'neither Jews nor Greeks', 'slaves nor free men' exist any longer. It makes visible what Roman society fundamentally lacks: boundary-transgressing solidarity. Paul pins his hope on the effect of this real solidarity that exists within the community. It will convince the world that a kingdom other than the Roman one is possible.

The 'principle' of the community strategy is:

---

[31]   Here I am following Gerhard Jankowski, to whose insightful commentary on Paul's writing I owe a great debt: 'the other peoples, the Goy, and the people of Israel. That is the great problem. Some want to solve it by turning everyone into a Jew, others want to achieve autonomy by force, at least in Erez Yisrael, which at the time is a Roman Province called Judea, and still others would love to stay out of everything and live in a degree of peace equipped with certain privileges in the midst of the mass of non-Jews' (Jankowski 1998, pp. 57 f.).

Do not let yourself be conquered by evil,
but conquer evil with goodness.
    Rom 12:21

In church theology, the following paragraph concerning the 'rulers' (Rom 13:1–7) fatally assumed an existence of its own as the 'Christian doctrine of the state', in which the highest commandment was 'being subject to the authority', as Luther then translated Rom 13:1. Not until Karl Barth's *Epistle to the Romans* was its original revolutionary content returned to Paul's *Politeia* [doctrine of the state], which began with Rom 12:21. Then it also becomes obvious that Rom 13 concerns evil that has to be conquered.[32]

This tenet discards the strategy of fighting evil (the Roman Empire) with its own means, armed rebellion. This is not only hopeless; it would also obliterate what the community intends to represent: the boundary-transgressing solidarity between Jews and Goy. For good is:

Owe nothing to anybody –
except for being solidary with each other.
    Rom 13:8

The community should not get involved in a direct confrontation with the Roman state. This has nothing to do with a lack of courage on the part of the members of the community. But they know that this would only furnish the state with a reason to take legal action against the community. To a certain degree, the state is justified to proceed against 'terrorists': destroy what destroys you. The community's revolutionary strategy is constructive:

That is why it is necessary to be 'subordinate'
not only because of the anger [of the state], but also because
of the knowledge [of your own cause].
    Rom 13:5

This 'subordinate' [*hypotassein*], which Luther translated as 'subservient', is meant strategically. The community makes a virtue of the necessity of their factual subordination: their subversive strategy.[33] And they can do this because they know:

---

32   'Contemporary power states are diametrically opposed to God's intentions, they are *per se* evil' (Barth 1985, p. 501).

33   Ernst Troeltsch, who ascribes a 'conservative attitude to social questions' to Paul, still

there is no power apart from God

the existing power has been put in place by God.

    Rom 13:1

Everything else that is said of the rulers is also strategy – with a heavy dose of irony. For those who live in the order of Rome's *kyrios* know that while it rewards evil with evil, it most decidedly does *not* reward good with good, as the church in allegiance with the state read Rom 13:3: 'If you do not want to fear the authorities, then do good; thus they will laud you' (in Luther's translation). When Paul issues the instruction 'the state does not carry the sword for nothing' (Rom 13:4), then that is by no means the positive recognition of the state monopoly on violence, but a realistic warning: those who rebel against the state face its police and that can strike a proper blow.[34] This is rather ironic: those who want to subvert this state do well to be as inconspicuous as possible in their role as citizens of the state. If the state still makes their alternative life impossible for the community, it should be clear: it is this alternative that the state cannot stand. It only persecutes good citizens because they, amongst themselves and in their deeds, do not acknowledge its order of rule, but wish to live free from domination. This persecution produces martyrs, i.e. witnesses (*martyros* = witness) of the right life in the wrong one.

They comply with the state's demands on its citizens: they pay their taxes, they respect high officials (Rom 13:7). So they owe nothing to the state. But they do all this only so that the community has the space to do what it owes, in a positive sense, to the world: demonstrating solidarity that breaks through the barriers that separate humans from one another – the ideological barrier (between Jews and Greeks = Goy), the class barrier (between free men and slaves).

    The practice of this solidarity is manifest above all in the *communal feast*.

Next to this 'breaking of the bread' with which the communal feast opened, there was also the 'doctrine of the apostles': the announcement of the liberating word, 'communality': the practice of solidarity within the community, and the 'prayer' (Acts 2:42): 'Hallowed be your NAME, your kingdom come, your will be done, as it is in heaven so on earth'. Membership in the community was bestowed through *baptism*:

---

has to concede its subversive character: 'That is why, in spite of all its submissiveness, Christianity did destroy the Roman state by alienating souls from its ideas' (1931, p. 82).

34 'The way in which he [Paul] speaks of the Roman authorities clearly shows how much it is part of the realm of evil in his eyes! Anger, revenge, fear, police weapons, these are the words he uses, and in a public plea for the sober dealing with the terrifying state power, at that: not by running one's head against a wall, but instead of a bloodbath a path between turmoil and capitulation' (Kroon 1982, p. 15).

the submergence under and re-emergence from the water (of death) symbolised the sinking of the old and the rising of the new human – into the new world of the Messiah's body. This is the radical opposite of the later baptism's 'entry ticket' into the society with which the church had meanwhile made its peace.

In those days, feasts of hospitality were events that vividly enacted the dominant order. The seating order was structured according to the hierarchy of master, clientele and others: the master acted as the benefactor who proved his paternal benevolence through this feast that he had organised and seated his guests according to their social status, high or low, at the table. Things were completely different at the community's feast. Here, there was only one 'Lord', one *kyrios*, who specifically refused to be a lord. His 'body', i.e. his society, knows no hierarchy: Jews and Goy, free men and slaves sit and eat together without one presiding over the other, demanding of the other to subordinate themselves to him. Here, the food is not 'granted' but shared: each according to their needs. Here the fact that everyone could have everything together was made evident to all.

This is why Paul reacts so harshly when he hears of the Corinthian community where 'everyone just eats their own meal so that some stay hungry and others are drunk' (1 Cor 11:21):

> All those, who do not do justice to the body of the Messiah during the meal,
> call judgement upon themselves through their eating and their drinking.
>   1 Cor 11:29

The community's 'nature', to be a messianic community, depends on the fact that their feast exists as the representation of a new humanity. If this feast is only celebrated as the liturgical dressing up of normal relations – religion as a private matter in messianic form – then 'judgement' is due. For it is worse to celebrate the feast in such a way that humans mistake its caricature for real than not to celebrate it at all.[35]

The fact that the order of Jews and Goy in the community was one of equality must have been a terrible provocation for Jewish self-understanding. Admittedly, Goy were not excluded from salvation. On the contrary, there was a place

---

35   Paul's solution to the problem is a compromise: 'when you come together to eat, wait for each other. But is somebody hungry, may he eat at home so that you do not come together for judgement' (1 Cor 11:34). Already, the shift from a feast where everyone really shares everything to a more symbolic representation of communality begins.

for them in the Torah, in the so-called Noachidic Laws: 'the Jewish Torah for Goy' (Marquardt), which was the foundation for a 'Goy' justice.[36]

There are seven of these: the law of the administration of justice, the injunction to idolatry, blasphemy, fornication, bloodshed, robbery and eating of limbs from live animals (according to the Tosevta Avoda zara 8:4).[37]

One thing this Torah did not command was circumcision. Should a Goy wish to join the Jewish community, though, he had to be circumcised. The order of Jews and Goy, which was a subordination of Goy to Jews, remained intact. The messianic community presented an absolute novelty with respect to this relation that was so crucial to Jewish self-understanding: the Goy were made members without having to be circumcised![38] And the big question was: is this novelty a new deed done by God the liberator that creates new relations in which the Jews, that is his chosen people, have been sublated [*aufgehoben*], or is this a reprehensible novelty that will dissolve Jewish identity into total assimilation? Paul was convinced: the novelty is the great breakthrough in a deadlocked history that will save 'all Israel' (Rom 11:26). The majority of Jews, as we in the meantime know, arrived at the opposite conclusion: the messianic community meant their demise, the end of Jewish identity.[39]

It is impossible to reconstruct the original conversation between Jews who avowed Jesus as the Messiah and Jews who rejected this avowal as un-Jewish. In any case, it was a matter of internal Jewish debate, whose harshness can only be explained by the fact that this was an encounter between 'antagonistic *brothers*'. Despite their mutual investment in socialism, communists and social democrats did not spare each other, either. Except that they could well deny the other's socialism. Just as Paul can write against his, doubtlessly Jewish, opponent: 'For he who shows it only publicly is not a Jew' (Rom 2:28). This is harsh, perhaps too harsh, but it is not anti-Jewish.

---

36 Marquardt 1993, p. 200.

37 The final law refers to ritual slaughter.

38 For Paul, the community is not constituted by the so-called 'Noah's covenant', but by Abraham as the father of *all* believers (Crüsemann 2003, p. 294).

39 Joseph Klausner speaks for this Judaism: 'This inevitably brought it to pass that his people, Israel, rejected him. In its deeper consciousness the nation felt that then, more than at any other time, they must not be swallowed up in the great cauldron of nations in the Roman Empire ... Two thousand years of non-Jewish (German: *heidnisch*), Christianity have proved that the Jewish people did not err' (Klausner 1947, pp. 390 f.).

All we can say is that the now purely Goy church has demanded total assimilation of the Jews. Judaism had lost its right of existence, had been replaced by the church as the 'true Israel'. Its downfall (Hebrew: *shoah*) could hence be seen as punishment for their insistence on continuing to exist. The Jew had no option but to say no to the Messiah – for the sake of hallowing the NAME![40]

Because Paul was convinced that this was the great breakthrough, he could not help himself but agitate strongly against the conception that the Goy should be circumcised in order to become full members of the community. His critique, incidentally, is directed at the messianic community itself in the first instance, not the synagogue. For it was precisely here that he discovered to his dismay the strong tendency to 'make Jewish' (Gal 2:14): Jews, but probably Goy, too, thought it best that Goy should be circumcised. Then the problem was, so to speak, solved: everybody had become a Jew who avowed Jesus the Messiah. Even this was new enough: a community in which the free man and the slave had equal rights. Wholly in the spirit of their *kyrios*, who had taught:

> Among you things shall not be as they are [among the Goy].
> Those who wish to be great among you, shall serve you
> and whoever wishes to take the top seat,
> shall be your slave.
> For the Son of Man did not come
> in order to be served,
> but in order to serve.
>   Mt 20:26–28

But was the exemption of a Goy who wanted to participate in this breakthrough from the command of circumcision also in his spirit? For Paul everything hinged on the fact that even this opposition between Jews and Goy was broken down – precisely because it was so deeply ingrained and had been so determining for the relation between the two up until this point. If circumcision really had been intended as a *salutary* distinction of the Torah project that was oriented towards freedom from domination from the Goy deification of power, then it could now no longer be employed as the defence against the unific-

---

40   'the Jewish no is their protest against the idolisation of Jesus Christ, which impacts on
      pagan legislation [making faith in Jesus Christ into the law]. Thus it is loyalty to the first
      commandment which protests in the Jewish no' (Marquardt 2009, p. 246).

ation, free of domination, of Jews and Goy in the messianic community. For then circumcision is turned into a sign of domination. It is a matter of saying explicitly:

> Neither circumcision nor foreskin is anything,
> but new creation.
>> Gal 6:15

New creation! *Creatio ex nihilo* – out of the nothingness in which the project 'Israel' had been caught up. The new exodus which Paul dares announce in all its power and all its radicalness – first to the Jews, because it occurred for their salvation first and above all:

> I dare publicly pronounce the Gospel.
> It is God's power
> to liberate all who trust in it,
> *Jews first* and then also Greeks.
>> Rom 1:16

This truly is extraordinarily bold. Certainly, it is not unthinkable; the prophets had thought it:

> Yes see: I [God the liberator] create a new heaven and a new earth.
>> Is 65:17

But that was the final exodus from this world into the world to come, while the time of the Messiah takes place in this world:

Judaism distinguishes between deliverance in the world to come (*olam-ha-ba*) and the days of the Messiah, which belong to life in this world (*olam-ha-ze*).[41] The discussion primarily revolves around the question of how much salvation will already be a reality in the days of the Messiah. There are both minimalists and maximalists with respect to this issue. Paul was a maximalist.

---

41 In this finally delivered world, Judaism agreed on this much: the Torah's regulations were really suspended. For example, the dietary laws: 'God will declare all animals, which are unclean now, clean in the time to come ... [I]n the time to come he will allow everything that is now forbidden' (Sjocher Tov in reference to Ps 146).

Paul does not deny this, either: the community is a community *in* the world. Calling it a new creation, though, means that just as creation was the beginning of 'Israel's becoming in the midst of the Goy', so Jesus the Messiah is the beginning of 'the community's becoming in the midst of a world torn apart by insurmountable differences'. A 'becoming' that really does end 'Israel's becoming', 'abolishes it', leads it to its goal: an entirely new (hi)story has begun. This is why Paul dares to claim that in the figure of the Messiah not only the opposition between Jews and Goy as well as that between free men and slaves is surmounted, but in him is also:

> not 'male and female'
> Gal 3:28

Paul cites the creation story:

> God created the human in his image,
> in God's image did he create him,
> *male and female* he created them
> Gn 1:27

There, 'male and female' is the condition for the *toledoth* (the 'begettings'), 'Israel's becoming'. The fact that *not* 'male and female' is in the Messiah can hence only mean that Paul intends to say: these 'toledoth' have fulfilled their purpose. The human 'in his image' has appeared.

Does this mean that 'the difference of being human according to creation' has been suspended?[42] Men and women no longer exist? But what does 'according to creation' mean here? Creation is qualitatively different from nature. 'Naturally', there are male and female bodies. 'According to creation' this natural 'male and female' becomes constitutive of the not at all natural but salvation-historical *toledoth*. This is what Gn 1 tells us. The 'cultural' consequence of this sexual differentiation – the development of men and women as well as the (hierarchical) relation between them – is another story. This story is told in Gn 2 and 3. Whether sexual difference itself, (misunderstood!) as the relation between men and women, albeit 'liberated from all polar dichotomy and all hierarchies',[43] cannot (may not?) be transgressed, is not deducible from the creation story. Could a society that was truly free of domination not bring about a much

---

42   Frettlöh 2002, p. 29.
43   Ibid.

more richly differentiated condition than we can even imagine? Why should the 'male and female' ultimately determine our humanity?

Whether this 'not male and female' led to equal rights for women within the community is unclear. The translation of this 'male and female' as 'man and woman', in any case, is over-determined. The fact that women wanted to have equal rights, though, is certain. How else could we explain Paul's insistence, when he brings out the big exegetic guns,[44] that: women should not behave like men in the community, but stay women by wearing their hair long or covering their head (1 Cor 11:4–10)? This 'headscarf debate', however, only takes place because the women pray like the men in the service, and are allowed to 'prophesy' (preach) (1 Cor 11:4–5).[45] Paul had already 'christologically' (messianologically) relativised the superordination of the man:

> but I want you to know
> that the head of each man is: the Messiah,
> and the head of the woman: the man,
> and the head of the Messiah: God
>
> 1 Cor 11:3

Here, the hierarchical logic of domination (woman → man → Christ → God) is disrupted by the fact that the order articulated by 'the woman's head is the man' is framed by the Messiah's being-head at the start and the Messiah's servitude towards God the liberator at the end of the sentence. This amends the man's 'superiority' to servitude. Paul argues in similar fashion in his letter to the Ephesians (5:21–33) when he calls upon the men to be solidary with their women as the Messiah is solidary with his community (25). For they are 'limbs of his body' (30). It is specifically in this context that he cites from biblical anthropology (Gn 2:24): 'that is why [!] the human will leave his father and his mother and follow his wife' (31); in other words that is, the reversal of the 'normal', patriarchal relation between men and women! And he closes with the commandment:

---

44   He even allows 'nature' as an argument (1 Cor 11:4: 'and does not nature teach you?') – as though 'natural theology' had something to say here!

45   The fact that it really should have been Paul, who, in the same letter that explicitly says that women are allowed to pray publicly and to preach, also commands women to remain silent during community gatherings (1 Cor 14:34), is so unlikely that we must assume that this sentence was foisted upon him by somebody for whom this equality went too far.

Everyone is to be solidary with his wife, (she is) *like him*
>   Eph 5:33

With Respect to the Jews: A Strategy of Jealousy

For Paul, the thought that the 'new creation' should destroy the first creation –
as though it were the nothingness from which humanity is liberated – is entirely
far-fetched:

> So I ask:
> Has God cast out his people?
> Impossible!
> >   Rom 11:1

The Jews with whom Paul argues may have missed the *kairos* by thinking the
commandment to separate themselves from the Goy was still in place. That was
their big mistake: being blind to the breakthrough that occurred right in front
of their eyes. But the fact remains:

> they are Israelites,
> to them is given the Son
> and the honour
> and the covenant
> and the gift of the Torah
> and the service of God
> and the promises;
> theirs are the fathers
> and from their midst comes the Messiah.
> >   Rom 9:4–5

But whether this is really a matter of *kairos* cannot be settled theoretically. It
has to prove itself in practice. Here, too, Paul is thinking strategically. The path
followed by the community will convince the Jews that they are faced with a
breakthrough that causes not their demise, but their salvation. They are wary;
they will be 'jealous'. So this should be the community's strategy:

> to make them jealous
> >   Rom 11:11

It is understandable that most Jews could not follow this 'firebrand' there. And it was not long before his 'wild thought' was falsified.[46] This renders Jacob Taubes's twentieth-century recognition of this strategy, and with it of Paul as a good Jew, all the more surprising.[47] Paul does something that Moses specifically did not do: he accepts rather than rejects God's offer of starting a new people with him.[48] Through his rejection, Moses remains loyal to his people and forces God to do the same. By accepting, has Paul betrayed his people? Taubes reminds us that such a 'strategy of jealousy' is thoroughly biblical. After all, Moses sings at YHWH's behest:

> They made me jealous with a non-god
>
> ...
>
> which is why I will make them jealous with a non-people.
>> Dt 32:1

But Jacob Taubes also can only reclaim Paul as a Jew by radically removing him from Christianity.[49] From the year 70 onwards – the destruction of the temple by the Romans – 'was all smooth sailing', when the Empire's brutality was 'interpreted ... as punishment of God'.[50] That is how quickly the Pauline project of 'community' came to an end, according to Taubes!

The aim of the Pauline strategy is for nobody to be lost. And this means first and foremost that Israel is not lost. For if Israel is lost then this 'nobody' is a pious abstraction. Paul's hope is that:

---

46 'His handling of "Scripture" is that of "wild thought" ... He destroys the old text, to which the highest authority has been assigned, in order to salvage something of sense from it ... Often his one-sidedness positions him on or beyond the boundary to heresy' (Reeling Brouwer 2002, pp. 114 f.).

47 'This is the point at which little Jacob Taubes comes along and enters into the business of gathering the heretic back into the fold, because I regard him – this is my own personal business – as more Jewish than any reform rabbi or any Liberal rabbi, I ever heard in Germany, England, America, Switzerland, or anywhere' (Taubes 2004, p. 11).

48 'Moses as an advocate for the people of Israel, Moses who rejects, twice rejects the idea that with him begins a new people and that the people of Israel should be eliminated – and of Paul, who accepts this idea' (Taubes 2004, p. 2).

49 'the word "Christian" – this I ask you to get into your heads – does not yet exist for Paul. This modernization, these anachronisms are the ruin of any venture into sensible textual study' (Taubes 2004, p. 21).

50 Ibid.

the fullness of the Goy come in
> Rom 11:25

But he hopes for this not least – or even specifically above all – because:

thus all Israel will be saved
> Rom 11:26

What matters here is to understand 'Israel' not as a metaphor (e.g. for the 'church' as the 'true Israel'), but literally as the name of that people that avows: Hear, Israel, YHWH, our God, YHWH is 'one'! As Paul emphasises, however, these are the Jews who should not settle for simply being a 'remainder', but who should hold fast to the idea that no one may be lost from Israel, either: '*all* Israel' will be saved! Only then can we truly speak of 'humanity' in the sense of the humanisation intended by God the liberator.

What Paul imagined this salvation to look like specifically, and how it relates to the project of the 'community of Jews and Goy', is not entirely clear (at least, not to me). But it will certainly not be a uniform humanity, forced into line! Just as the notion that 'God is all in all', which becomes a reality in the finally successful humanisation, does not mean the end of all difference. This may be the case for the 'philosophers' god': undifferentiated unity as the highest conceivable idea. The God of the Bible, however, is no enemy of difference, but of hierarchy: the people of Israel number twelve tribes, and Judah is not like Benjamin; there are four gospels, and Matthew is not like Luke is not like Mark is not like John; Jesus has twelve apostles, and Peter is not like Paul; the body of the Messiah also has many limbs (1 Cor 12:12). But the last one will be the first one, and 'you shall honour the other higher than yourself' (Phil 2:3).

The Church and the Kairos

The messianic community, in which Paul believed, was unable to sustain itself. It turned into the church, which was well capable of serving two *kyrioi* and of respecting the ruling interests of the Empire.[51] It happily let itself in on the 'historical compromise' that the Emperor Constantine offered it: to become

---

51   Bloch writes the following on the 'given Church': 'It bristles at see-through blouses, but not at slums in which naked children starve, and, above all, not at the relations that hold three-quarters of mankind in misery. It damns desperate girls who abort a foetus, but it sanctifies war, which aborts millions. It has nationalized its God, nationalized him into an

religio licita (permitted religion) on condition of forthwith praying for the preservation of the Imperium Romanum.

The status of *religio licita* also enabled the church to acquire land. Before long it was the empire's largest landowner and had its own ruling interests to protect.

But the church did not simply betray the project of a messianic community, it also passed it down.[52] For it incorporated Paul's political theology into its canon. In practice it then de-politicised his theology, dogmatised it, spiritualised it – and, not least, gave it an anti-Jewish interpretation. But his treatises, which founded the project of organised freedom from domination, could be read. It was possible to draw on them and to employ them as church critiques against the real church.

Thus Luther rediscovered the Roman letter as the treatise of the 'freedom of a Christian' (1520), which consists of 'loving each other' – against the asocial freedom, which he saw spreading throughout early-capitalist Germany. Against a church, too, that had turned the 'good works' into a business (*selling* of indulgences). Except that he, unfortunately, adopted this church's anti-Jewish reading of Paul without critique, even increasing its harshness.

Karl Barth then rediscovered the Roman letter as an explicit 'political theology': 'Only by renouncing the *methods* of the extant world will you serve its true, radical revolutionising'.[53] And he radically defused the anti-Jewish reading of this theology by consistently reading the 'Law' as 'religion' and the 'Jews' as 'church'.[54] This reading, too, critical of religion and the church, was not unproblematic: now the Jews did not appear at all in the Roman letter. Paul's concern was to explain to his fellow Jews: The messianic community is the great breakthrough to your benefit.

---

ecclesiastical organization, and it has inherited the Roman Empire under the mask of the crucified' (Bloch 1986a, p. 278).

52   'Certainly, for long swathes of time Christianity served to sanction the dominant order from a religious perspective. But deep down inside it is the great narrative of Israel, which was the stimulus for the messianism of the gospels and the apostolic writings ... The 'Aufhebung' (sublation) of messianism is specifically the safeguarding of the great narrative of Israel' (Veerkamp 2007, p. 144).

53   Barth 1985, p. 498.

54   In the second version of his *Epistle to the Romans*. In Rom 7, Barth declares the 'Law' to be (the 'frontier', 'meaning' and 'reality' of) *religion*. Rom 9–11 (Paul's fundamental consideration of the future of Israel), according to Barth, is about '"tribulation", "guilt" and "hope" of the *church*' (Barth 1968).

The messianic community was not the great breakthrough that permanently changed the course of history. The movement, which Paul supplemented with his critically constructive letters, turned into literature: the resurrection of the crucified is a textual reality; as event it has been lost. The real feast, which demonstrated how close, how graspable a society free from domination was, turned into liturgy, in which more often than not, even if only symbolically, there was no trace of freedom from domination. The faith that Paul could tie to the 'real changing fact' of the community turned into the avowal of an 'invisible church', whose becoming visible can only be waited for.[55]

And yet still! This literature exists and it still has the power to move people to hope for the event of the resurrection of the crucified. The liturgy exists and it can keep the longing for a society free from domination alive, even if 'only' (but why 'only'?) symbolically. And the avowal exists: I believe in a catholic (worldwide) *ekklesia*, a communality of 'holy ones'. The declaration of its invisibility is not the final word on the matter – so long as people exist who believe a different church from the real one is possible!

The (hi)story includes this 'yet still' actually happening, too: the *kairos*. Paul saw what everything looked like after it: the project 'Israel' has run its course, it is over and done with. And then it happened, the 'still' of the *kairos*! And was it not also a *kairos* when the small Christian communities developed in the particularly hierarchical Roman-Catholic church of Latin America, and a theology of liberation allied itself with the practice of the oppressed?

It may well be that this *kairos*, too, is over and has passed into the time of the so apolitical Pentecostal churches. Is that reason to give up the hope for a new *kairos*? Is it even entirely impossible that despite everything that speaks against it the time of the Pentecostal churches could turn into a *kairos*?

The Community and the Jews

History will not, however, repeat itself. Jews no longer fight about the novelty of a community in which Jews and Goy demonstrate solidarity and have

---

55   'What God according to His Word wills with men and from men is that they should and must hear, believe, know and reckon with this ... in the totality of their existence as men, that they should and must live with the fact that that not only sheds new light on, but materially changes, all things and everything in all things – *the fact that God is*' (Barth 1956b, p. 258). But this God is not without his people, his community. He creates in the people, as it were, the facts that will really change the world!

equal rights, as they did during Paul's time. Even if the *kairos* existed in the church, where people organised themselves as a grassroots community, this community will not consist of Jews and Goy. It will hence be unable to demonstrate to the synagogue it faces the breakthrough that can make it see: See, everything is new, for your benefit.

But is the 'Jewish question', so burning for Paul, not now a thing of the past? Surmounting the opposition between the Jews and the Goy may have been crucial for the future of the project 'Israel' in the context of the time, but in our time it is solely the 'social question', because it remains unresolved, that has become crucial for the future of this project. Is it not sufficient simply to say: Neither free man nor slave is in the Messiah? The fact that in modern society Jews and non-Jews are equal before the law is hardly contested and does not need to be explicitly demonstrated in the community.

Whether the Jews see things this way is doubtful. Was it not precisely in the centre of modern Europe, which had inscribed the equality of all people in its constitution, where the decision was made to finally resolve the 'Jewish question' by wiping out the Jews? Is theology after Auschwitz, if at all possible, possible without placing this question in particular at the centre of all its considerations? And does a community that avows the Jew Jesus as the Messiah not have to do its utmost to demonstrate to the Jews that they have found in them a trustworthy friend?

But it is the case that the Jews encounter little sympathy especially from leftist Christians, who make the exodus project of the delivery from slavery into the foundation of their liberationist theology. They associate 'Jewish' with the Jewish state of Israel, and there is no state in the world, apart maybe from the USA, that is more spitefully criticised. They have good arguments for this criticism, too: the politics of the state of Israel are terrible. And it is true that the Jewish state is certainly not the state of all Jews. But the language of the criticism is revealing: it favours words that must insult all Jews. The Israeli army's violence against the Palestinians is called 'Holocaust', the prime minister a Hitler, anti-Israel demonstrations never lack the swastika, Zionism is simply racist. Thus the Jews are paid back for what they have suffered – Holocaust, Hitler, swastika, racism. We are relieved of our guilt by finding that they are not much better themselves. The immeasurable exaggeration shows that this is a matter no longer of criticism but of the anti-Semitic complex that is deeply rooted in our cultural subconscious.[56]

---

56 The Shoah further strengthened this complex. It produced the 'secondary antisemitism'

A community that excommunicated the Jews cannot be humanity's avant-garde, where there is space for everyone. Its idealism is deadly for those who disappoint it: the Jews first, with their Jewish state, but then also the Communists with their Stalinism, and sooner or later probably the Palestinians, too, with their suicide bombers. Such a community operates a pure culture of beautiful souls instead of solidarity with real people, who could say to us, those 'born later':[57]

You who will emerge from the flood
In which we have gone under
Remember
When you speak of our failings
The dark time too
Which you have escaped.

For we went, changing countries oftener than our shoes
Through the wars of the classes, despairing
When there was injustice only, and no rebellion.

And yet we know:
Hatred, even of meanness
Contorts the features.
Anger, even against injustice
Makes the voices hoarse. Oh we,
Who wanted to prepare the ground for friendliness
Could not ourselves be friendly.

(Adorno), which was terribly accurately conceptualised by the Jewish doctor Zwi Rix: 'The Germans will never forgive the Jews for Auschwitz'.

57   As a black man, Frantz Fanon felt a particular bond with the Jews: 'my brother in misery'. He wrote: 'At first thought it may seem strange that the anti-Semite's outlook should be related to that of the Negrophobe. It was my philosophy professor, a native of the Antilles, who recalled the fact to me one day: "Whenever you hear anyone abuse the Jews, pay attention, because he is talking about you"' (Fanon 2008, p. 122). Ideally, all humans are equal, regardless of whether they be white, black or Jewish. But in their specific, often ugly and hateful otherness, black people and Jews (and now also, of course, Muslims) remain hated by us, with our clean, idealist hands. And let us make no mistake: the others are very sensitive to this!

But you, when the time comes at last
And man is a helper to man
Think of us
With forbearance.[58]

---

58   Brecht 1976, p. 319 f.

Though He Liberated Others, He Could Not Liberate Himself

Instead of a Christology: A Meditation

Jesus is the Messiah, his people's promised liberator (*Yehoshua* = YHWH liberates)? The image we have of him is when he has been crucified. Is it not impossible to reconcile such an image with the idea of a liberator? The messianic community did it. They avowed that Jesus is *kyrios* – as the master who renounces acting as lord. And they avowed it in their practice of a lifestyle free of domination. It could seem all too easy for us to believe this avowal, which was so practical – if we too readily began to avow that the crucified one is risen and has ascended into heaven, there to establish his rule.[1] He is the *elevated Kyrios*. Our avowal – the *crucified one* is risen – would be nothing but the tracing of his movement upwards without us as a community being brought into the movement of the trace by the crucified one. But to avow is to do what he modelled for us to do. This doing is the power of the resurrection, which brings about the role model of the crucified one. That is why Paul can write:

> I decided to know *nothing* while with you
> *except for Jesus the Messiah*, and him *crucified*
> 1 Cor 2:2

The perspective is determining: are we seeing the image of the crucified from above or from below? Where images are concerned, this is a matter of aesthetics. Looking at the image from below is the task of 'aesthetics of resistance'. Peter Weiss opens his novel of the same name with such a viewing from below.[2] The year is 1935 in Hitler's Germany. Three young antifascists are standing in front of the famous Pergamon-Altar in the museum – a recognised pinnacle of Greek culture. The frieze depicts a battleground where the Greek gods are holding down the barbaric Giants with the use of extreme violence. The three

---

1 Cf. Bonhoeffer: 'Whoever wishes to be and perceive things too quickly and too directly in New Testament ways is to my mind no Christian' (2010, p. 213).

2 Weiss 2005.

men can see this, too, but they see it through the eyes of those who suffer from this violence themselves: 'The subjugation of the Gallic tribes invading from the north and turned into a triumph of aristocratic purity over wild and base forces, and the chisels and mallets of the stone carvers and their assistants had displayed a picture of incontestable order to make the subjects bow in awe'.[3] The view from below exposes the view from above – as just that: a view from above.

The image of the crucified one can also be viewed from above in this way. Then we might see a human who suffers the insufferable, who sacrifices his life to a bloodthirsty God so that we can celebrate that as our deliverance. The view from below is different: here, we see a victim of the Roman rule of violence, executed because he interfered with this rule. Only those who see like this can even begin to understand what it means to avow this human as *kyrios*. They will also be able to see how a sculptor might imagine letting the crucified one descend from his cross in order to make him into his liberator, as well as the liberator of this like him. By doing this he would also be following the Torah's aesthetics of resistance: the cry of the slave people (my God, my God, why have you abandoned us) which triggers their exodus.

In the ruins of the Franziskaner-Klosterkirche in Berlin, there is a sculpture by the GDR sculptor Fritz Cremer, who designed the memorial in the former concentration camp Buchenwald, among other things. The sculpture is called 'He who is detaching himself from the cross'. It shows a well-built man who is in the process of descending from the cross to which he has been nailed. With his right hand he pushes the crown of thorns from his head. The cross already appears to be falling down behind him.

We know this man. We know him from Christian art: Jesus nailed to the cross, the head bent to the side under the crown of thorns, finally dead after infinite suffering. Jesus Christ caught in an aesthetic of suffering, the 'Man of Sorrows' who delivered us through his suffering, who died for our sins.

This image of the crucified Christ contradicts what the Romans were intending to demonstrate through him. After all, it is an image intended to provoke sympathy. The Romans, however, wanted to make an example of him: a rebellious slave has no chance, see him hanging there, he wanted liberation from slavery, forget about it, those of you watching now. Those who rebel against their fate end up on the cross. Simultaneously, though, the Christian image of the man stapled to the cross (fixed to the cross = crucifixion) reinforces the moral of the Romans: the crucified Christ does not resist but remains passive,

---

3   Weiss 2005, p. 5.

FIGURE 1   *Cremer*

endures, suffers, dies; and delivery lies beyond all these earthly occurrences. Those who look at the crucifix need no real crucifixion executed by Roman soldiers in order to know that they should not rebel against the dominant order. They willingly carry out what was enforced on the slaves through the crucifixion: to endure suffering in imitation of his Lord.

Fritz Cremer 'cites' this image by depicting the well-built man who detaches himself from his cross with one powerful movement. This 'Christ' can no longer bear to endure for ever and ever as humans are tortured and executed – 'only' because they no longer wished to be slaves, but wanted to become humans. The crucified one must not remain caught within an aesthetic of suffering; his image must visualise the resistance that has been suppressed in Christian art: aesthetics of resistance.

Smashing the Cross: Devotion to the End

Whilst producing this sculpture, Fritz Cremer might have been thinking of Ernst Bloch's words: 'the cross was to be *smashed*, not to be carried'.[4] Bloch is saying this against the Christian doctrine of Christ, which no longer understood the death on the cross as the execution of Jesus but as 'voluntary sacrifice', as if 'this death had itself arisen from love and was, as Paul put it, the price which Jesus paid God to redeem men from sin'.[5] Thus the world that murdered Jesus successfully avoids responsibility. The fact that 'the death on the cross came from without, not from within, from Christian love' was forgotten.[6]

For Bloch, the death on the cross had another dimension, though, apart from shattering the cross. For this death specifically demonstrates that Jesus remained loyal to his own, the 'the poor and the despised', remained faithful to death, his 'devotion to the end'.[7] Had Jesus been spared this death, or had he spared himself this death, something essential would have been missing, i.e. the realisation of 'a love which no longer wanted anything for itself, which is prepared to give its life for its brothers [sisters do not figure in Bloch]'.[8] Only as the crucified one, i.e. only as the human who was willing to pay the price of his own life for the 'cause' of the liberation from slavery, was Jesus the embodiment of the human as the 'Highest Being' for the human. He did what not even the God of the Exodus did, nor could do: 'For the Yahweh of Moses and the prophets could never suffer death; among the infinite qualities of his infinite goodness one, after all, was missing: devotion to the end. Logically only a mortal *man* could possess and prove this, not a god

---

4 Bloch 1986b, p. 1271.
5 Bloch 1986b, p. 1262.
6 Ibid.
7 Bloch 1986b, pp. 1260, 1265 f.
8 Bloch 1986b, p. 1261.

immeasurably remote from and unassailable by fear of death and torment'.[9] Thus Jesus 'put himself as the Son of Man into this Above [where up to now the gods made the decisions]'; but that means: 'He did not put in existing man but the utopia of something humanly possible whose core and eschatological fraternity he exemplified in his life [again the sisters do not figure]'.[10] In Jesus the word of the new human has become flesh, but part of this becoming flesh, as emphasised by Bloch, is the *'crucifixus sub Pontio Pilato'* (crucified under Pontius Pilatus, the Roman proconsul).[11] Fritz Cremer's sculpture depicts a man who is descending from the cross. His movement, though, is one of ascension. He detaches himself from the cross in order to set out to deliver others who still remain caught in the aesthetics of sufferance. I suspect Bloch would have enjoyed this image. But for Bloch the *'crucifixus sub Pontio Pilato'* was important not only because it reminds us of the fact that Jesus was a rebel who was executed by the Romans, but also because Jesus's death on the cross revealed his devotion to the end. Had Jesus descended from the cross, the question would remain as to whether he really was prepared to go all the way. The crucified one that Fritz Cremer shows us was evidently able to detach himself from the cross, he possessed that power. Thus he can become other people's deliverer: he liberates himself in order to enable himself to liberate others. But will he also do that? Will he, when they come for him, not give preference to the possibility of saving his own life and hopelessly abandon the others? How many deliverers have there been who ultimately delivered themselves above all. Not that they had planned it that way. But once they realised that the project intended to bring about the delivery from slavery of *all* humans was not feasible, they turned into realists who knew that the priority was to save themselves – perhaps even sincerely justifying their actions by arguing that only those who could stand their own ground stood a chance of helping others.

But Bloch sees the crucified one as the human who did not want anything for himself and thus opened the way for a vision of unconditional solidarity. This is perhaps also the vision he is referring to with the phrase 'smashing of the cross'. After all, this is not necessarily only an act of violence. Bloch could also have been imagining this unconditional solidarity, which radically 'smashes' the fatal necessity that humans be crucified at its root. To me, in any case, Bloch reinforces once again the phrase that plays such an important part in the story

---

9   Bloch 1986b, pp. 1265f.

10   Bloch 1986b, p. 1260.

11   Ibid.

of Jesus's suffering: 'though he liberated others, he could not liberate himself'
(Mt 27:42; Mk 15:31; Lk 23:35).

Jesus: The Messiah, Who Could Not Liberate Himself

The phrase 'though he liberated others, he could not liberate himself' is a
phrase *about* Jesus. In the first instance, it wants to acknowledge that he *did*
liberate others. By word and by deed he showed others that poverty and misery
are not necessary and that need can be turned around. With that he also
awakened the hope that God's Kingdom is close by and provoked the avowal:
You are Christ, the Messiah, the son of the living God. That is also why he was
condemned to death by a great coalition of church (the Sanhedrin) and state
(Pontius Pilate). That is the fate of a son of this God and Jesus knows this. He
reacts as follows to the avowal of his messianity: 'The Son of Man has much
to suffer and must be condemned by the elders and the high priests and the
scribes and must be killed' (Mk 8:31). This has nothing to do with fatalism;
it is the consequence of the path he is walking: liberating others. God is not
inflicting a fate on him; he demands he does Torah.

Doing Torah means: 'Hallow the name'. And Israel knows first-hand that this can mean
sacrificial death. They have read the story of 'Isaac's binding' (Gn 22:1–13) from the
perspective of the son, who is prepared to sacrifice his own life 'for the sake of hallowing
the divine name'.[12]

Now he is hanging on the cross, his project of liberation has failed. The assertion
'though he liberated others, he could not liberate himself' states this failure. It
is an assertion made by high priests and scribes, i.e. Jews. It is also a Jewish
assertion, which is not necessarily directed against the failed man's sincerity
per se. It is directed against his avowal as the Messiah. For the Messiah is the
liberator, and who can this crucified one liberate?

The idea of a suffering and ultimately also killed Messiah was not alien to Judaism. It
knew a Messiah Ben-Joseph, who went to war for Israel and fell in battle. He was a
hero, but that by no means made him a liberator. Liberation remained the Messiah
Ben-David's prerogative, with whom the days of the Messiah begin – unmistakably,
noticeably, visibly. And Maimonides writes in his *Mishne Torah*: 'Rabbi Akiva ... and
all the sages of his generation thought [Bar Kochba who rose against the Romans] was

---

12   Gradwohl 1995, p. 86.

the Messiah King, until he was slain in his guilt. And after he was slain they all know that he was not the Messiah King'.[13] The voice of the suffering Messiah, on the contrary, signified an appeal to speed up his coming as the liberator by listening to his voice. One Midrash narrates how a rabbi finds the Messiah at the entrance to Rome, among the poor, like them covered in wounds. The rabbi asks him: when will you come? The Messiah replies: today. The rabbi returns to the prophet Elia, who had told him where to find the Messiah: 'the Messiah deceived me and lied to me for he said: I will come today and he did not come'. To which Elia replied: 'This is what he meant to say: *today – when you listen to his voice*' (Ps 95:7) (Sanhedrin 98a).[14]

Certainly, he used to liberate, temporarily; but what else is left to those who see the crucified one but the realisation that – once again – the hope for final liberation has been disappointed? The call for Jesus to descend from the cross is not pure cynicism. For it is unimaginable that God would abandon his Messiah in this desperate situation. As one Midrash says: 'He [the just one] calls himself a Child of the Lord ... He boasts of God as his father. Let us see whether his words are true, and test what end it takes. For if the just one is God's son then he will attend to him and save him from the clutches of his enemies'. But no God appears to save him here. Jesus is hopelessly lost. He can only cry out: '*Eli, Eli, lama sabachthani* [translated this means: My God, my God, why have you abandoned me?]' (Mk 15:34).

The Jewish 'no' to the Christian claim that Jesus is the Messiah is spoken most recently from the first-hand experience of the Shoah. After Auschwitz we can no longer say that the cry 'my God, my God, why have you abandoned your beloved people' was answered by him.[15] It is possible to see, as most Jewish people probably do, the State of Israel as the rescuing of the surviving Judaism. But even then it must still be said: 'this time [in Auschwitz], however, it [the rescue] came too late'.[16] Since Auschwitz, the religious Jew knows 'that a God who did not or could not prevent the Holocaust cannot be counted

---

13   Hertzberg 1991, p. 218.

14   Bonhoeffer interprets similarly: 'People go to God when God's in need, / find God poor, reviled, without shelter or bread, / see God devoured by sin, weakness, and death, / Christians stand by God in God's own pain' (2010, p. 461).

15   'There were those in Auschwitz who died in the gas believing, who uttered the prayer Sch'ma Israel: ss murderers have testified this, as have survivors. Under no circumstances, however, may this still be theologised because such an interpretation [giving meaning to this catastrophe] could encourage the next Auschwitz. Any such interpretation has to be refused' (Marquardt 1988, p. 129).

16   Fackenheim 1987, p. 36.

on'.[17] If Jews still obstinately insist that the Messiah has yet to come, then this is not a sign of their disobedience, but a demonstration of their loyalty.[18]

The aesthetic of this representation of the crucified one is not simply an aesthetic of suffering. Jesus's cry bears witness to god-forsakenness protesting itself. He, too, now wants to see his messianic project affirmed by God; he, too, is calling on God: attend to me and save me from the clutches of my enemies! That is most certainly an aesthetic of resistance. But this resistance falls on deaf ears; it ends in resounding silence. Thus, all that is left in the end is the aesthetic of suffering, the representation of the bent dead body as an indication of a possible life after death. The question, however, as to whether there is also life before death remains unanswered.

Karl Marx exposed this idea, which refers the people's longing for deliverance into an afterlife, as just 'the *fantastic realisation* of the human essence'. When we see the crucified one we are really seeing '*religious* distress' that is 'at the same time the *expression* of real distress and also the *protest* against real distress'. We should not sugar coat what is terrible: religion 'is the sigh of the oppressed creature'. But if this sigh breaks our heart, this could be a motivation to protest against *true* misery and 'to establish the truth of *this* world'.[19]

But what would have happened if Jesus had proved his messianity by heeding the call to descend from the cross? Let us assume for a moment that he really would have been able to do this. As materialist Bible-reading discerned, the Bible contains a mythological code, which narrates liberation by means of the idea of a God in heaven who sends his only son to earth, a son who in accordance with his heavenly nature has the power to work miracles.[20] Why should such a miraculous Son of God not be able to descend from the cross and return to his Father? Had he done this, though, would that not have meant that he had extricated himself from the events he had involved himself in at the last minute? While his fellow sufferers have to face the final consequences of their engagement, he takes off in the nick of time? Is that what we should

---

17   Fackenheim 1987, p. 217.

18   Marquardt 1981.

19   Marx 1975b, p. 76.

20   This 'code' presumes the schema 'heaven / earth / river (= hell)', where 'mythical' beings like angels, etc. live (Clévenot 1978, p. 85). The Bible itself offers the possibility of a materialist reading by demythologising itself (Clévenot 1978, p. 87).

expect from a Messiah? A deliverer who, when the going gets tough, detaches himself from the cross, delivers himself from the burden of solidarity?

In his play *Der Auftrag* [*The Mission*], the GDR writer Heiner Müller tells the story of the son of a Haitian landowner who is sent to Haiti by the young French Republic in order to organise the revolution there with two other men. Once it becomes evident that the revolution will fail, the son abandons the revolution in order to return to his father and the estate. Müller subsumes what happens there into a single sentence that says it all: 'In times of betrayal landscapes are beautiful'.[21] This is what would have happened to Jesus, too: the memory of the overwhelming beauty of the heavenly landscape and the temptation to return to his father.

Now, arguably the people with whose liberation Jesus was concerned had long since withdrawn from danger and, as Luke tells us, were only watching when Jesus was crucified (Lk 23:35). Why should Jesus not also detach himself from the cross and run off into the heavenly distance? This, though, would only confirm to the people what they already knew: in an emergency, save yourself. That is also why they prefer to watch when the powerful reckon with their enemies once again.

I wonder, though, whether we necessarily have to read the phrase 'though he liberated others, he could not liberate himself' through the lens of the mythological code. The synoptic gospels tell the life of Jesus as the life of a human who cannot depend on direct heavenly interventions, a human who is wholly dependent on earthly conditions. The mythological story of the 'temptation in the desert' demythologises the idea of a God-man who would be elevated above simply living on the word of God.

In the story of the temptation (Mt 4:1–11; Lk 4:1–12) Jesus refuses Satan's offer to behave like a God-man empowered by God. Jesus does not want to be a mythical being, but to become human and stay solidary.

This Jesus really cannot liberate himself. He relies entirely on others acting in solidarity with him and so producing togetherness which really will liberate. Jesus liberated others by practicing this togetherness, by demonstrating his solidarity – his 'devotion to the end'. Where this togetherness, this solidarity is absent, he is hopelessly lost.[22]

---

21   Müller 1998, p. 45. He is referring to Anna Seghers, whose novella *Das Licht auf dem Galgen* [*The Light on the Gallows*] was the inspiration for this play.

22   As Brecht has a proletarian mother say in a lullaby to her new-born son: 'And so, my son,

Maybe that is precisely how he is the Messiah. For where did humans get the fatal idea that they have to liberate themselves? Is it not because they cannot believe that solidarity between humans is even possible to the last? They have experienced the betraying of solidarity too often – not least by themselves. Post Christum Christians, in any case, can no longer make this case: there was *one* person who embodied this solidarity.[23]

Of course, we might ask: what is the significance of one person remaining solidary to the end? But the Talmud knew that 'when one person saves one life it is as though they had saved the whole world' (Sanhedrin 4, 6). For this one human proved that it really is possible to be solidary to the last.

Jesus is this one human, but he is not the only one of his 'kind'. It is the 'kind' of people who, as Slavoj Žižek remarks, 'regularly [appear] in the memoirs of concentration camp survivors[:] that one ..., that one person, who *did not break down* and in the midst of unbearable conditions, which reduced everyone else to the selfish fight for survival, who retained and exuded "irrational" generosity and dignity in a miraculous way ... Even here, there was the one person, who maintained the minimal solidarity, which defines the social bond in its true sense, in opposition to collaboration as survival strategy'.[24] Nor is it an issue of Jesus having to be the only one, for the sake of the dogma. The issue is that we are not missing this one human. Had he not existed, we would be lost.

Deliverance instead of Final Solution

The phrase about Jesus, 'though he liberated others, he could not liberate himself', is then a *Christological* assertion: this is precisely what makes him the Messiah.

This Christological assertion is also a *theological* one. For the God who gave humans the Torah engaged himself in the realisation of the Torah. He takes pleasure in the people

---

stay close to your own people | So your power, like the dust, will spread to every place. | You, my son, and I and all our people | Must stand together till there are no longer two unequal | Classes to divide the entire human race' (Brecht 1976, p. 191).

23   'if the earth was deemed worthy to bear the human being Jesus Christ, if such a human being like Jesus lived, then and only then does our life as human beings have meaning' (Bonhoeffer 2010, p. 515). In other, biblical, words: then life is not without promise ('The unbiblical term "meaning" is, after all, only the translation of what the Bible calls "promise"', ibid).

24   Žižek 2000, p. 73 [translated R.P.].

doing Torah; he is pained when they do not do Torah. When the people, when his son, suffers 'for the sake of hallowing his name', he suffers, too. This is why we can dare to say: 'Jesus's death and resurrection constitutes the final stage of the transformation of fate into a God who became human, a God who can feel pain and who is ready to feel pain. God is not inflicting violence but suffering violence in order to abolish violence for ever'.[25]

Representing Christ as 'detaching himself from the cross' misses the crucial point: the representation of his solidarity to the bitter end. But Christian art, too, inasmuch as it fixes the crucified one into the image of a human who lets his head hang, falls short. This image invites the viewer too readily to let their own head hang. Maybe the aesthetic of resistance embodied by the crucified one cannot be fixed in *one* image anyway. It is necessarily complex, just as the narration of the Passion in the gospels is complex. Depicting this story as an object of visual art can then only be a multi-layered composition of meaningful details – as is the case for the artworks that Peter Weiss has commented on in his *Aesthetics of Resistance*.

But can the phrase about Jesus which says that he could not liberate himself really be a christological assertion, if the cry 'My God, my God, why have you abandoned me' remains unanswered – because there is no one, neither a God nor a human, who liberates him? As noted at the beginning, the problems are solved too quickly if we follow the church by referring to the answer that God himself gave: the Resurrection. And it would not be harmless to add that Christian art does not exclusively cultivate an aesthetic of suffering, but also an aesthetic of victory: Christus Triumphator, the World's Judge who executes the Final Judgment, the 'final solution' according to which good people will enjoy eternal bliss in paradise, evil people will suffer eternal damnation in hell.[26] Where would this victory leave solidarity? Where would the humans go who joined in solidarity, the solidarity of which Jesus set an example? Why, where would those humans go without whom the God with whom Jesus was concerned does not even want to be God?

The gospels tell of such a (hu)man. He is, of all things, a Roman officer, who, when he sees that Jesus 'has surrendered his spirit' (Greek: *exepneusen*) in 'that way' – i.e. in this solidarity – says: 'truly, this man was God's Son' (Mk 15:39). Or, in the words of another of the gospel writers: 'this man was a just

---

25   Füssel 2003, p. 58.

26   'What is fatal about this [the image of the Last Judgment] is the expectation that [it] will bring about a *final*, eternal decision ... a clean final solution ... a [-] final [-] radical [-] *cleansing*' (Marquardt 1996, p. 167).

one' (Lk 23:47). Is this not already something akin to a resurrection? Here, where a man from the world of the Goy, who never really knew what to do with the world of Judaism, says of this Jew, who does Torah, he was a Son of God, a just one (a *tzaddik*)? Are the gospels perhaps trying to tell us that God consciously restrains himself from avowing Jesus in order to give humans the opportunity to avow him without knowing in advance that God is by his side? Is this also the point of the *exepneusen* that they employ in order to say that Jesus 'passed away' (as some translations still render this word): he surrendered his *spirit* (Greek: *pneuma*), the *spiritus*, which 'inspires' people?[27] Are they trying to prevent an all too triumphant understanding of the resurrection, one that fixes on Jesus in heaven instead of orienting itself towards the community as 'the earthly-historical form of His own existence' (Barth)?[28] And we could ask further: does an aesthetic of victory, which shows us Jesus as the executor of the Final Judgment, not obscure the solidarity that he lived to the end? Should deliverance not be depicted as the end of a world in which people win and are defeated, rather than a 'final solution' with winners and losers?

The Crucified One Walks Away

This question can also be posed to the aesthetic of resistance practised by the modern labour movement. Has the rhetoric of victory not also suppressed the vision of humanity no longer in need of winning because all enmity has been defeated? And what is the significance of the fact that in this aesthetic the protagonists of liberation are all represented as muscular men and women, bursting with strength? Fritz Cremer's man detaching himself from the cross also makes the impression of being a strong type, who is not much exerted by liberating himself from this cross. Is the message of this aesthetic not that only the strong ones can liberate themselves and that a politics of strength is imperative for the 'poor and despised' – instead of trusting the strength of the weak? Had their aesthetic not been more liberating, had they also shown their movement's weakness, and had they not repressed the desperation to which solidarity can lead.

To be sure, such an aesthetic exists: Peter Weiss's *The Aesthetics of Resistance*. Here, nothing is silenced; it commemorates those people who fall silent,

---

27   The Gospel of John is more explicit: *paredokè to pneuma*, he handed over his spirit (Jn 19:30), that is, to his disciples, i.e. the community.

28   Barth defines the community this way in the principles of the §§ 62, 67 and 72 of his Church Dogmatics (Barth 1956b).

because the suffering they see renders them speechless, those people, who can see no other way out but self-selected death. At the end, his book speaks of a 'sweeping movement with which they [who rebelled against their superiors] can finally wipe away the terrible pressure that rested on their shoulders'.[29] But, like Bloch's 'smashing of the cross', this 'sweeping away' does not have to be thought of as an act of violence. It could also be the subversive force of solidarity that 'sweeps away' the pressure of the dominant non-solidary relations and points towards a world without a cross. Perhaps then the final sentence of Bloch's 'Principle of Hope' comes true and 'there arises in the world something which shines into the childhood of all and in which no one has yet been: homeland'.[30]

Indeed, there is an aesthetic of *resistance*, at best. All liberation to date has been temporary; even where there was community there is now church, and the aesthetic of limitless solidarity has turned into an aesthetic that has made a virtue out of the necessity of suffering. What remains is the image of the crucified one who resisted the temptation to relinquish solidarity and *thus* surrendered his spirit. A Christian aesthetic of resistance will be inspired by this image. For this, it would have to have an eye again for the crucified Jesus as the Jew Schalom ben-Chorin sees him.[31] He wants nothing to do with 'the exalted *kyrios*, the Lord, indeed to the *Christos Pantokrator*, the ruler of the universe, he is hidden from our view'. And then he writes (another final sentence): 'Let us, instead, look once more upon the Jew Jeshua Ben-Yosef of Nazareth, as he hangs, despised and rejected, there on the cross. His countenance, distorted by pain, is crowned with a diadem of thorns. The martyred body bleeds from countless wounds. Thus we see him once again, the Jew on the cross. His voice carries down through the centuries: Just as you did to one of the least of these my brothers, so you did to me'.[32]

One last remark on Fritz Cremer's sculpture. Can we be certain that the image is trying to say that the crucified one is detaching himself from the cross, because it is beneath his dignity to be weak and abandoned by God, and he can only imagine liberation as an act of violence? The image is, after all, a quotation. The point of the quotation is to criticise the Christian aesthetic of suffering. We read this quotation as the commanded alternative: instead of hanging on the cross, Fritz Cremer's crucified one heeds the call: descend from the cross and liberate yourself. But there is another way of reading the quotation. The

29   Weiss 1983, p. 268.
30   Bloch 1986b, p. 1376.
31   Ben-Chorin 2001.
32   Ben-Chorin 2001, p. 88.

crucified one does not descend from the cross, but walks away – from an aesthetic that reduces him to his suffering. With his image Fritz Cremer is not criticising the Jesus of the gospels, who categorically refuses to liberate himself. The view of this Jesus is precisely what the Christian aesthetic of suffering has obscured for Cremer. His crucified one, on the other hand, expresses: I want nothing to do with this aesthetic anymore. Thus Jesus throws off the shackles of an ideology that renders him unrecognisable. I had the idea of reading the image in this way from Imre Varga's Lenin memorial in the Hungarian city of Mohács. This memorial showed Lenin stepping off the pedestal on which he stood. I do not think that Varga was trying to say that Lenin was giving up on his bond with the proletariat that he wanted to liberate. His Lenin is walking away from the part which the aesthetic of Soviet Communism foisted on him: the *Übermensch*, the *Máximo Líder*, the elevated *Kyrios*. He descends: to his people, from whom the 'proletarian' ideology had separated him. It is, understood correctly, a very Christian image, full of messianic meaning. Fritz Cremer's image could be read as equally Christian.

I walk around the ruins of the Franziskaner-Klosterkirche in Berlin. I regard Cremer's image. It is in the right place, here, in this ruined church. Jesus descends from the cross so as to be with his own, the condemned of this earth, again, and to stay with them.

FIGURE 2   *Lenin*

References

Adorno, Theodor W. 1974 [1951], *Minima Moralia: Reflections from Damaged Life*, London: Verso.

Adorno, Theodor W. and Max Horkheimer 2002 [1947], *Dialectic of Enlightenment: Philosophical Fragments*, Stanford, CA: Stanford University Press.

Althusser, Louis 1984, 'Reply to John Lewis', in *Essays on Ideology*, London: Verso.

Assmann, Jan 2000, *Herrschaft und Heil: Politische Theologie in Ägypten, Israel und Europa*, München/Wien: Carl Hanser Verlag.

Badiou, Alain 2003, *Saint Paul: The Foundation of Universalism*, Stanford, CA: Stanford University Press.

Baeck, Leo 1964, *This People Israel: The Meaning of Jewish Existence*, New York: Holt, Rinehart and Winston.

Barnard, Willem 1987, *Bezig met Genesis: Van ark en altaar*, Voorburg: PSLectuurvoorlichting.

——— 2004, *Stille duif in de verte: Gepeins bij psalmen*, Zoetermeer: Meinema.

Barth, Karl 1956a, *Church Dogmatics, Vol. I/2*, Edinburgh: Clark & Clark.

——— 1956b, *Church Dogmatics, Vol. IV/1–3*, Edinburgh: Clark & Clark.

——— 1957, 'The Christian's Place in Society', in *The Word of God and the Word of Man*, New York: Harpers & Brothers Publishers.

——— 1959, *Dogmatics in Outline*, New York: Harpers & Brothers Publishers.

——— 1968, *The Epistle to the Romans*, London: Oxford University Press.

——— 1985, 'Der Römerbrief (Erste Fassung) 1919', in *Karl-Barth-Gesamtausgabe II*, H. Schmidt (Hg.), Zürich: Theologischer Verlag Zürich.

——— 1957, *Church Dogmatics, Vol. II/1*, Edinburgh: Clark & Clark.

Ben-Chorin, Schalom 2001, Brother Jesus. *The Nazarene through Jewish eyes*, Athens GA; London: University of Georgia Press.

Benjamin, Walter 2003a, 'On the Concept of History' [1940], in *Selected Writings, Volume 4 (1938–1940)*, Cambridge, MA: The Belknap Press.

——— 2003b, 'Central Park', in *Selected Writings 4 (1938–1940)*, Cambridge, MA: The Belknap Press.

Bloch, Ernst 1969, 'Thomas Münzer als Theologe der Revolution', Vol. 2, in *Ernst Bloch Werkausgabe*, Frankfurt am Main: Suhrkamp.

——— 1986a, *Natural Law and Human Dignity*, Cambridge, MA: MIT Press.

——— 1986b, *The Principle of Hope*, 3 Vols, Cambridge, MA: MIT Press.

Boer, Theo De 2001, 'Zoek het Koninkrijk', in *Wie God zegt ... Spreken over God in een wereld zonder God*, Kampen: Kok.

Bonhoeffer, Dietrich 1998, 'Sanctorum Communio', in *Dietrich Bonhoeffer Works, Vol. 1*, Minneapolis: Fortress Press.

———— 2001, 'Discipleship', in *Dietrich Bonhoeffer Works, Vol. 4*, Minneapolis: Fortress Press.

———— 2010a, 'Barcelona, Berlin, New York: 1928–1931', in *Dietrich Bonhoeffer Works, Vol. 10*, Minneapolis: Fortress Press.

———— 2010b, 'Letters and Papers from Prison', in *Dietrich Bonhoeffer Works, Vol. 8*, Minneapolis: Fortress Press.

Boyarin, Daniel 1997, *A Radical Jew: Paul and the Politics of Identity*, Berkeley, CA: University of California Press.

Braun, Volker 1976, *Gedichte*, Leipzig: Reclam.

Brecht, Bertolt 1965, *The Messingkauf Dialogues*, London: Methuen.

———— 1976, *Poems 1913–1956*, edited by John Willett and Ralph Manheim with the help of Erich Fried, London: Eyre Methuen Ltd.

———— 1979, 'Threepenny Opera', in *Collected Plays, Vol. 2 Part 2*, edited by John Willett and Ralph Manheim, London: Eyre Methuen Ltd.

———— 2003a, 'A Necessary Observation on the Struggle against Barbarism', in *Brecht on Art and Politics*, edited by Tom Kuhn and Steve Giles, London: Methuen Publishing Ltd.

———— 2003b, 'The Days of the Commune', in *Brecht's Plays, Poetry and Prose: Collected Plays Vol. 8*, edited by Tom Kuhn and David J. Constantine, London: Methuen.

Breukelman, F.H. 1992, *Bijbelse Theologie* I/2, Kampen: Kok.

———— 1999, *Bijbelse Theologie* IV/2, Kampen: Kok.

Buber, Martin 1949, *The Prophetic Faith*, New York: Macmillan.

———— 1956, *Tales of the Hasidim*, London: Thames and Hudson.

———— 1993, 'Kirche, Staat, Volk, Judentum', in *Der Jude und sein Judentum: Gesammelte Aufsätze und Reden*, Gerlingen: Verlag Lambert Schneider.

Bultmann, Rudolf 1958, *Jesus and the Word of God*, New York: Charles Scribner's Sons.

———— 1963, 'Prophecy and Fulfilment', in *Essays on Old Testament Hermeneutics*, edited by Claus Westermann, Richmond, VA: John Knox Press.

Butting, Klara 1994, *Die Buchstaben werden sich noch wundern. Innerbiblische Kritik als Wegweiser feministischer Hermeneutik*, Berlin: Alektor Verlag.

Casalis, Georges 1980, *Die richtigen Ideen fallen nicht vom Himmel. Grundlagen einer induktiven Theologie*, Stuttgart-Berlin-Köln-Mainz: Kohlhammer Verlag.

Clévenot, Michel 1985, *Materialist Approaches to the Bible*, New York: Maryknoll.

Cohen, Hermann 1995, *Religion of Reason: Out of the Sources of Judaism*, Atlanta, GA: Scholars Press.

Crüsemann, Frank 2003, *Kanon und Sozialgeschichte. Beiträge zum AT*, Gütersloh: Gütersloher Verlagshaus.

Deurloo, Karel 1988, *De mens als raadsel en geheim. Verhalende antropologie in Gen. 2–4*, Baarn: Ten Have.

———— 1998, *Genesis*, Kampen: Kok.

Deurloo, Karel, Evert van den Berg and Piet van Midden 2004, *Koning en Tempel* (Kleine Bijbelse Theologie 11), Kampen: Kok.

Diebner, Bernd Jørg 2003, 'Kurskorrektur: Plädoyer für einen anderen Zugang zum "Alten Testament"', *Transparent: Zeitschrift für die kritische Masse der Rheinischen Kirche*, 69(3): 1–18.

Engels, Fredrick 1987 [1877–8], 'Anti-Dühring, Herr Eugen Dühring's Revolution in Science', in *Marx and Engels Collected Works*, Volume 25, Moscow: Progress Publishers.

Fackenheim, Emil 1987, *What is Judaism? An Interpretation for the Present Age*, New York: Summit Books.

Fanon, Frantz 2008, *Black Skin, White Masks*, London: Pluto Press.

Feuerbach, Ludwig 1989, *The Essence of Christianity*, Buffalo, NY: Prometheus Books.

Frettlöh, Magdalene 2002, *Wenn Mann und Frau im Bilde Gottes sind. Über geschlechtspolitische Gottesbilder, die Gottesebenbildlichkeit des Menschen und das Bilderverbot*, Wuppertal: Foedus.

Freud, Sigmund 1991a [1929–30], 'Civilization and Its Discontents', in *The Penguin Freud Library*, Vol. 12, London: Penguin Books.

———— 1991b [1933], 'New Introductory Lectures on Psychoanalysis', in *The Penguin Freud Library*, Vol. 2, London: Penguin Books.

Füssel, Kuno 2003, 'Rückkehr der Rachegottheit?', in *Gott und die Katastrophen. Eine Debatte über Religion, Gewalt und Säkularisierung*, edited by Michael Jäger et al., Berlin: Edition Freitag.

Gradwohl, Roland 1995, *Bibelauslegungen aus jüdischen Quellen*, Bd. I, Stuttgart: Calwer Verlag.

Gramsci, Antonio 1971, *Selection from the Prison Notebooks*, New York: International Publishers.

Groot, Gerrit de 1979, 'Het scheppingsverhaal', *Opstand*, 4.

Hegel, Georg Wilhelm Friedrich 1977 [1807], *Phenomenology of Spirit*, Oxford: Clarendon Press.

Hertzberg, Arthur 1961, *Judaism*, London: Prentice Hall International.

———— 1991, *Judaism: The Key Spiritual Writings of the Jewish Tradition*, New York: Simon & Schuster.

Heym, Stefan 1973, *The King David Report: A Novel*, New York: Putnam.

Holloway, John 2002, *Change the World Without Taking Power*, London: Pluto Press.

Jankowski, Gerhard 1998, *Die grosse Hoffnung. Paulus an die Römer. Eine Auslegung*, Berlin: Alektor Verlag.

Jenni, Ernst and Claus Westermann 1976, *Theologisches Handwörterbuch zum Alten Testament*, Vol. 2 (Art. 'Abbild'), München/Zürich: Kaiser Verlag/Theologischer Verlag.

Kant Immanuel 2006, 'Toward Perpetual Peace: A Philosophical Sketch', in *Toward*

Perpetual Peace and Other Writings on Politics, Peace, and History, New Haven, CT: Yale University Press.

———— 2009, *An Answer to the Question: 'What is Enlightenment?'*, London: Penguin.

Kautsky, Karl 1897, *Communism in Central Europe in the Time of the Reformation*, translated by J.L. Mulliken and E.G. Mulliken, London: Fisher and Unwin.

———— 1976a [1895–7], *Vorläufer des neueren Sozialismus I: Kommunistische Bewegungen im Mittelalter*, Berlin: Dietz.

———— 1976b [1895–7], *Vorläufer des neueren Sozialismus II: Der Kommunismus in der deutschen Reformation*, Berlin: Dietz.

Kautsky, Karl and Paul Lafargue 1977 [1922], *Vorläufer des neueren Sozialismus III: Die beiden ersten grossen Utopisten*, Stuttgart: Dietz.

Klausner, Joseph 1944, *From Jesus to Paul*, London: Allen and Unwin.

Kroon, Kleijs 1982, *Romeinen 13*, Voorburg: Interkerkelijk Vredesberaad.

Lenin, Vladimir I. 1960, 'The State and Revolution', in *Collected Works*, Vol. 25, Moscow: Foreign Languages Publishing House.

———— 1960, 'The Three Sources and Three Component Parts of Marxism', in *Collected Works*, Vol. 19, Moscow: Foreign Languages Publishing House.

Levinas, Emmanuel 1996, 'Nameless', in *Proper Names*, London: The Athlone Press.

Lucebert 2013, *Collected Poems Vol. 1*, Kobenhavn/Los Angeles: Green Integer.

Marquardt, Friedrich-Wilhelm 1972, *Theologie und Sozialismus. Das Beispiel Karl Barths*, München-Mainz: Kaiser-Grünewald.

———— 1988, *Von Elend und Heimsuchung der Theologie. Prolegomena zur Dogmatik*, München: Kaiser.

———— 1993, *Was dürfen wir hoffen, wenn wir hoffen dürften? Eine Eschatologie 1*, Gütersloh: Kaiser/Gütersloher Verlagshaus.

———— 1996, *Was dürfen wir hoffen, wenn wir hoffen dürften? Eine Eschatologie 3*, Gütersloh: Kaiser/Gütersloher Verlagshaus.

———— 1997, *Evangelische Freude an der Tora*, Tübingen: Theologischer Verlag Tübingen.

———— 2009, '"Feinde um unsretwillen" Das jüdische Nein und die christliche Theologie', in *Auf einem Weg ins Lehrhaus. Leben und Denken mit Israel*, Frankfurt/Main: Verlag Otto Lembeck.

Marx Karl 1975a [1844], *On the Jewish Question*, in *Marx and Engels Collected Works*, Volume 3, Moscow: Progress Publishers.

———— 1975b [1844], *Contribution to the Critique of Hegel's Philosophy of Law. Introduction*, in *Marx and Engels Collected Works*, Volume 3, Moscow: Progress Publishers.

———— 1976a [1845], *Theses on Feuerbach*, in *Marx and Engels Collected Works*, Volume 5, Moscow: Progress Publishing.

———— 1979 [1852], *The Eighteenth Brumaire of Louis Bonaparte*, in *Marx and Engels Collected Works*, Volume 11, Moscow: Progress Publishers.

———— 1987 [1857–8], *Economic Manuscripts (First Version of Capital)*, in *Marx and Engels Collected Works*, Volume 29, Moscow: Progress Publishing.

———— 1996 [1867], *Capital, Vol. 1*, in *Marx and Engels Collected Works*, Volume 35, Moscow: Progress Publishers.

Marx, Karl and Fredrick Engels 1975c [1845], *The Holy Family*, in *Marx and Engels Collected Works*, Volume 4, Moscow: Progress Publishers.

Marx, Karl and Fredrick Engels 1975d [1845–6], *The German Ideology*, in *Marx and Engels Collected Works*, Volume 5, Moscow: Progress Publishers.

Marx, Karl and Fredrick Engels 1976b [1848], *Manifesto of the Communist Party*, in *Marx and Engels Collected Works*, Volume 6, Moscow: Progress Publishers.

Miskotte, Kornelis H. 1967, *When the Gods are Silent*, New York: Harper and Row.

———— 1968, *The Roads of Prayer*, New York: Sheed and Ward.

———— 1983, 'Edda en Thora. Een vergelijking van Germaanse en Israëlitische religie', in *Verzameld Werk* 7, Kampen: Kok

———— 1997, *Biblisches ABC. Wider das unhistorische Bibellesen*, Wittingen: Erev Rav.

Mönnich, Conrad W. 1966, *Antiliturgica. Enige kanttekeningen bij de viering van kerkelijke feesten*, Amsterdam: Ten Have.

Monshouwer, Dirk 1983, *Leviticus. Verklaring van een bijbelgedeelte*, Kampen: Kok.

Müller, Heiner 1998, 'Motiv bei A.S.', in *Werke 1 (Die Gedichte)*, Frankfurt/Main: Suhrkamp.

Naastepad Thomas 1975, *Salomo. Verklaring van een bijbelgedeelte*, Kampen: Kok.

———— 1979, *Rondbrief van Maart*.

———— 1986, *Rondbrief van April*.

———— 1989, *Rondbrief van Mei*.

———— 1999, *Rondbrief van October*.

———— 2001, *Van horen zeggen. Uitleg van het boek Deuteronomium*, Baarn: Ten Have.

———— 2003, *Naar Mokum. Uitleg van Exodus 1–34*, Baarn: Ten Have.

Nietzsche, Friedrich 1990, *Beyond Good and Evil: Prelude to a Philosophy of the Future*, London: Penguin.

———— 2005, *Thus Spoke Zarathustra: A Book for Everyone and Nobody*, Oxford: Oxford University Press.

Oosting, Berthil 2004, *Verzoening als verleiding. Een nieuwe toegang tot de wondere woorden van het boek Leviticus*, Vught: Skandalon.

Osten-Sacken, Peter von der 1994, *Katechismus und Siddur. Aufbrüche mit Martin Luther und den Lehrern Israels*, Berlin: Institut Kirche und Judentum.

Pascal, Blaise 1966 [1669], *Pensées*, Harmondsworth, Middlesex: Penguin Books.

Ragaz, Leonhard 1972 [1929], *Von Christus zu Marx – von Marx zu Christus. Ein Beitrag*, Hamburg: Furche Verlag.

Reeling Brouwer, Rinse 1992, 'Verantwoordelijkheid in de christelijk-sociale traditie en bij Mozes', *Opstand*, 18(2).

———— 2002, 'Lied van Paulus', in *Liedje dat ik niet laten kan. Verzamelde opstellen over de liederen van Huub Oosterhuis, doctor ecclesiae*, Kampen: Gooi en Sticht.

Rosenzweig, Franz 2005, *The Star of Redemption*, Madison, WI: University of Wisconsin Press.

Steffensky, Fulbert 2007, 'Warum sollen die Linken fromm sein und die Frommen links?', *CfS-Circular*, 1: 6.

Strack, Hermann und Billerbeck, Paul 1928, *Kommentar zum Neuen Testament aus Talmud und Midrasch, Band IV-1 (Exkurse zu einzelnen Stellen des Neuen Testaments*, München: C.H. Becksche Verlagsbuchhandlung.

Taubes, Jacob 2004, *The Political Theology of Paul*, Stanford, CA: Stanford University Press.

Ter Schegget, Bert 1975, *Het lied van de Mensenzoon. Studie over de Christuspsalm in Fillipenzen 2: 6–11*, [Baarn]: Wereldvenster.

Tillich, Paul 1952, *The Courage to Be*, New Haven, CT: Yale University Press.

Troeltsch, Ernst 1931, *The Social Teaching of the Christian Church*, London: Allen & Unwin Ltd.

Van der Leeuw, Gerardus 1986, *Religion in Essence and Manifestation: A Study in Phenomenology*, Princeton, NJ: Princeton University Press.

Veerkamp, Ton 1992, *Autonomie und Egalität. Ökonomie, Politik und Ideologie in der Schrift*, Berlin: Alektor Verlag.

———— 1996, 'Weltordnung und Solidarität oder Dekonstruktion christlicher Theologie. Auslegung des 1. Johannesbriefes und Kommentar', *Texte und Kontexte*, 71/72.

———— 2001, Art. 'Gott', in *Historisch-Kritisches Wörterbuch des Marxismus*, Vol. 5, Hamburg: Argument Verlag

———— 2005, *Der Gott der Liberalen. Eine Kritik des Liberalismus*, Hamburg: Argument Verlag.

———— 2007, 'Der Abschied des Messias. Eine Auslegung des Johannesevangeliums', II. Teil, *Texte und Kontexte*, 113/115.

Völker, Klaus 1979, *Brecht: A Biography*, London: Marion Boyars Publishing Ltd.

Weiss, Peter 1983, *Die Ästhetik des Widerstands Bd. 3*, Frankfurt: Suhrkamp Verlag.

———— 2005, *The Aesthetics of Resistance*, Vol. 1, Durham, NC: Duke University Press.

Wielenga, Bastiaan 1981, *It's a Long Road to Freedom: Perspectives of Biblical Theology*, Madurai: Tamilnadu Theological Seminary.

Wilsdorf, Till 1990, *Der diskrete Charme der kirchlichen Bürokratie. Religionskritische Texte gegen die formierte Gesellschaft*, Stuttgart: Plakat Verlag.

Žižek, Slavoj 2000a, *The Fragile Absolute, or, Why is the Christian Legacy worth fighting for?*, London: Verso.

———— 2000b, *Das fragile Absolute. Warum es sich lohnt, das christliche Erbe zu verteidigen*, Berlin: Volk und Welt.

Zuurmond, Rochus 1983, 'De ethiek van de bergrede', *ACEBT (Amsterdamse Cahiers voor Exegese en Bijbelse Theologie)*, 4.

Index of Authors

Index of Biblical References